the
Romans in the Age of Augustus

The Peoples of Europe

General Editors: James Campbell and Barry Cunliffe

This series is about the European tribes and peoples from their origins in prehistory to the present day. Drawing upon a wide range of archeological and historical evidence, each volume presents a fresh and absorbing account of a group's culture, society, and usually turbulent history.

Already published

The Etruscans
Graeme Barker and Thomas Rasmussen

The Byzantines
Averil Cameron

The Normans
Marjorie Chibnall

The Norsemen in the Viking Age
Eric Christiansen

The Lombards
Neil Christie

The Serbs
Sima Ćirković

The Basques*
Roger Collins

The English
Geoffrey Elton

The Gypsies
Second edition
Angus Fraser

The Bretons
Patrick Galliou and Michael Jones

The Goths
Peter Heather

The Franks*
Edward James

The Romans in the Age of
Augustus
Andrew Lintott

The Vandals
Andy Merrills and Richard Miles

The Russians
Robin Milner-Gulland

The Mongols
Second edition
David Morgan

The Armenians
A. E. Redgate

The Britons
Christopher A. Snyder

The Huns
E. A. Thompson

The Early Germans
Second edition
Malcolm Todd

The Illyrians
John Wilkes

In preparation

The Irish
Michael Herity

The Spanish
Roger Collins

The Picts
Benjamin Hudson

The Angles and Saxons
Helena Hamerow

The Celts
John Koch

*Denotes title now out of print

the

Romans in the Age of Augustus

Andrew Lintott

WILEY-BLACKWELL

A John Wiley & Sons, Ltd., Publication

This edition first published 2010
© 2010 Andrew Lintott

Blackwell Publishing was acquired by John Wiley & Sons in February 2007. Blackwell's publishing program has been merged with Wiley's global Scientific, Technical, and Medical business to form Wiley-Blackwell.

Registered Office
John Wiley & Sons Ltd, The Atrium, Southern Gate, Chichester, West Sussex, PO19 8SQ, United Kingdom

Editorial Offices
350 Main Street, Malden, MA 02148-5020, USA

9600 Garsington Road, Oxford, OX4 2DQ, UK

The Atrium, Southern Gate, Chichester, West Sussex, PO19 8SQ, UK

For details of our global editorial offices, for customer services, and for information about how to apply for permission to reuse the copyright material in this book please see our website at www.wiley.com/wiley-blackwell.

The right of Andrew W. Lintott to be identified as the author of this work has been asserted in accordance with the UK Copyright, Designs and Patents Act 1988.

Wiley also publishes its books in a variety of electronic formats. Some content that appears in print may not be available in electronic books.

Designations used by companies to distinguish their products are often claimed as trademarks. All brand names and product names used in this book are trade names, service marks, trademarks or registered trademarks of their respective owners. The publisher is not associated with any product or vendor mentioned in this book. This publication is designed to provide accurate and authoritative information in regard to the subject matter covered. It is sold on the understanding that the publisher is not engaged in rendering professional services. If professional advice or other expert assistance is required, the services of a competent professional should be sought.

Library of Congress Cataloging-in-Publication Data

Lintott, A. W. (Andrew William)
  The Romans in the age of Augustus / Andrew Lintott.
    p. cm. – (The peoples of Europe)
  Includes bibliographical references and index.
  ISBN 978-1-4051-7655-2 (hardcover : alk. paper) – ISBN 978-1-4051-7654-5 (pbk. : alk. paper) 1. Rome–History–Augustus, 30 B.C.-14 A.D. 2. Augustus, Emperor of Rome, 63 B.C.-14 A.D. 3. Rome–Civilization. I. Title.

  DG279.L48 2010
  937′.07–dc22

                         2009032178

A catalogue record for this book is available from the British Library.

Set in 10 on 12.5pt Sabon by Toppan Best-set Premedia Limited
Printed and bound in Malaysia by Vivar Printing Sdn Bhd

I 2010

4301926

Contents

Figures

Maps

Preface

When I was originally approached by the editors of the *Peoples of Europe* series about writing this book, I was hesitant. It seemed impossible to convey in the space allowed the nature of a people, which came to dominate the ancient Mediterranean world and whose history spanned more than a thousand years, with the richness of detail which characterizes and gives life to other volumes in the series. A short history was perhaps possible, but the people of Rome themselves were liable to disappear in a blur. I was also aware that I was not the first to be asked to write this book. A snapshot of Rome in a significant epoch offered some kind of solution and the age of Augustus was one of the obvious candidates. Referees consulted by the publishers on this offered wildly divergent advice. It was all kindly meant and I must apologize for the extent that I disregarded, as was inevitable, a great deal of it. The one recommendation that I took to heart above all was that the publishers had better give me my head and see how it turned out. The conventional disclaimer excusing the author's advisers for errors in the work should be extended to excusing them for the fact that the work is there at all.

Much of my writing has been closely connected to my teaching. The reign of Augustus was the first historical subject I taught, when I was at King's College, London. Since then I have specialized in the history of the Roman Republic, but continued to teach subjects centered in the period of the emperors. In particular I have found myself dealing with pupils who had little or no background in Roman history but were beginning with Augustan Rome, some of them because they were combining the study of the ancient world with that of the medieval and modern worlds. I became used to providing a quick introduction to the growth of Rome, without which Augustus, his city, and his empire, are incomprehensible. This is the raison d'être of chapters 2 and 3. Another influence has been the undergraduate City of Rome course held annually by the British School in Rome, where the directors have not only to guide their flocks round monuments and sites but provide historical background in evening talks. I hope this book may give some help and stimulus to those who are visiting Rome and Italy for the first time. I am conscious that the Romans in the empire are but briefly mentioned in this volume. The general need for selectivity aside, my excuse would be that, as people, they are best understood in conjunction with the indigenous inhabitants of the provinces whose lands they came to share.

It is a pleasure to thank James Campbell for his encouragement both before and after he read what I wrote, and Ed Bispham and Jo Quinn for their thoughtful comments on the text. I am also indebted to my editor, Jennifer Speake, and the staff of Wiley-Blackwell in Oxford for their help and their patience.

Worcester College
Oxford
June 2009

Abbreviations

Abbreviations of periodicals in general follow the system of *L'Année Philologique*.

ANRW   *Aufstieg und Niedergang der römischen Welt*, Festschrift J.Vogt, ed. H. Temporini and W. Haase (Berlin and New York, 1972–)

Braund   D. C. Braund, *A Sourcebook on Roman History 31 BC–AD 68* (London, 1985)

CAH   *Cambridge Ancient History*

CIL   *Corpus Inscriptionum Latinarum*

EJ²   V. Ehrenberg and A. H. M. Jones, *Documents Illustrating the Reigns of Augustus and Tiberius* (2nd edn. with addenda, Oxford, 1975)

FIRA   S. Riccobono, *Fontes Iuris Romani Anteiustiniani* (2nd edn., Florence, 1968)

GC   A. H. M.Greenidge and A. M. Clay, *Sources for Roman History 133–70 BC* (2nd edn. rev. E. W. Gray, corrected, and augmented, Oxford, 1986)

HRR   H. Peter, *Historicorum Romanorum Reliquiae*, 2 vols. (2nd edn., Stuttgart; repr.1993)

ILLRP   A. Degrassi, *Inscriptiones Latinae Liberae Rei Publicae*, 2 vols. (2nd edn., Florence, 1966)

ILS   H. Dessau, *Inscriptiones Latinae Selectae*, 4 vols. (Berlin, 1892; repr. 1955)

Inscr.Ital. A. Degrassi, *Inscriptiones Italiae, xiii: Fasti et Elogia*, 3 vols (Rome, 1947–63)

LTUR   E. M. Steinby (ed.), *Lexicon topographicum urbis Romae*, 6 vols. (Rome 1993–2000)

MRR   T. R. S. Broughton, *The Magistrates of the Roman Republic*, vols. I and II (2nd edn., New York, 1960), vol. III (Atlanta, Ga, 1987)

OGIS	W. Dittenberger, *Orientis Graeci Inscriptiones Selectae*, 4 vols. (Leipzig, 1903; repr. Hildesheim, 1960)
ORF	H. Malcovati, *Oratorum Romanorum Fragmenta*, 2 vols. (4th edn., Turin, 1976–9)
POxy	B. P. Grenfell, A. S. Hunt et al., *Oxyrhynchus Papyri* (London, 1898–)
RDGE	R. K. Sherk, *Roman Documents from the Greek East* (Baltimore, 1964)
RE	Pauly-Wissowa, *Real-Encyclopaedie der classischen Altertumswissenschaft*
RG	P. A. Brunt and J. M. Moore, *Res Gestae Divi Augusti* (Oxford, 1973)
RGE	R. K. Sherk, *Rome and the Greek East to the Death of Augustus* (trans. Docs. G & R 4, Cambridge, 1985)
RRC	M. H. Crawford, *Roman Republican Coinage*, 2 vols. (Cambridge, 1974)
SEG	*Supplementum Epigraphicum Graecum*
Syll³	W. Dittenberger, *Sylloge Inscriptionum Graecarum*, 4 vols. (3rd edn., Leipzig, 1915; repr. Hildesheim, 1960)
THerc	*Tabulae Herculanenses*; cf. G. Rowe, *Studia Classica Israelica* 20 (2001), 235–42
TPSulp	G. Camodeca, *Tabulae Pompeianae Sulpiciorum*, Vetera 12 (Rome, 1999)

1

Introduction

The Indian Embassies

When the emperor Caesar Augustus was on the island of Samos in 20 BC after organizing his eastern provinces and making a settlement with his neighbors the Parthians, he received an embassy from an Indian king named Poros or Pandion, who seems to have lived in the area of the mouth of the Indus.[1] His message, written in Greek, a language known in India for three centuries since Alexander the Great's invasion, was carried by the three envoys who had survived the journey. It read that, although the king ruled over 600 princes, he nevertheless set great store on becoming a friend of Caesar and was ready to grant him free passage and to cooperate with him as far as was appropriate. Eight slaves accompanied the envoys, clothed in nothing but scented loincloths, charged with conveying the king's gifts: tigers, a human "herm" born without arms, a number of large snakes, including a python, an enormous river-turtle, and a partridge larger than a vulture. There was also with them a Brahman called Zarmanochegas from Barygaza – from the class whom the Greeks called naked philosophers – who, when the party later visited Athens, was initiated into the Eleusinian mysteries and subsequently cremated himself alive on a pyre. The Athenians showed due respect and gave the ashes a tomb with a commemorative inscription saying that he had committed suicide according to his ancestral tradition. Augustus is said to have accepted King Poros as a friend of the Roman people, though we know nothing of any embassy in return. He refers nevertheless in his official autobiography to frequent embassies from the Indians, perhaps from different rulers. Furthermore, there was by now regular commercial contact with India by sea, thanks to the exploitation of the monsoon winds.[2]

For the Indian kings Caesar Augustus was one of the great rulers of the world. Even if Roman military power was too remote to assist

North Sea

BRITANNIA

GERMANIA

Atlantic Ocean

Rhein
Batavi
Cherusci
Sigambri
Ubii
Mosel
Seine
Neckar
Main
Elbe
Marcomanni
Danube

Loire

GALLIA
COMATA

LUGDUNUM   Arausio

GALLIA
NARBONENSIS

RAETIA   NORICUM

GALLIA
TRANSPADANA

VENETIA-
ET HISTRIA   PANNONIA

Drau

Astures   Cantabri

HISPANIA TARRACONENSIS

Duero

LUSITANIA

Emerita   Tajo

BAETICA

Gades

Tingis

Ebro

Barcino
Tarraco

Massilia   Forum
Iulii

LIGURIA   2●   ●3
●1

Rubicon

Salonae

ILLYRICUM

Adriatic

ETRURIA

4●   UMBRIA

Roma

●5   SAMNIUM

CORSICA

CAM
6●PANIA●7
●8
9●

Mediterranean Sea

SARDINIA

10●   ●11

12●

13

Cirta   Carthago   SICILIA

Gaetuli

AFRICA PROCONSULARIS

0   500 km

Garamantes

1 Mantua   8 Nola
2 Mutina   9 Misenum
3 Bononia   10 Tarentum
4 Perusia   11 Brundisium
5 Velitrae   12 Naulochus
6 Circei   13 Mylae
7 Beneventum

Map 1   The Roman Empire in the age of Augustus

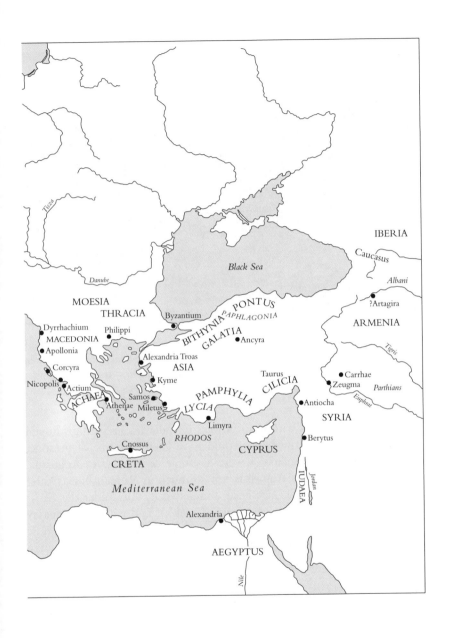

IBERIA

Caucasus

Albani

?Artagira

ARMENIA

Black Sea

MOESIA

THRACIA   Byzantium   PONTUS

                                      PAPHLAGONIA

Dyrrhachium   Philippi   BITHYNIA   GALATIA

MACEDONIA   Ancyra

Apollonia   Alexandria Troas   Carrhae

Corcyra   ASIA   Zeugma   *Parthians*

Nicopolis   Actium   Kyme   Taurus   CILICIA

        ACHAEA   PAMPHYLIA   Antiocha

    Athenae   Samos   LYCIA   SYRIA

            Miletus   Berytus

                    Limyra   CYPRUS

        Cnossus   *RHODOS*

CRETA

Mediterranean Sea   IUDAEA

                    Alexandria

            AEGYPTUS

Tisza

Danube

Tigris

Euphrat

Jordan

Nile

Figure 1   The Forum Romanum from the slope of the Capitol. In the foreground is the temple of Saturn (the public treasury); in the right background the three surviving columns of the temple of Castor stand out against the Palatine hill.

Poros in any struggles with rival powers in India (as he perhaps hoped it would), Augustus' friendship would have been a source of prestige, as indeed the Indian embassies were a source of prestige to Augustus. Poros may have viewed Augustus not so much as Roman but as ruler of that world which had once been dominated by Alexander the Great and with which he shared a language, Greek. If and when his embassy returned, they would have had much to tell him of the people who now ruled in place of Alexander and his Macedonians and what was Roman rather than Greek. The writing of ethnographies, accounts of foreign peoples and their societies, especially the more exotic, was one aspect of the reaction of Greeks and later Romans to the alien world around them.[3] We do not know if the Indians wrote anything similar. If such a work about the Romans or Greeks existed, it would be immensely precious as an account of Western civilization at that time by a complete outsider. For a European to write now an ethnography of the Romans in Augustus' time is to be an outsider in time but not in space nor entirely in culture. The envoys can be no more than a starting-point – what they might have written lies beyond even speculation; for the present reader modern research and modern perceptions are more relevant. Nevertheless this book's priorities, I hope, will be those that the envoys' might have been: to pick out the important sources of Roman wealth and strength, to suggest what it was like to live among them, and to stress the features of their society that would have seemed exotic to a foreigner.

First Impressions

The embassy did not sail, as traders from India regularly did, up the Red Sea to Berenice or Myos Hormos on the east coast of Egypt,[4] but arrived in Syria. They probably had sailed into the Persian Gulf (called by the Romans Arabian) and then followed the Euphrates from southern Mesopotamia (now Iraq) up to Zeugma – the town at the river-crossing, where the Euphrates emerges from the mountains, which is little more than 100 miles from the Mediterranean coast. The eastern bank of the river was the westernmost outpost of Rome's powerful neighbors, the Parthians, a northern Iranian people whose Arsacid dynasty had taken over the control of what is now Iran and Iraq in the second century BC from the Macedonian dynasty of Seleucids, who were descended from one of Alexander the Great's successors. As the Indians journeyed from there to Samos, Athens, and then presumably Rome, they would have noticed the characteristic Mediterranean landscape and cultivation – olives, vines, nut-trees, aromatic plants – and realized the importance of that sea for the empire. They would also have been conscious of a compression of space, a compactness of civilization compared with the vast distances of the Iranian empire and Indian subcontinent, accentuated by the multiplicity of cities.

Roman rule had initially spread from the peninsula of Italy to the other peninsulas, islands, and coasts of the Mediterranean. Before 100 BC the greatest territorial acquisitions had been in the Iberian peninsula and Anatolia (modern Turkey). More recently Julius Caesar's conquest of Gaul had created a continental empire as far as the English Channel and the Rhine, and Augustus himself was about to extend this to the east as far as the Danube. Nevertheless, it remained to a great extent a maritime empire or, more precisely, one based on water. In North Africa, Roman rule was limited by the Sahara, except in Egypt, where, south of the Delta, the Nile provided a narrow salient of civilization, for the most part no more than a few miles wide on either side of the river, whence a road led from Coptos east through the mountains to the stone quarries and the Red Sea. In the East, Roman rule was limited by the Euphrates and the Arabian desert. Expansion to the north had in part been facilitated by the great rivers of western Europe, especially impressive when compared with those of peninsular Italy and Greece. Indeed when Augustus'commanders conquered the Balkans, they seem to have accomplished this by an initial advance to the Danube and then the exploitation of its tributaries south and westward back toward the Mediterranean.[5]

Mediterranean civilization had been chiefly based on an abundance of towns or cities (the main exception was the complex of habitation associated with a great temple, found in Egypt and other parts of the Near East). Cities had grown up in the Greek world, early Italy, and among the Semitic peoples of the eastern Mediterranean; thence they had spread through Greek and Phoenician settlement to Sicily, North Africa, Spain, the shores of the Adriatic, and southern Gaul. However, it was not simply a matter of colonization: urban settlement was also the practice of those Iberians and Celts who were nearer their Greek and Phoenician neighbors. Even later in the course of Roman history Gaul south of Lugdunum (Lyon) was characterized by a far greater number of towns than the north. As they journeyed through Mesopotamia the Indian envoys would have had some foretaste of this through the Greek cities there, especially in the south and near the border-crossing in the northwest. These were not simply collections of people living and trading together but had civic institutions. The Parthian authorities dealt with them in much the same way as a Roman emperor dealt with his subordinate cities, as we can see from a letter of Artaban III to Susa (Seleuceia on the Eulaios) of 21 AD.[6] Nevertheless the increase in number of cities as the envoys traveled westward through the Roman empire would have been striking.

This was also an empire where commerce was essential. Several areas were not regularly self-sufficient in basic foodstuffs, and even those which were would not have been self-sufficient in raw materials. Sources of metal were widely dispersed; good-quality timber was not universally available. Civilization, moreover, had created its own demands in more specialized raw materials (for example fine stone for architecture and sculpture), luxury foodstuffs, and manufactured goods. Movement, on the other hand, though frequent, was not fast. Merchant vessels reached a considerable size; freighters of 350–500 tons were not unusual and there were some monstrous vessels. However, their average speeds over a long journey, even under favorable conditions, would barely reach four knots. Though it is wrong to think that the lateeen rig was unknown to the Romans, and something similar could be achieved by a brailed spritsail, we do not know how frequently these rigs were used. When Pliny gave estimates of the number of days' sail Ceylon (Sri Lanka) was from the Ganges, it was 20 days for "boats of papyrus and the rigging found on the Nile," compared with seven days for "our ships." The papyrus boats may have been rigged like a modern felucca. They were presumably considerably shorter than "our ships," which would explain their comparative lack of speed. A square-rigged vessel tacking against the wind would have found it difficult to point higher than 75° to it. The galleys of war-fleets, mainly under oars, would travel faster over short distances, but over a long journey would not exceed three knots.[7]

Some winds in the Mediterranean could be anticipated with considerable regularity. For example in the warmer months the hot air rising over the Sahara sucks in cooler air from the north, producing a variety of northerlies depending on the region: the Greek *bora* or *meltemi*, the *tramontana*, and the mistral. From time to time there is a reaction from North Africa in the form of a strong and arid southerly, the sirocco. It was thus difficult to sail into the northern Aegean, up the Adriatic, or up the Tyrrhenian in the summer, but the winds could assist voyages east and west along the length of the Mediterranean. In the winter the eastward procession of Atlantic depressions over this sea created winds that were both violent and of swifly varying direction, making sailing a more unpredictable and dangerous business.

Heavy and bulky merchandise would have been moved by water as far as possible. For communication by land there were a number of well-maintained roads. The Indians on their journey would have followed one of the main routes of the old Persian empire of the Achaemenids into Syria and, if they had wished, they could have pursued it westward over the Taurus mountains into central Anatolia and thence down the Maeander valley to Ephesus. The Romans built or rebuilt roads in a characteristic fashion in the areas that came under their control. These roads consisted of a linear mound (*agger*) running between two ditches, whose base would include large stones for drainage. Superimposed on the *agger* were close-packed layers of gravel, flint, or other material, which might be surmounted with paving stones (those with a basalt surface are particularly durable). This raised the surface of the road high above possible flooding.

The Romans' conquest of Italy was accompanied and facilitated by these arteries. Major roads had also been built outside Italy under the Republic. After his conquest of southern Gaul in 121 BC, Cn. Domitius Ahenobarbus built the *via Domitia* from the Rhône to the Col de Perthus in the Pyrenees, and it was extended down the Spanish coast to Cartagena

(New Carthage); one of his milestones can be seen in the museum at Narbonne (Narbo Martius). In the same period the proconsul Gnaeus Egnatius turned into a Roman road the artery that ran from the Adriatic over the Pindus mountains eastward into central Macedonia (near modern Thessaloniki).[8] This was subsequently extended through eastern Macedonia and Thrace to Byzantium and the crossing over the Bosphorus into Asia Minor. More recently, in Gaul, Caesar Augustus's most distinguished marshal, and later son-in-law, Marcus Agrippa, had built a road along the east bank of the Rhône and then northwards, which ultimately reached the English Channel, and another from Lyon to Aquitaine.[9] Many others were constructed during Augustus' reign. Their milestones commemorate the commander and the legions responsible for their construction. However important they might be commercially, the primary purpose of the roads was to facilitate the movement of troops and those on official business. This is especially clear from a road like the Augustan *via Sebaste* in Asia Minor (Pisidia), which improved communication in an area hard to control, or that in the semi-desert at the edge of the Sahara leading from the legionary winter-quarters at Tacape (Gabès) to Capsa (Gafsa) and beyond.[10]

The legions marched; others rode or used one of several types of two- or four-wheeled carriage; goods traveled in carts. No long or relatively fast journey would have been possible without relays of horses, mules, or other animals. The Achaemenid dynasty had established in the Persian empire a system of requisitioning men and beasts, which the Greeks had inherited and called *angareia* – used as an illustration in Christ's Sermon on the Mount.[11] Augustus developed a similar system throughout the Roman empire called the *cursus publicus* or *vehiculatio*. This is best attested in a series of inscribed documents from the first three centuries AD, which show Roman authorities seeking to repress abuses of the system. The earliest, from the beginning of the reign of Augustus' successor Tiberius, is an edict of Sextus Sotidius Strabo, governor of Galatia, found at Burdur (Sagalassus in Pisidia) in Asia Minor, which illustrates both this system and road transport in that area: "The people of Sagalassus must provide a service of ten carts and the same number of mules for the legitimate purposes of people passing through and receive from the users ten *asses* [bronze coins worth 1/16th of the silver *denarius*] per *schoenus* [i.e. a Persian parasang, roughly five miles] and four *asses* per *schoenus* for each mule." The extent of the responsibility of the Sagalassians is defined by two towns on either side. To escape this obligation, they had to pay a neighboring town or village at the same rate. This service, the edict continues, is not available to everybody. Those who can profit from it are the imperial procurator (an official in charge of finance, taxes, and imperial estates in the province), those on military service, and those with a warrant (*diploma*), using up to ten carts, or three mules in place of each cart, or two donkeys in place of each mule; a Roman senator could get one cart or its mule or donkey equivalent; a knight in the imperial service three carts or their equivalents, and so on. The service is not available for those transporting grain or anything similar for commercial purposes or for their own use.[12]

The Indians would have experienced both sea and land transport of this kind on their travels. However, their first impression was perhaps more of a question. Where were the Romans, and what made this the Roman empire? They had come from the region east of the Euphrates, where Greek and Syriac were spoken, to one where the chief languages were again Greek and another Semitic language, Aramaic. At the frontier crossing there would have been tax-collectors, mainly locals under Roman supervision, the latter perhaps invisible. No doubt there were also some soldiers nearby, but possibly only a unit of local auxiliaries under a Roman commander or soldiers detached from the legions to keep a watch on the area (*stationarii*). This was an era when, especially in potential danger areas, the legions were a field army rather than a static garrison. The Syrian legions had winter-quarters by cities like Antioch and Laodicea on the coast: in the summer they would have been frequently either carrying out minor campaigns against rebels or bandits or engaged in a construction project. At Antioch, the headquarters of the imperial *legatus* (deputy) who governed Syria, there would have been the Romans who formed his entourage and the imperial procurators and their staff. Otherwise, the nucleus of what was Roman was the new Augustan *colonia* of Berytus (Beirut), which in time would become the location of an important school of Roman law. Some Romans had no doubt settled in the province for business reasons. There were also locals who had been rewarded with Roman citizenship for services rendered, notably Seleucus from the autonomous city of Rhosos, who had served the emperor as an admiral during the preceding civil wars, and his whole family.[13] Nevertheless, in general this was a region of mixed Greek and oriental culture with a small Roman superstructure.[14]

If the envoys had moved by road westward towards their rendezvous with Augustus on Samos, they would have found an essentially Greek world but many more Romans settlers living in the towns or on their estates. These had been numerous enough 30 years before for a governor of Cilicia (Cicero) to recruit from them a substantial reinforcement for his weak legions when faced with a Parthian threat.[15] Augustus, moreover, in the course of his reign settled time-served legionaries in *coloniae* in Asia Minor. Western Asia Minor had already been full of Roman citizens in 88 BC; on one, probably exaggerated, estimate some 80,000, when King Mithridates VI of Pontus successfully invaded the area and subsequently massacred them.[16] By Augustus' time it is likely that the Romans had returned in numbers – businessmen, estate-owners, employees of the companies of tax-collectors, not to forget their agents, usually freedmen (manumitted slaves) but sometimes actually slaves. When Cicero reached Samos on the way to his province in 51 BC, he was greeted by a large reception committee of such people, as well as local Greeks to whom he was well known.[17] Indeed, his brother Quintus, while governor of the province of Asia (effectively western Asia Minor) had created a monument to their family in one of the most prestigious religious sanctuaries of the ancient world, that of the temple of Hera on Samos, only some 25 meters from the steps of the temple itself. By 20 BC the emperor Augustus and his family too were developing a close relationship with the Samians, as attested by a complex series of decrees inscribed in the sanctuary of Hera, unfortunately only preserved in fragments.[18]

It would have been a similar story at Athens, where Romans went not merely for commercial purposes but to live there as expatriates enjoying its intellectual society and ancient fame; they even became Athenian citizens and subsequently members of the oldest Athenian political and judicial council, the Areopagus. Moreover, Rome and the imperial family were making a big impact on the physical appearance of Athens. A new Roman agora was created to the east of the original Athenian one; a temple to Rome and Augustus was built to the east of the Parthenon; Marcus Agrippa was responsible for the building of the Odeion, an auditorium, on the south side of the Agora, and a monument to him was placed outside the Propylaea on the Acropolis.[19]

Only, however, when the envoys at last crossed the Adriatic to Italy, perhaps to Brundisium, would they have felt that they were in an overwhelmingly Roman world. The Latin language had by now effectively supplanted, for both public and private purposes, the varied languages once spoken in Italy; a Roman pattern of town-planning and public architecture had largely come to dominate local traditions. The same process was occurring in North Africa and the western provinces, though there the speaking of local languages had not been eliminated. Above all there was the city of Rome itself which the emperor had been rebuilding so that it could appear worthy to be a capital of the world and strike awe into foreign visitors. As the Greek friend of Augustus, the geogra-

Figure 2 The northwest end of the Forum Romanum. In the foreground are the Augustan Rostra. Behind this are the temple of Saturn (left) and the Republican basilica, now known as the Tabularium, incorporated into a medieval palace (right background).

pher Strabo wrote, "Again, if, after arriving in the old Forum, you were to see first one and yet another Forum extending beside it, and the basilicas and temples, if you were to see the Capitol and the architecture there and the building on the Palatine and in the Macellum of Livia, you could easily forget foreign places. Such is Rome."[20]

2

The Growth of
an Empire

The Beginnings of Rome[1]

Rome was a city before it was an empire, and a group of villages before
it was a city. For Romans in the age of Augustus the southwestern corner
of the Palatine hill nearest the river Tiber was associated with the beginnings of Rome. Below this there was the Lupercal shrine, the fig-tree with
the statues of the founder twins Romulus and Remus (according to some
accounts), and the cave of the shepherd Cacus, and from there a stair
was constructed to the summit, where in an area of antique cisterns and
wells a representation of the hut of Romulus was still exhibited. Modern
archeology has revealed post-holes from the eighth century BC in the tufa
here, a few yards away from the site Augustus chose for his residence.[2]
The man who refounded Rome became a neighbor of Romulus by buying
at least two late-Republican houses and combining the resulting property
with a new temple complex dedicated to Apollo (the temple podium is
an infill into part of a house).[3]

   In fact evidence of human presence in the form of burials on the
Palatine and Esquiline hills and in the area of the later Forum Romanum,
most strikingly in the form of urns shaped like huts, goes back well
beyond the eighth century. The physical evidence for the creation of a
city, however, is later. Although the Palatine hill had in the eighth
century what seems to be a boundary wall and ditch, it was only toward
the end of the seventh century that the marshy area of the Forum
Romanum (which was a receptacle for the water running off the surrounding hills) was drained, infilled, and acquired a gravel paving. In the
century following, the evidence for public and private building increases:
the earliest *comitium* (assembly area) at the northwest end of the Forum;
at the opposite end the earliest versions of the *regia*, the royal house,
later the headquarters of the *pontifex maximus* (chief pontiff); the first
temple in the Forum Boarium under the Capitoline hill on the site of the

later temples dedicated to Fortuna and Mater Matuta; grand houses with lower stories in stone at the foot of the Palatine on the Sacred Way; shrines on the Palatine itself; and the first temple to Jupiter on the Capitoline hill. We can infer from this an organized and urbanized society ruled by a king. Terracotta architectural decorations found at Rome show men in chariots or on horseback, presumably the city's aristocracy. There is evidence for heavily armed infantrymen, like the Greek hoplite, in similar decorations from neighboring Latium and Etruria, and it seems likely that these too would have been part of the Roman army at the time.[4] In what was then the Roman countryside some two miles north of the center of ancient Rome the remains of a farmhouse have been found, which was expanded at the end of the sixth century to become an impressive country residence. This shows that the so-called Roman villa had its origins at the end of the regal period.[5]

The word *rex* (king) appears on the foot of a broken bowl found on the site of the *regia*. Other examples of an archaic form of the Latin language survive on stone, metal, and pottery from Rome and elsewhere in Latium.[6] Ancient Latium was an area of coastal plain extending southeastward from the Tiber, incorporating on its northeastern boundary the territories of Tibur (Tivoli) and Praeneste (Palestrina) at the edge of the mountains of central Italy, and to the southeast the Alban hills. The language of its peoples, Latin, was but one of the Italic dialects spoken over most of the rest of the peninsula. The Latin peoples had originally a joint military organization, permitted intermarriage and migration between cities, and shared some legal practices and religious cults – the last best exemplified now by the double row of altars at Lavinium (Pratica del Mare), which are oriented on a line pointing to the summit of the Alban hills, itself the site of the cult of Jupiter Latiaris and the great spring festival of the Latins. Lavinium has also produced fourth-century BC dedications to "Lar Aeneas" and "the *kouroi* Castor and Pollux," the Greek heroes regularly identified with the Roman house-gods called *penates*. About 100 meters east of the altars a seventh-century funerary mound, reconstructed in the fourth century, has been identified as a *heroon*, a shrine dedicated to a dead human being. It has been argued that the hero honored here was in fact Aeneas, the Trojan exile who was said to have settled in Latium.[7]

In a circle from the north to the southeast the Latins were hemmed in by other Italic peoples, living chiefly in the Apennines – Umbrians, Sabines, Marsians, Aequians, Volscians, Samnites – who spoke various branches of the Oscan language, which was related to Latin. To the north and west of the Tiber were the Faliscans and Etruscans, the latter

Map 2   Italy and the central Mediterranean

a league of highly developed and urbanized peoples with a reputation for war and luxurious living. Although Etruscan bore no relation to any other Italic language, Etruscan culture had similarities to that found in Latium, and Etruscan influence on Rome was as great as or greater than that of any other neighboring people. To complete the register of peoples in what is now Italy, there were Gauls, Ligurians, and Venetic peoples in the north, while in the south the native Oscans and Messapians had a frequently uneasy relationship with the Greek colonies established there, such as Taras (Tarentum), Poseidonia (Paestum), Neapolis (Naples), and Cumae.

There was no Roman history written until shortly before 200 BC. Some public record of events before that time existed in the form of a list of the consuls of the Republic, to which were attached, from a date that we cannot determine, *annales*, notices of important events of the year, such as wars, plagues, and famines. In addition the Romans possessed the texts of early laws and treaties, and monuments to great men.[8] There is not the space here to discuss properly the credibility of the version of early Roman history that had been created by Augustus' time and is accessible to us principally in the histories of Livy and Dionysius of Halicarnassus. Accounts of Rome's origins were a far from consistent texture of strands of myth or folklore which had grown up over many centuries. For a long time Romulus or Romus, the founder of Rome, was thought to be the grandson of Aeneas the Trojan exile and hero of Latium, until consideration of chronology revealed a 400-year interval between the Trojan war, reputedly in the early twelfth century, and the founding of Rome, dated to the mid-eighth. This necessitated the invention of a long line of kings of Alba Longa.[9] The history of the early Republic was to a great extent created from the stories handed down about the members of aristocratic families, perhaps in the form of ballads, certainly through the panegyrics delivered at the funerals of great men. The latter commemorated not only the man who had just died but also his ancestors and had a reputation for pious but unscrupulous invention.[10]

"Rome was once ruled by kings," is the first sentence of the *Annals* of Rome's greatest historian, Cornelius Tacitus, born some 40 years after Augustus' death in 14 AD. The statement is certainly true, but from what date kings ruled, even how many kings there were, is far from certain. Aside from the physical development of the city, which can be detected on the ground, some of the achievements ascribed to the kings by later historians are plausible: the creation of a senate from the leading men, the institution of public religion, the earliest military organization, perhaps the earliest popular assembly. It is also likely that under the kings Rome had expanded its territory in Latium so as to annex that of some immediate neighbors. However, at the maximum its boundaries then would not have been much more than 15 miles from the center of the city.

According to Roman tradition, the last three kings of Rome, including Tarquin the Proud whose family provoked the overthrow of the monarchy, were Etruscan. Etruscan tradition knew of other warrior heroes, who seem to have temporarily seized power in Rome – Aulus and Caelius Vibenna, Mastarna, even Lars Porsenna who, according to the Etruscans, was not defeated but paid to withdraw from Rome. At all events it can hardly be a coincidence that the year of the founding of the Republic that the Romans later deduced from their consular lists (509 BC) is very close to that in which the Etruscan domination of Latium was fatally weakened by Aristoboulos, the Greek tyrant of Cumae, at the battle of Aricia (505 BC). The Republic, therefore, was not merely a Rome free from monarchs but a Latin city free from Etruscan overlords. The Augustan writers portray a coup d'état that was bloodless, which may or may not be true. However, the subsequent hostility to monarchy in any shape or form implies a genuine revolution rather than a peaceful transition.[11]

In the accounts of the early Republic in the annalists there are two themes – wars against Rome's neighbors, both the peoples surrounding Latium and Rome's Latin rivals, and the conflict between the aristocracy and the plebs in the city. The themes are linked in so far as Roman historians suggested that a city, which otherwise might have torn itself apart, survived because of the need to unite against external menaces. Much of the detail must be invented reconstruction on the model of later events. The question is whether the general picture given by the annalists is true. Archeology is unfortunately of no help. We have almost nothing, neither architecture nor artefact, which can be dated to the period between the beginning of the Republic and the sack of Rome by Gauls in the early fourth century; this may in fact indicate a period of poverty and weakness after the prosperity under the Etruscan rulers.

The Institutions and Society of the Early Republic[12]

Perhaps the best evidence for the early Republic is the institutions and traditions that are found later on. In place of a permanent ruler the Romans had two elected annual senior magistrates, eventually called *consules*, whose tasks were to lead armies and preside over the civic and religious life of the city. Their insignia were an inheritance from the kings and from Etruria: the bundles of rods (*fasces*), carried by lictors, each of which, at least outside the city, included an ax. The consuls were elected in an assembly, the *comitia centuriata*, which was essentially the army, organized in centuries and with a relative preponderance given to the cavalry and the more wealthy infantrymen. Monarchy was placed under a curse; a *rex* could be killed on sight with impunity, and the same fate awaited anyone judged to have similar aspirations. So, according to a tradition that was still invoked at the end of the Republic (the assassination of Julius Caesar is one instance), populist leaders who had done nothing treasonable but were suspected of pursuing personal power were killed with or without any form of legal process.

The Romans did, however, invent a temporary supreme magistrate, called the *dictator*, mainly to deal with military emergencies. Such a man was expected to abdicate as soon as the particular crisis was over and, until the late Republic, always held office for less than a year. Other magistracies of the people were allegedly created in the first century and a half of the Republic: the *praetor* as junior colleague of the consuls with military and judicial functions; two (*curule*) *aediles*, matching the two chosen by the plebs (see below), to care for the fabric and people of the city; *quaestores* to assist senior magistrates with a particular care for finance; two *censores* – the one regular magistracy that was not annual – to produce a census of the population and wealth of the citizen body and to register the more important in their appropriate rank (*ordo*).

Even in the annalists there is no evidence of a major division in the citizen body under the kings. However, the aristocratic families that seized power from them and constituted the senate (or *patres*, fathers) of the new Republic, seem to have swiftly sought to entrench a class distinction, in order to separate themselves, the patricians (*patricii*), from the rest of the citizen body, the *plebs*. Conflict arose allegedly from economic oppression, debt, and shortage of land among the plebeians, who could not be ignored because they constituted the bulk of the army. Apart from smaller disputes, the plebeians are said to have "seceded" on three occasions (the word *se-cessio*, like *se(d)-itio*, means simply "going apart"). The first time, in 494 BC, they went from the city itself to a hill just outside Rome (either the Mons Sacer to the northeast or the Aventine to the southwest). In their new base they elected *tribuni*, tribunes of the plebs, to act as their spokesmen and swore an oath to take the life of anyone who physically harmed these tribunes.

Under this protection the tribunes were termed sacrosanct, and in due course they exploited this immunity to interpose their persons in order to block the acts of patrician magistrates, whether as a form of political obstruction or as a defense for citizens when they were under threat of physical coercion by a magistrate or his attendants. Appeals for this sort of protection are associated in our sources with what the Romans termed *provocatio*, which seems in origin to have been a cry for help and physical support, directed to people in general, but, after it was eventually backed by statute in 300 BC, became a guarantee for the citizen against execution without trial, at least in theory. This right was to be extended by a law of Marcus Porcius Cato in the second century to include a total ban on the flogging of citizens in civilian life. *Provocatio*, as recognized by the law, was regarded as one of the cornerstones of republican liberty.

The office of tribune developed over a long period. Their number was increased from two to 10; these were given two assistants called *aediles*, who looked after the more material concerns of the plebs. The tribunes came to hold assemblies both informally and, formally, in order to hold elections, pass resolutions (*plebiscita*), and to prosecute offenders against the rights of the plebs. They were eventually allowed to attend meetings of the senate and declare their opposition to decrees of that body which they did not approve. The Hortensian law, enacted after the third secession of 287 BC, is normally regarded as the end of the "Struggle of the Orders," in that it granted to plebiscites the same authority as statutes enacted in assemblies of all the citizens.

Perhaps the one completely authentic source on Roman society in the fifth and fourth centuries would have been the first and only comprehensive law code of the Republic, the Twelve Tables, drawn up by a commission of 10 (the *decemviri*).[13] This generated a wealth of colorful stories in the annalists. They represent it as a reaction to plebeian agitation, but one that did not operate ultimately in the plebeian interest. For it introduced *inter alia* a total ban on intermarriage between patricians and plebeians. The commission, so it was said, extended its office into a second year and became tyrannical. It was only overthrown by a second secession of the plebs to the Aventine and (according to Cicero) a return under arms to seize the Capitol. The office and powers of the tribunes of the plebs had to be reintroduced afterwards. Unfortunately, the text of the laws survives only imperfectly in quotations and paraphrases by later sources. On this evidence the code was concerned primarily with relationships between individual citizens, what Romans called the civil law. It did not supersede certain earlier laws, on homicide and religion, which Romans ascribed to the kings.

The legal procedure the code prescribed reflected the extra-legal procedures which existed previously for settling disputes. Private force was accepted as a remedy in an emergency: one could kill on the spot a thief who came by night or by day with a weapon, though one was expected to call on one's neighbors to assist and bear witness to the justice of the reprisal. Private force was also recognized as a means of bringing a man to court and of punishment or compensation, whether by the "eye for eye" procedure of the *lex talionis* or private imprisonment for some thieves and debtors. Society was by then clearly based on the individual household and nuclear family, though some importance still lay with wider groupings. The code provided for inheritance by will, but there were inevitably also rules for intestate succession: in that case the estate was divided among the so-called *sui heredes*, the children and the wife of a deceased man, the latter only if she had been subject to her husband's power; if these did not exist, the estate fell to the males in the father's line or, if there were none, the members of the *gens*, those who shared the deceased's family name. We find rules for relationships between neighbors, boundary walls, overhanging trees, and, for the city, the width of roads between properties. There is also the earliest reference to the characteristic form of Roman verbal contract, the *sponsio*, a solemn promise requested in a formula called *stipulatio*, which was to be the foundation of much of Roman commercial law. Other provisions reflect more particularly fifth-century society, for example the penalty for moving crops from a field by magic or that against *occentatio*, the Roman equivalent of "rough music," that is, organized chants that defamed and threatened an unpopular person.[14]

The establishment of written law is an important step in the development of any society, since it restricts the arbitrariness of magistrates and judges and makes justice public property. How far the Twelve Tables actually benefitted the *plebs* is another matter. The ban on intermarriage between patricians and plebeians was to be repealed within a few years. The rules about property were for propertied persons. The law about debtors was harsh: "on the third market-day let them cut the parts." Even if there were no actual Shylock-like dissection, debtors could be retained in bonds or sold as slaves across the Tiber. Above all, access to the law remained difficult for the majority of the plebs, while elements in procedural law, as opposed to substantive law, remained unpublished until, at the end of the fourth century, Gnaeus Flavius, an aedile who had worked as a scribe, took action. Before that time all but the aristocracy would have been to some degree dependent on the patronage of their superiors. Relations between patrons and clients were a vital part of Roman society then as later. The Twelve Tables enacted that the patron who injured a client was *sacer* – outlawed and liable to be killed on sight. It is not clear, however, how this was to be proved. Another problem is how to reconcile patronage with the conflict between patricians and plebs; here the easiest solution is to suppose that patronage was not confined to patricians but was also exercised by wealthy plebeians. It is in any case true that a man could be both a patron of others and himself a client of someone superior to him.

The Conquest of Italy[15]

Roman annalists filled their texts on the early Republic with accounts of wars. There can be little doubt that in that period the Romans frequently engaged in fighting. The details of a few wars were elaborated in legend, for example that in which the Roman exile Coriolanus joined a Volscian army in attacking Rome or that in which the Fabii as a clan tried to stem an attack from Etruscan Veii. For the rest, even if we accept the fact of a war, we must admit that we can really know little or nothing about it, not even the result of most of them. In many wars the Romans must have participated as members of the Latin League, not necessarily under the supreme command of a Roman. Perhaps the best evidence for this are the early dates ascribed to certain Latin *coloniae* (fortress settlements) in southern Latium or Volscian territory, such as Antium (Anzio), Cora, and Norba, which implies that they were Latin, not Roman foundations. However, at the end of the fifth century the capture or recapture from the Etruscans of Fidenae near the east bank of the Tiber is likely to have been a purely Roman affair, as was the much more important capture in the early fourth century of Veii, a powerful city beyond the Tiber in southern Etruria but only some 10 miles from the center of Rome. Veii was systematically looted and almost totally destroyed; its territory, probably stretching to Lake Bracciano to the north, became Roman public land which could be used to satisfy the needs of the Roman people as a whole, including the plebeians.

However, before full advantage could be taken of this, a historical accident led to a crisis that nearly overwhelmed the city. In 387/6 (according to the chronology of the second-century Greek historian Polybius; that of the later antiquarian Varro gave 390) a group of Celtic warriors, intending to take mercenary service with Dionysius I, tyrant of Syracuse, came southward through Italy. They attacked Etruscan Clusium, defeated a Roman army at the river Allia, 11 miles north of Rome, and captured the city apart from the Capitoline hill. When they had acquired enough booty they moved on, leaving the sacked city to be recovered by Marcus Furius Camillus and an army of those who had previously escaped. This disaster, which produced an ingrained hostility at Rome to Celtic peoples, was also a stimulus to political and military activity which transformed the Republic.

The Romans rebuilt their city, providing it for the first time with a circuit wall about seven miles long (the so-called Servian wall, parts of which can be seen today, and which is constructed from tufa from the Grotta Oscura in Veientine territory). After a period of agitation they opened the consulship to plebeians and created the magistracies of praetor and curule aedile: these changes were the starting–point for a series of constitutional and religious reforms occurring at intervals down to 287, which eliminated patrician dominance of magistracies and priest-hoods. The tribunes, who in the 360s had secured the access of plebeians to the consulship, also introduced restrictions on an individual's exploi-tation of public land for agriculture and grazing, in order to make that land as widely available as possible. As for debt there is evidence for statutes on usury and interest rates and for a *lex Poetelia*, usually ascribed to the late fourth century, which forbad voluntarily contracted debt-servitude. However, such servitude to a creditor could still result from a legal judgment, and indebtedness remained a problem. The final seces-sion of the *plebs* to the Janiculum hill in 287, which led to plebiscites being recognized as binding on both patricians and plebeians without further ratification, is said to have arisen from a crisis over debt.

This same century after the Gallic sack was also a period of astonish-ing Roman expansion abroad, such that the city became dominant over most of peninsular Italy. Initially Rome came under attack from both non-Latin and rival Latin neighbors, as well as from further Gallic raids. Military victories enabled Rome to remodel the Latin League as an organization subordinate to itself and to acquire new dependent cities both southeast of Latium and in Etruria. The most dramatic develop-ment, however, arose from its relations with the Samnites, an Oscan-speaking people composed of at least four tribes, who lived in the central Apennines, and with the cities of Campania, the region south of the river Volturnus with its fertile plain and volcanic coastline, then inhabited by a mixture of Greeks, as at Neapolis (Naples), and Oscan-speaking Sabellians. The Romans were guilty of double-dealing, as even our Roman source, Livy, admits, first defending the Campanians against their former allies the Samnites and then resuming this alliance to the detriment of the Campanians. The Campanians revolted in conjunction with discontented Latin cities but were defeated in 340 and two years later a new settlement was imposed on the Latins and Campanians.

Some Latin cities were simply absorbed into Roman territory, becom-ing country towns in a state whose capital was Rome. The warships of Latin Antium (Anzio) became Rome's first fleet, apart from those whose *rostra* (beaks, i.e. rams) were used to decorate the speakers' platform in the Forum Romanum. Other cities retained at this time both a domestic independence and their close interrelation with Roman society as Latins: the chief elements in this were intermarriage, the right to migrate, and the right to acquire land in the territory of other Latin cities and to behave in legal matters like a citizen of those other cities. Needless to say, in external relations Latin cities were subordinate to Rome. A new status, the *municipium*, was devised for the Campanians and Volscian cities outside Latium. Their people had the private rights of Roman citizens, but not the public rights of voting and holding public office. They did, however, have the public duties of Romans, especially service in the Roman army. Their administration seems originally to have retained some local independence, but eventually they were expected to conform to Roman practice and became subject to Roman law.

In this way the Romans created a complex and flexible system for both the articulation of their existing power and the management of further expansion, the effectiveness of which was demonstrated in the next 50 years or so. They readily used their increased manpower in further wars up and down the peninsula, which in theory were defensive – they were either protecting their own territory or that of new allies, many of whom had been required to hand their territory over formally to the Romans – but in fact led to the subordination in different degrees both of their defeated enemies and their new allies. In the territory they subjected they established as strong-points either Roman *coloniae* (small fortresses of Roman citizens) or Latin *coloniae*, new cities with a similar relationship to Rome as the surviving members of the old Latin League. These colonies and other schemes for land distribution enabled many Romans and Latins to acquire new homes. Other foreign cities could be turned into Roman *municipia* like those of the Campanians, or left as allies under treaties which bound them in varying degrees of subordination to give military aid to Rome.

Roman expansion was also facilitated by technical advances. Apparently learning from their conflicts with the peoples of the Apennines, they created an infantry army, in which the three main ranks had a screen of skirmishers in front; only the last rank had the heavy spear such as was used by the Greek hoplite, the two front ranks having a lighter spear which could be used for either throwing or thrusting. Military movement was facilitated by the earliest road-building (see chapter 1 above): the *via Appia* running southeast to Campania was begun by the censor Appius Claudius in 312, the *via Valeria* eastward through the Apennines by the censors of 307. In one of the colonies that guarded the roads (Terracina, founded 327) there is the earliest evidence for centuriation, the orthogonal land division that is characteristic of Roman settlement and is still to be seen embedded in the landscape today.

Physical evidence for Roman life in this period is comparatively scarce, but significant: the Servian wall; the subterranean remains of the first aqueduct, the Aqua Appia named after the censor of 312; the remodeling of the *comitium* in the Forum; the rebuilding of the Forum Boarium sanctuary as two temples; the earliest phases of two temples in the "Field of Mars" (now to be found in the Largo Argentina) and of the temples of Hercules Invictus and Portunus near the Tiber. The clan of the Cornelii, who, unlike most Romans, inhumed rather than cremated their dead, are represented by some imposing sarcophagi. There are impressive examples of bronze-working from Latium: the boxes (*cistae*) engraved with mythological scenes (they are associated especially with Praeneste, but one of the finest was made at Rome) and engraved bronze mirrors of similar workmanship to the more common Etruscan products. Good-quality decorated and black-glaze pottery was produced at Rome by the early third century. Perhaps third-century also is a fragment of a historical wall-painting from a tomb on the Esquiline, the earliest Roman example of this form of decoration. The Romans were far from being a purely agricultural society, uninfluenced by the culture of more sophisticated peoples such as the Greeks and Etruscans. However, their greatest achievements in this period were the resolution of internal conflict and their phenomenal expansion, each in this period assisting the other.

In the 20 years from 310 to 290 Rome faced a series of challenges to its rising power from Etruscans, Umbrians, Gauls, and Samnites, which left her in a dominant position in most of peninsular Italy, including Lucania and Apulia in the south. A major revolt by Etruscans and Gauls in 284 was put down after two years' fighting. Meanwhile Rome supported an oligarchic faction in the Greek city of Thurii against democrats backed by not only the city's Greek neighbor Taras (Tarentum) but by a coalition of Samnites, Bruttians, and Lucanians who wished to drive Rome from the south of Italy. The Romans were successful in the field and were seeking to negotiate a settlement with the Tarentines in 281, when the latter decided to protect their independence by summoning Pyrrhus, king of Epirus, and his army from the other side of the Adriatic.

The war that followed, though it was to an extent eclipsed in importance by the later conflicts with Carthage and in the east, may be rightly regarded as the one that redefined Rome as a Mediterranean power. Pyrrhus, was one of the Macedonian "successors" who had contested over the empire of Alexander the Great; he had at one point even been ruler of Macedonia itself. His army was modeled on those that had marched with Alexander as far as Samarkand and the Indus and included elephants. Of course, Greek colonies had existed in Italy since before the time Rome became properly a city, and both Greek and oriental cultural influences in Rome and Latium are a datum throughout the city's history; Spartan armies had even campaigned west of the Adriatic. Nevertheless, Italy, although it allegedly had formed part of Alexander's "last plans," had remained isolated from Alexander's power and the ambition of his successors. The Romans, on the other hand, could not have been ignorant of the Macedonian-dominated world, though our sure evidence for Roman and Italian traders in Greece and the eastern Mediterranean is from later in the century. However, there is evidence for diplomatic relations with the island of Rhodes from around 300 BC and the Pyrrhic war was to bring similar contact with Egypt in 273.[16] By fighting to drive Pyrrhus from the west, the Romans confirmed themselves as the leaders of Italy and acquired the rank of a Mediterranean power.

The Subjection of the Western Mediterranean[17]

The story of the defeat of Pyrrhus became an important element in Roman historical mythology. Initially the king was victorious, though allegedly at the cost of heavy losses in men (but Roman and Greek estimates of the casualties vary greatly). After defeating the Romans at Heraclea in southern Italy in 280 he marched as far as Praeneste (Palestrina) in Latium. Here he offered terms, the liberation by the Romans of the Samnites, Lucanians, and the Greek cities and their acceptance of his own hegemony, but the senate, encouraged by the aged and blind Appius Claudius (the censor of 312), rejected them. A further victory by Pyrrhus the next year at Ausculum was followed by another offer of peace, also rejected. Rome instead made a new alliance with the city of Carthage (now a seaside suburb of modern Tunis; see figures 4a and 4b) which had dependent cities in Sicily. Further campaigning by Gaius Fabricius restricted Pyrrhus to southern Italy and induced him to turn his energies to aiding the Greek cities of Sicily against Carthage. Here he was unsuccessful and unpopular with his allies and, after returning to Italy, he was at last defeated in 275 by Manius Curius at Beneventum. Tarentum eventually fell to the Romans in 272. One of those captured and taken to Rome as slaves was a boy who was to be educated there and subsequently liberated. He became the first Roman to write plays and poetry following Greek models, Livius Andronicus.

Rhegium (Reggio di Calabria) and Messana (Messina) were two Greek cities which faced each other across the narrow but dangerous straits between Italy and Sicily. The former had been seized by some Campanian mercenaries, theoretically fighting for Rome against Pyrrhus, but it was recaptured and its captors executed in 270 BC. Meanwhile Messana had also been seized by Campanians, formerly in mercenary service with the tyrant of Syracuse Agathocles. The new king of Syracuse, Hiero II, tried to expel them, and in 265 they appealed for help both to Carthage and to Rome. Before the Romans could take a decision, the citadel of Messana was handed over to the Carthaginians. Up to this point Carthage would have regarded itself as the single most powerful city in the western Mediterranean. Founded by the Phoenicians, according to the archeological record in the eighth century, the city's people spoke a Semitic language and had Phoenician religious cults, political institutions, and social practices, but had also been influenced by the Greeks. Carthage's wealth was based on a rich agricultural hinterland and the city's prime location for commerce. It had contested control of Sicily with Greek Syracuse, was dominant in Sardinia, and had links with the Phoenician cities in Spain. Its commercial and diplomatic relations with Italian cities including Rome went back at least to the sixth century. When Rome decided in the end to assist the Campanian mercenaries, it broke a long-lasting peaceful relationship.

The senate, we are told, were afraid that Carthage would dominate all Sicily (as indeed it had in the early fourth century) and would be a dangerous neighbor across the straits. On the other hand they persuaded the assembly to back the war by pointing to the profits that would accrue and compensate for the people's sufferings in recent campaigns. Neither side could have expected that 23 years would elapse before a final peace treaty, thus making this the longest continuous war in ancient Mediterranean history. Most of the fighting took place in the first 15 years. Hiero originally supported the Carthaginians, but, after Messana was liberated by the Romans and they went on to besiege Syracuse, he changed sides. The Greek city of Agrigentum was liberated from Carthage after a long siege and the Romans decided to take the campaign to the west of the island previously dominated by Carthage. Up to this time Rome's war-fleet had been provided by its allies, such as Neapolis, Velia, Locri, and Tarentum, but under Roman command. However, now the Romans judged it impossible to obtain and secure control of all Sicily without a fleet of their own. A large fleet was rapidly built, using a captured Carthaginian vessel as model – a plausible story, inasmuch as we know that Punic ships were built from prefabricated parts.[18] At the same time crews were apparently trained on land to row. The Romans, however, introduced an innovation, a spiked gangplank called a *corvus* (crow), which enabled them to lock ships together and thus board enemy vessels the more easily. This led to an initial Roman victory at Mylae under Gaius Duilius, who commemorated this with a column decorated with the rams (*rostra*) of enemy warships. The column itself unfortunately does not survive, but we possess in a damaged state an inscribed block commemorating Duilius, which seems to have been an ancient replacement for its original base.[19]

Roman progress in subduing the Punic-dominated west of Sicily by land was slow. Meanwhile Rome used its new naval capability with more boldness than success, attacking first Punic dependencies in Sardinia, then Malta, and finally the Carthaginian homeland in Africa (a move pioneered 50 years before by Agathocles, tyrant of Syracuse). Marcus Atilius Regulus successfully landed on the Cape Bon peninsula near Clupea (Kelibia), an area with an immensely productive agriculture. The coastal settlement excavated at Kerkouan, a so far unique piece of evidence for Punic urban life outside Carthage, was destroyed about this time. However, the following year Regulus was induced to risk a pitched battle in the plain against a Punic force with good cavalry and elephants (the Carthaginians had taken advice from a visiting Spartan mercenary). Defeated, Regulus became first a prisoner, then a Punic envoy to Rome, and finally a myth on account of his return to Carthage and death there after dissuading his compatriots from making peace. By 249 Rome controlled most of Sicily: only two Punic cities, Lilybaeum (Marsala) and Drepanum (Trapani) held out. However, they had suffered heavy losses at sea not only through the Carthaginians but their own bad seamanship. There was then a stalemate for several years, while both sides rebuilt fleets; the Romans through shortage of public money used a private finance initiative. Finally, under Gaius Lutatius Catulus, they secured a decisive naval victory at the Aegatian Isles west of Sicily in 242.

The peace treaty required the Carthaginians to evacuate Sicily and the islands between Sicily and Italy, to cease war with Syracuse, and to pay Rome an indemnity of 2,200 silver talents. However, worse was to come for Carthage. Because it had not the money to pay off its mercenaries, they revolted with the support of some African cities, formerly subject allies of Carthage. The resulting bloodthirsty conflict, the subject of Flaubert's novel *Salammbo*, lasted more than three years. Hiero of Syracuse backed Carthage; the Romans remained neutral, but in 238, when the Punic mercenaries in Sardinia offered to surrender the island to them, they accepted and punished Carthaginian protests by declaring war and exacting a further indemnity of 1,000 talents. The Romans then began a decade of campaigning in Sardinia and Corsica which led to the full subjection of these islands. Meanwhile Hamilcar Barca, the last Punic land commander in Sicily who had himself remained undefeated, had been sent out to govern the Carthaginian dependencies in Spain, taking with him his nine-year-old son Hannibal.

According to Polybius, the Greek historian of the second century BC who described Rome's rise to dominance, the experience of the first Punic war gave the Romans both the courage and capability to acquire a Mediterranean empire.[20] They had become a maritime power, in spite of the colossal loss of 700 ships. War expenditure must also have been enormous, but the indemnities imposed on Carthage would have allowed the Romans to repay their war loan and restock their treasury. Fittingly, it is in this period that we first have evidence of large-scale issues of silver and bronze coinage. Originally, like most of the Etruscan cities, the Romans used bronze bars for money. There were small issues of silver at the end of the fourth century and some silver and bronze about the time of the Pyrrhic war. After some experiment, by the 220s they were using a range of coins of full metallic value. On the reverse of the silver coins, weighing two Greek drachmas, was Jupiter driven by a goddess of victory in a four-horse chariot; the reverse type of the bronze was appropriately the prow of a warship, while among the deities on the obverse Janus, the two-faced god of money-lenders, appeared frequently.[21] The Romans had a traditional dislike of professional money-lending, but the series of laws from the fourth century onwards controlling the practice are evidence that it became recognized as a necessary evil.

The Romans attributed their second decisive war with Carthage to Hannibal and Punic revanchism; a longer view might see it as the product of Rome's own expanding horizons. Apart from its operations in Corsica and Sardinia, Rome consolidated its hold on the Adriatic coast and northern peninsular Italy. A major counterattack by the Gauls was defeated in 225; communications with the north were improved by the construction of the *via Flaminia* up the Tiber valley, across Umbria to the Adriatic, and then up the coast to the Latin *colonia* of Ariminum (Rimini), an area by then heavily settled with Roman citizens. At the beginning of the war with Hannibal in 218 the Romans were creating their first *coloniae* in Cisalpine Gaul, Cremona and Placentia (Piacenza), and a settlement at Mutina (Modena). At the other end of Italy, Brundisium (Brindisi) had become a Latin *colonia* in 244 during the first Punic war; fifteen years later the Romans intervened against the Illyrians, notorious in the Greek world for their piracy, and established a protectorate on the Dalmatian coast. However their protegé, Demetrius of Pharos, changed his allegiance in favor of Philip V of Macedon and the Romans duly expelled him in 219, retaining the island of Pharos (Hvar) as their ally.[22]

The expansion of Punic power in Spain by Hamilcar and his successors Hasdrubal and Hannibal did not affect the Romans directly. However, it was a potential threat to a longstanding ally, the Greek city of Massilia (Marseilles), which possessed a string of trading stations in southern France and the Costa Brava, and any revival of Carthaginian power could be seen as ultimately a challenge to the Romans' new position in the western Mediterranean. In 225 they made an agreement with the then Punic commander in Spain, Hasdrubal, that he should not cross the Ebro northward under arms and about the same time they took under their protection the town of Saguntum south of that river. In 221, after the murder of Hasdrubal by a Celt, Hannibal was given the Punic command by popular acclaim and his vigorous military activity, though south of the Ebro, was eventually directed at Saguntum.

Polybius treated the second Punic war as the contest which decided who was to rule the world about which he wrote: it is still rightly regarded as one of the critical wars in world history because it was the *sine qua non* for the creation of the Roman empire. It resembled a modern world war in taking place in a number of theaters simultaneously, and had consequences that could not have been imagined by the participants at the start. It was occasioned by Hannibal's siege and capture of Saguntum in 220/19. While Polybius and other pro-Roman sources held the deeper cause to have been Punic bitterness over their losses through the first war and more particularly the desire for revenge in Hannibal's own family, Polybius admits, nonethelesss, that the Romans were anticipating a new contest with Carthage and planning to fight it in Spain with Saguntum as a base.[23] In the event they did not send help during the eight-month siege, but exploited Saguntum's capture as a breach of treaty, by sending an embassy to Carthage to demand the surrender of Hannibal and his advisers – a demarche unsurprisingly opposed by the Carthaginians. In the early summer of 218, while Rome was thus maneuvering to take the moral and religious high ground in a "just war," Hannibal was probably already over the Ebro on his march to Italy.

There were three elements in Roman policy initially, which remained important for most of the war: the defense of Italy, the control of Sicily, Sardinia, and the sea, and the disruption of Punic power in Spain. Hannibal's remarkable journey across the Pyrenees and Alps and his subsequent military success meant that for long time the Italian front eclipsed the others. Although he arrived in Italy with only 20,000 infantry, 6,000 cavalry, and a single elephant (albeit soon reinforced with Gallic allies), he was victorious in two battles in the Po valley in 218. Though inferior to the Romans in infantry, his army had superb Numidian cavalry, fine light-armed troops, and above all himself as a general. The way south now lay open: in 217 he entrapped the consular army of C. Flaminius between the mountains and Lake Trasimene and was able to march into southern Italy, though avoiding Rome. The Romans began the policy associated with Quintus Fabius Maximus of shadowing Hannibal's army without risking pitched battle, but unwisely abandoned this to suffer another crushing defeat at Cannae in Apulia (August 2, 216), which induced most of Rome's allies in the south to defect. Some historians portrayed this as the point when Hannibal could have marched on Rome and taken it. Rome, however, was even then a great city, and Hannibal did not have the resources for a long siege. We should also remember that in this war neither side aimed for the extermination of the other or even its unconditional surrender. Hannibal wanted to dismantle the Roman empire, not Rome itself.

At this time of military catastrophe Rome, according to Polybius, was saved by its political fabric. Magistrates, senate, and people worked together in a series of emergency measures.[24] To remedy the shortage of manpower both underage boys and slaves bought from their masters were recruited, while criminals and debtors were released from imprisonment to serve as soldiers. Rich men were ordered not only to supply slaves for naval service but to pay them. Military contractors were required to supply arms and clothing on credit. A limit was placed on private holdings of precious metal and jewelry, even displays of wealth by women were banned by law, and a new monetary system was devised. The bronze coinage became fiduciary, the *as* being devalued to half its weight, while a new silver coin of full metallic value, the *denarius*, was introduced: this weighed about four grams and was deemed to be worth ten *asses*.[25]

Apart from one landing of elephants, money, and grain in 215, Carthage failed to support Hannibal, partly on account of Roman naval power, partly because of alternative strategic concerns. Hasdrubal Barca was forced to defend the empire in Spain, instead of joining his brother Hannibal. The Carthaginians were successful in detaching Syracuse from its Roman allegiance after the death of Hiero in 216, but this, although it deprived Rome of important grain supplies, involved their committing forces to fight in Sicily. Hannibal made an alliance with Philip V of Macedon in 215, but, although the latter won victories in Illyria, he was unable to cross the Adriatic. In the longer run the effect of this last alliance was to draw the Romans deeper into the politics of the eastern Mediterranean. In Italy a war of attrition continued for several years. The Romans suffered another major defeat in the south and lost the port of Tarentum. In 211 after a long siege they recovered Capua and Campania, standing firm when Hannibal tried to divert the besieging army by his only direct march on Rome itself. This was a critical year in other respects. In Sicily Syracuse had fallen to the Romans after a plague broke out in the city, while in reaction to the defeat of Publius and Gnaeus Scipio in Spain the previous year, the Romans sent out the son of Publius (later surnamed Africanus), who was to be their best commander and a decisive factor in the rest of the war. In northwest Greece the Romans made an alliance with the Aetolian League in order to distract Philip from any attacks on their own territory. King Attalus I of Pergamum (in western Asia Minor) and other Greek communities were incorporated into this alliance, which for the next five years waged somewhat incoherent warfare against Philip and other Greek targets with the backing of Roman fleets.

The young Scipio embarked on an aggressive policy. In 209 he captured the Punic stronghold of New Carthage (Cartagena) and the next year he was victorious in the Baetis (Guadalquivir) valley in Andalucia. This induced Hasdrubal Barca to leave Spain in 207 to join his brother in Italy. Scipio exploited Hasdrubal's absence to win a second victory and subsequently complete the subjection of Punic Spain before returning to Rome in 206. The Punic army from Spain was no more successful in Italy. When its path was blocked at Ariminum, the Romans managed to withdraw half the army shadowing Hannibal and the combined force defeated Hasdrubal at the Metaurus river (June 23, 207). This left Hannibal still a threat but isolated in the south of Italy. The Romans and their allies were exhausted even before this victory. When Publius Scipio was elected consul for the year 205, he was given the command against Hannibal but with permission (apparently grudged by some senators) to invade Africa with a volunteer force. After securing in advance the cooperation of the Numidian prince Masinissa, with whom he had contact while the latter was serving with the Carthaginians in Spain, he landed in Africa in 204.

A Roman victory in the Bagradas (Medjerda) valley in 203 enabled Masinissa to seize the Numidian throne from the pro-Punic incumbent Syphax and induced the Carthaginians to seek terms. These were accepted at Rome but rejected at Carthage; instead Hannibal and his veteran army were summoned back to fight Scipio. Hannibal landed at Hadrumetum

(Sousse) in 202 and the decisive battle was fought on the plain of Zama, about 100 miles southwest of Carthage. The Numidian cavalry on either side fought a separate action, Hannibal's elephants were rendered innocuous, and the outcome was a long and bloody infantry battle, in which the Romans proved superior. The terms imposed were a more severe version of what had been on offer the previous year. Carthage was to give up its empire, its sovereignty being confined to what is now northern and eastern Tunisia; it was to recognize the independence of the Numidian kingdom and to subordinate its foreign policy to Rome's; its war-fleet was to be reduced to a token 10 ships and it was to pay an indemnity of 10,000 silver talents (worth 60 million *denarii*) over 50 years. Two republics with similar constitutions had fought for empire in the western Mediterranean. Naval superiority, political coherence, and sheer bloody-mindedness had saved Rome; ultimately manpower, strategic imagination, and tactical effectiveness in some close-fought land battles gave it victory also.

The Dominance of the Eastern Mediterranean[26]

Although the Romans had made peace with Philip V of Macedon in 205, they still regarded him with great suspicion. There were claims that he was still meddling with Roman allies in Illyria and that Macedonian volunteers had aided Hannibal at Zama. In the event, within two years of their treaty with Carthage they were at war with him again, profiting from the opportunity offered by the unstable relations between the great powers in the eastern Mediterranean world. The result of this was to be a reorientation of Rome's international relations such that for 50 years it was to be more concerned with that world than with the western Mediterranean it had so recently conquered. Polybius thought that from one point of view the establishment of Roman dominion over his world was the work of fortune (*tuchê*).[27] This makes sense, if we understand it as the outcome of the meshing of various sequences of events through coincidence in time and space.

The throne of one of the great powers, Egypt, had passed in 203/2 to a minor, Ptolemy V Epiphanes. Wishing to exploit this, the monarchs of the two chief rival powers, Philip V and Antiochus III of Syria, made an agreement not to obstruct one another in extending their respective empires over cities in the Aegean and Asia Minor. Antiochus' planned expansion was to be at the expense of Egypt, which had helped Rome with grain in the second Punic war, and of Rhodes, a longstanding friend of Rome; Philip's most directly threatened Rhodes. Both kings' aims were against the interests of Attalus I of Pergamum. After a series of appeals from their friends the Romans sent an embassy which urged Philip to leave Attalus and the Greeks alone, threatening war, if he refused. The consul had to try twice before the popular assembly would vote for war. However, in the end Roman confidence after Zama prevailed over war-weariness.

The Romans' attempts to fight their way through the mountains and enter Macedonia from the west were unsuccessful, but an attack on Philip's stronghold at Acrocorinth brought the Achaean League, a federation of cities in the Peloponnese, into the war on their side in 198. The Aetolians were by then fighting Philip on their own account. Philip sought peace but was faced with escalating demands from the Romans for the liberation of Greek cities from subjection. The following year Titus Quinctius Flamininus defeated Philip in a pitched battle at Cynoscephalai in Thessaly; the formidable Macedonian army, which had dominated Greece and the Near East since the days of Philip II and Alexander the Great more than a hundred years before, came off second best to the more flexible Roman force on uneven ground. The peace terms demanded by the Romans in effect substituted their authority over Greece for Philip's. Philip was required to pay an indemnity of 1,000 talents, surrender his fleet, and evacuate his extra-territorial fortresses in Greece and Asia Minor. The Romans proudly proclaimed the "liberation" of Greece at the Isthmus of Corinth in 196. However, this liberty was not very different to that granted to Greek cities by the monarchs who had succeeded to power in various parts of Alexander the Great's empire. The cities were to be autonomous in the sense of having their own laws and political systems, and to be free of garrisons and Roman taxes. However, they were treated as Roman military allies even when there was no formal treaty, and it became quickly apparent that Rome would encourage the creation of local constitutions of which it approved (normally oligarchies, i.e. republics dominated by the wealthier citizens) and similarly would back individual Greek politicians whom it trusted. For example, its former ally, Nabis, tyrant of Sparta, who had joined Philip in the war, was deposed and Sparta became a republic. Flamininus became the first Roman to have his head on Greek coins and to be celebrated by a victory ode and festivals in his honor.

The legions were withdrawn in 194, but soon had to return. The Aetolians had fought Philip in the hope of adding cities to their league but the "liberation" left no place for this and they were discontented. The Romans meanwhile were drawn into a confrontation, initially diplomatic, with Antiochus III of Syria. Unaffected by Roman operations in Greece, in 197 he had taken control of cities in Asia Minor north and south of Pergamum and then moved into Europe, seizing cities formerly subject to Philip in the Chersonese (Gallipoli peninsula) and on the coast of Thrace. He was a threat to Rome's allies, Rhodes and the new king of Pergamum, Eumenes II, and potentially would present the Romans with an awkward choice: either the newly liberated Greeks would be free to join Antiochus or Rome would have to use force to retain them as her allies. Accordingly, the Romans used the "freedom of the Greeks" as a diplomatic weapon against Antiochus, arguing that Greek cities everywhere, including Asia Minor, should be free, and that Antiochus had neither any right to Philip's cities nor any proper interest in Europe. Antiochus replied that he was merely resuming control of ancestral dependencies, where he had more right to intervene than the Romans, and a stalemate ensued, made more uneasy when Hannibal, driven from Carthage by his pro-Roman political opponents, arrived at Antiochus' court in 195. In 192 the Aetolians finally fomented a revolt against Rome and requested Antiochus to liberate Greece.

Antiochus obtained little support in Greece and was certainly not going to receive any from Macedon. So, when a Roman army arrived under Acilius Glabrio in 191, it was no great problem to defeat the comparatively small Syrian army at Thermopylae. The Aetolians, faced with a demand for unconditional surrender, continued to fight for their independence, but their strongholds were captured one by one during the next two years. Meanwhile the Romans and their allies Pergamum and Rhodes carried the war into Asia. There were naval victories (perhaps the occasion for the dedication of the famous *Victory of Samothrace*, now in the Louvre) and a major victory on land at Magnesia by Mount Sipylus in 190. The Romans were led by Lucius Scipio, brother of Publius the conqueror of Hannibal, who took Publius with him on his staff. After Magnesia the peace terms Rome demanded were simple but far-reaching: Antiochus should pay an indemnity of 15,000 talents to Rome and one of grain to Eumenes, and should evacuate Asia Minor north and west of the Taurus mountains. The cities that had not voluntarily joined the Roman side were divided between Pergamum and Rhodes; the greater part of Asia Minor was left to the various kings and dynasts there. The year following, in the interest of Pergamum, the Roman commander Gnaeus Manlius Vulso subdued the Galatians, a people descended from Celtic invaders of Asia Minor a century earlier.

Syrian power in the Mediterranean was now confined to the seaboard of the Levant. For the Greeks their freedom proved confusing, since, although there were no Roman commanders exercising direct authority, a city or people which believed itself being worsted in its external relations or had factional problems could appeal to Rome for diplomatic assistance. The Achaean League which tried to control internal politics in both Sparta and Messenia found its opponents there backed by Rome. This led a pro-Roman Achaean politician Callistratus, when on an embassy to Rome in 180, to urge the senate to make clear in advance the policies it expected its friends to pursue. For a time also the Romans tried to control Macedon indirectly. Philip seized towns outside his borders during the war with Antiochus but was forced to surrender these in 184–3. However, his son Demetrius, who had been developing a close friendship with the Romans, was executed on Philip's instructions in 180. After Philip's death in 179, his other son Perseus built up Macedonian military strength and became active diplomatically in Greece as an alternative focus to Rome. Roman hostility to him was aggravated by Eumenes II of Pergamum, who claimed that Perseus had tried to have him assassinated, and after a pretense of diplomacy Rome once again embarked on a war with Macedon in 172.

While Perseus was joined by Illyria and much of Epirus in the southern Balkans, Greek support for Rome was often lukewarm or not forthcoming: Rhodes in particular sought to play the honest broker between the two sides. Roman progress was at first slow but in 169 Quintus Marcius Philippus succeeded in forcing an entrance into lower Macedonia through the Olympus range and the following year Lucius Aemilius Paulus won a decisive victory at Pydna. Illyria was conquered by a separate expedition. Macedonia was divided into four independent republics, paying to Rome half of what had been paid to Perseus; Illyria similarly was divided into three. The Roman armies were then withdrawn. In 168 too Roman authority in the east was demonstrated, when the ambassador Gaius Popilius Laenas, armed only with the text of a decree of the senate, persuaded Antiochus IV of Syria to lead his army out of Egypt and cease intervention in the dynastic conflict there. This would not have passed unnoticed by the Hasmoneans in Judaea, who a few year later rebelled against Syria and sought an alliance with Rome (161 BC).

Some Greeks took the defeat of Perseus as the critical date when Rome ceased to be the benevolent liberator and became instead a ruthless imperial power of a traditional sort. In Epirus 70 towns were plundered and 150,000 people enslaved. Less enthusiastic allies were punished: 1,000 dissidents from the Achaean League, including the Greek historian Polybius, were taken into detention in Italy. The Rhodians were forced to condemn to death those politicans who had advocated that the city

Figure 3   The "Agora of the Italians," on Delos, an enclosed peristyle believed to have been used as a slave-market by Italian businessmen.

should be neutral and a mediator during the war. Moreover, Rhodes was stripped of dependent cities in Asia Minor and in 165 found its commercial supremacy subverted, when Rome set up Delos as a free port – one which was quickly frequented by Romans and Italians (the "Agora of the Italians," plausibly argued to be in fact a slave market, is their particular monument (figure 3).[28] Roman and Italian businessmen had already moved into Greece, especially Thessaly, and could be found in other parts of the eastern Mediterranean. Perhaps the most exotic piece of evidence for this is an Egyptian papyrus recording a maritime loan for a voyage to the "Scent–Producing Land," i.e. Somalia: one of the voyagers is a man from Massilia (Marseilles); among the guarantors are found another Massiliot and a Greek Carthaginian, while the organizing agent is called Gnaeus.[29]

While up to this time Rome sought to exercise power indirectly in the east, in the west it was a different story.[30] The Iberian peninsula was not to be fully subjected until Augustus' time, but from the second Punic war onward there were regular expeditions from the Romans' bases on the east coast and in Andalucia into the hinterland. Peoples were forced to submit; taxation gradually became more regular and systematic; above all the great resources of precious and base metals were exploited. Romans had been first settled at Italica near Seville at the end of the war with Carthage, and there seems to have been a significant flow of immigrants to Spain, drawn by the agricultural and commercial opportunities there, during the last two centuries of the Republic. The south coast of France was also known to Roman traders but no conquest occurred until late in the century. However, in Cisalpine Gaul – Liguria, Venetia, and the Po Valley – the Romans worked hard to consolidate their power. There were new colonies such as Bononia (Bologna) and the sea-port of Aquileia at the head of the Adriatic. The *via Aemilia*, begun in 187, was constructed from Ariminum northwestward to Bononia and Placentia, and Roman citizens were settled in numbers on plots on either side of the road (the "centuriated" land division is still visible on the ground and its extent can even be detected on a satellite photograph).[31]

In Africa Carthage prospered to such an extent that it paid off its vast indemnity to Rome. There had, however, been friction for some time with the Numidian king Masinissa (who lived to a venerable old age) over claims to territory, and arbitrations had been decided by the Romans in his favor. In 153 there was a fresh quarrel and Carthage decided to use force, contrary to her treaty with Rome. This was a convenient pretext for those at Rome who feared Carthage's reviving fortunes, in particular the veteran politician Marcus Porcius Cato (the Censor), and in spite of the fact that the Carthaginian expedition into Numidia had failed, a Roman force was sent to Africa in 149. The city of Utica joined Rome and the Carthaginians at first surrendered, but retracted this, when faced with a demand to move their city ten miles inland – which would have destroyed it as a center of commerce. The city held out under siege by land and sea for three years until finally in the spring of 146 another Scipio, the adoptive grandson of Africanus, succeeded in storming and capturing it after a week of house-to-house fighting. The city itself was burnt (the marks can still be seen on stone blocks surviving from the military shipyard (figure 4a), and the whole site put under a curse by Scipio.[32] The land now came under the direct rule of a Roman magistrate as a *provincia* and the Romans became the proprietors of Punic territory, assigning some of it to those who had helped them in the war.[33]

It was not entirely a coincidence that in the same year another ancient city was destroyed, Corinth, and with it the illusion of Greek freedom. In Macedonia the uprising of a pretender to the throne, Andriscus, had caused a Roman army to be dispatched there and this was victorious in 148. Meanwhile, a revival of the recurrent quarrel between the Achaean League and Sparta, which wanted to secede, led to an appeal to Rome.

Figure 4a One of the Carthaginian ship-pens used for the war-fleet on the "Admirals' island," destroyed by the Romans in 146 BC.

Figure 4b A residential quarter of Carthage on the north side of the Byrsa hill, destroyed in 146 BC; superimposed on this are the brick-faced piers and retaining wall which supported the Roman forum of the Carthage recreated by Augustus, following a project of Julius Caesar's.

Eventually a Roman embassy arrived in 147 with instructions that not only Sparta, but Argos, Corinth, and other cities should be detached from the league. This was rejected by the Achaean assembly with violent threats to the ambassadors. The next year Rome declared war, sending out a new army, and in spite of enthusiastic mobilization by the Achaeans crushed their forces. The cumulative consequence of this was that Macedonia became a *provincia* under a military governor, who also had responsibility for overseeing Greece; the city of Corinth was largely destroyed; the leagues were dissolved; some territory was annexed by Rome, and, while some cities and regions retained their former free status, in others oligarchic governments were installed. Later writers were to see the year 146 BC as the acme of Roman success, a point from which only decline was possible.[34]

3

The Crisis of the Late Republic

Rome and its Mediterranean Empire in the mid-Second Century BC[1]

The year 146 BC was taken by many Roman historians as the turning point in the history of the Republic, on the ground that up to then a combination of moral virtue and divine favor had granted the Romans an unparalleled run of successes. This very prosperity, however, in its turn was thought to have instilled in them collectively and individually a lust for power and money, which subverted their society, creating political strife at home and encouraging greed and brutality in the administration of their subjects. Nor, with the threat of Carthage removed, was there any external force to restrain them: it was indeed urged in debates in the senate at the time that a strong Carthage was desirable as a competitor in order to enforce discipline among Romans.[2]

This picture is obviously far too schematic. The desire for glory was embedded in the ethos of the governing class and of the whole city from early times, and wealth was required for the public display associated with this, to be found in the provision of public monuments, games, and dinners. Nor were the Romans averse to making money from their conquests. When, according to the Jewish writer of 1 Maccabees, Judas was admiringly cataloguing Roman imperial achievement, he began with "the wars and noble acts which they had been doing among the Gauls, and that they had conquered them and brought them under tribute, and what they had done in the country of Spain, to gain control of the mines of silver and gold which is there."[3] As for brutality, the traditional ruthlessness with which Romans sacked cities, when compared with the behavior of their Greek rivals, was a subject of special comment by Polybius.[4] Nevertheless, aspects of Roman behavior after the third Macedonian war and the treatment of Carthage and Corinth suggested to some critics at the time a hardening of public attitudes to empire.[5] Moreover, Romans were conscious of a change in private morality. Cato and the historian Calpurnius Piso denounced luxury among their contemporaries: a love of pickled fish from the Black Sea or Greek sideboards and one-legged tables may seem harmless, but the point was the expense involved. Luxury in its turn was linked with political ambition and the vainglory of conspicuous expenditure. It is no coincidence that the first sumptuary law of 182 controlling private expenditure, especially on dinners with a huge guest list, was followed in 181 by the first law on electoral bribery and in 180 by the first law regulating the ascent through the magistracies (*cursus honorum*), which laid down minimum ages at which certain magistracies could be held.[6]

Some modern scholars have seen the Romans as originally reluctant empire-builders, pointing to their unwillingness to impose direct rule after military victory, their minimalist approach in areas where they did impose direct rule, and their comparatively restrained attitude to the exaction of taxes. However, the standard implied here seems to be a modern one. By contrast, it has been argued that the concept of the *imperium* of the Roman people is essentially that of the *imperium* of an individual: it is a matter, not of total subjection at all times, but of the superior expecting to be obeyed when he chooses to give orders. This was still true in the age of Augustus.[7] The minimalist approach to direct rule continued to prevail then also, at least outside Italy. A province was an area where a governor with military authority operated. His primary tasks were security and the extraction, or the facilitation of the extraction, of revenue, and justice and local administration were left mainly to the various communities that already existed; the governor, or one of his few subordinates, only intervened when requested or when Roman interests required. In the second century BC, moreover, there was no question yet of Rome desiring to change the nature of the societies subjected by it or indeed their identity. Nevertheless, the seizure of the land in Africa in 146, when compared with the treatment of Macedonia in 168, does suggest a greater readiness to treat the empire as a possession of Rome to be exploited for its profit, and this is confirmed by the history of the late Republic. Furthermore, the massive expansion of Roman citizenship in this period was to lead to changes in Roman society, now extended throughout Italy, to which it was still adapting itself under Augustus, and which in due course would affect the provinces also.

We should consider first, however, the consequences for Rome and Italy of imperial expansion so far. Military success had brought financial rewards throughout society; so had the expansion of Italian commerce in the Mediterranean. Settlements on land in Italy had benefited plebeians. At the same time, continuous warfare, at home or abroad, had demanded a political and social coherence which tended to suppress the kind of class conflict that had characterized the early Republic. The patrician aristocracy had been replaced by one in which patricians were far outnumbered by plebeians: here certain "noble" families formed an almost permanent core but were surrounded by a more mobile periphery, whose fortunes changed. Wealth was a *sine qua non* for membership of this class but it was also an aristocracy of talent, open to "new men," as the Romans termed them. This was because the senate, which represented the aristocracy constitutionally, was largely composed of ex-magistrates, who had secured their magistracies through popular election. Here birth was still an important source of electoral appeal but could be subverted by moral turpitude or incompetence; careers were built on military victories or other popular achievements. Men stood for office as individuals and for the most part operated politically as individuals. Aristocratic groupings, based on family or friendship, might be important, especially electorally, but it is hard to assign them any consistent significance. Political connections could be broken as easily as made, even between relatives. So could patron–client relationships, equally important in elections, especially in an era in which wealth was clearly being deployed in electoral bribery.[8]

The constitution[9] was a *res publica*, something that belonged to the people, in that the popular assemblies (under the presidency of a magistrate) elected the magistrates, judged criminal cases in matters of public interest, and gave their approval to legislation. It was normally necessary to pass a statute in an assembly in order to make changes in most major matters that affected domestic politics and the life of the citizen: the numbers and powers of magistrates; grants of citizenship; colonization and land distribution; taxation and interest rates; the procedure of civil and criminal law, and even priesthoods and religious festivals. Popular assent was also normally required for major wars, but the minutiae of foreign and military policy and of economic management were left to the senate, which was the only deliberative council for political matters Rome possessed. As a body chiefly composed of ex-magistrates, it had considerable authority, and this was amplified by Rome's record of military success. No less important were the individuals under whose command the victories had been won. Rome traditionally allowed a great deal of discretion to its commanders in the field and in the provinces, thus making it the more easy for men to display excellence (*virtus*), to dominate the political scene, and so to achieve glory. This last was the ultimate aim in life and death for the aristocracy, as we find well documented in epitaphs of members of the Scipionic family and in early Roman drama.[10]

The domination of Rome by the new aristocracy, gradually but steadily being replenished from a wider circle, did not go without challenge. The conflicts of the "Struggle of the Orders" in the early Republic were a matter of history – of which in the 50 years since the second Punic war more and more was being written at Rome – but by the same token not forgotten and a source of political inspiration. For the plebs there were two great legacies from that struggle. The first was *provocatio*, the protection of the citizen from arbitrary execution, which was amplified in the early second century by the statute, proposed by Cato, forbidding the flogging of citizens except on military service. The second was the office of tribune of the plebs. Since the Hortensian law of 287 most legislation was passed as plebiscites in plebeian assemblies under the presidency of tribunes. We even find them from time to time passing laws contrary to the wishes of the majority of the aristocracy. Tribunes also conducted political prosecutions in an assembly of the plebs: in this period their judicial function was the greatest threat to a corrupt or incompetent magistrate once he had left office. However, what was perhaps more important for them as plebeian representatives were their negative powers, first their veto over acts of other magistrates, decrees of the senate, and even bills in an assembly, and secondly their capacity to protect individual Romans. In effect they were brokers between the plebs and either the senate or another magistrate. The whole college of 10 might even debate between themselves an issue in which they were asked to intervene. For example, they could block a prosecution by a magistrate and they also backed individual Romans who they believed to be justly resisting conscription.[11]

In a century from the fall of Carthage this political system was to be brought low by two civil wars, both preceded by a period of domestic political conflict in which violence often played a decisive part. Polybius was impressed by the "mixed" constitution that had seen Rome victorious over Carthage and in the east, but lived long enough to prophesy that the "democratic" element in the system would get out of hand, flattered by ambitious leaders into a sense of self-importance and driven by a sense of injustice to want more for itself than it should.[12] From another point of view, after the comparative concord of the middle Republic the class conflict of the early Republic, embedded as it was in the constitution, returned to haunt Rome at a time when its economic and social problems were more acute. What were these problems and how were they exploited by the ambitious?

The Army and the Land[13]

First, military demands created or exacerbated agrarian difficulties. Rome had become mistress of the Mediterranean through an army chiefly of peasant farmers, whether Roman citizens, Latin, or Italian. Roman citizens possessing a certain minimum property were compelled to perform six years of military service (so the manuscript text of Polybius, which should be respected[14]), not necessarily in one sequence. They might be required to do more in an emergency, and they could volunteer for more. When campaigns had been near home and intermittent, this had not been too disruptive to the civilian life of the soldier, but the Hannibalic war had squeezed Italian manpower and the subsequent fighting in the east, Spain, and Cisalpine Gaul maintained the pressure, especially on those who had just become adult and liable to serve. Absence abroad meant that a man could neither farm nor raise children. Conquest had of course also brought rewards. Land in Italy and Cisalpine Gaul was taken over for settlement by Romans in colonies or on individual allotments, especially by former soldiers, who also provided a convenient military reserve for defending the region. Nevertheless, this affected only a small proportion of Rome and Italy's manpower.

The demands of the army would not have been so burdensome if the economic basis of the peasantry had been more secure. Peasant farmers frequently would not have owned enough land of their own to provide adequate subsistence, but needed to rent cultivable land in addition. They also used public pasture land to graze beasts and exploited public woods to collect timber for fires and other purposes, to gather herbs as food and medicine, to hunt, and to graze their own pigs on the acorns. The Roman people had acquired a great deal of public land in their conquest of Italy. Parts of this were used for settlement or sold and thus became private; parts of this were rented on long- or short-term contracts but remained public land; other parts were made available to Latin and Italian communities for exploitation (in some cases this would have been to return land on loan, which had been taken from the communities in the first place). The remainder was left for general use, occupiers paying a ground rent proportional to their plot and graziers a tax on each animal. Limits had been established early in Rome's history on such occupation and grazing, but wealthy men tended to disregard these limits and in effect treated public land as their own private property. They also bought the private holdings of peasants. In disputed areas, or where occupiers were reluctant to sell or move, those who were expanding their properties used violence, and a series of special legal actions had to be created to repress this – on our evidence with limited success.[15]

A fundamental reason for the legal or illegal expansion of landhold-ings was the wealth that was flowing into Italy through war and commerce in the second century. In a society with no stock market, where land was the chief source of production, it was the safest place for capital investment and, moreover, a source of prestige, unlike money-lending or strongboxes full of silver. The landowners began to pursue a more rational approach to farming, mixing forms of agriculture and stock-raising on their estates and gearing production to the best market. This is attested in Cato's work on agriculture; another book on this topic by Mago is said to have been translated from Punic at about this time. Slaves had probably been used on the estates of the rich for centuries, but now they were freely available and cheap after Rome's victories and therefore economically preferable as a permanent labor force, although this prac-tice had its dangers, as a massive slave revolt in Sicily and south Italy, lasting five years (137–132 BC) showed, and free labor was still needed for harvests. Cumulatively, the activities of the rich drove some peasants off their land or reduced them to extreme poverty, and this became a political issue. However, archeological evidence from field surveys sug-gests that this was a feature of certain regions rather than of the whole of Italy. The decline of the peasantry was probably most pronounced where large-scale stock-raising prevailed – a particularly profitable enter-prise on account of the production of wool and leather, the latter being in particular an essential material for the Roman army.

Italy and Rome[16]

This agrarian problem would have affected both the Romans and their Latin and Italian allies. The allies however, also had problems of their own. They had assisted Rome to mastery of the Mediterranean world and by now provided between half and two-thirds of every major Roman army. Nevertheless, they were less well rewarded in land and booty, had no protection against Romans in authority through the institution of *provocatio* or the tribunate of the plebs, and had no part in the decisions that led to war. This was the price they had to pay for their theoretical independence in domestic matters, a condition that the Romans were happy to disregard if they believed it contrary to the general good (for example in their restriction of Bacchic rites throughout Italy in 186). Any Latin or Italian might lose his possession of what had been made Roman public land; any Latin or Italian might suffer at the hands of a Romans magistrate. The local aristocracies, however, had a special grief in that, although they might be as wealthy or, in their view, as noble, as their Roman counterparts, they were none the less subordinate. Moreover, non-Latin Italians had not even the right to intermarry with Romans or to own Roman land. Obviously, this would all change, if they became Roman citizens. However, such a change would bring with it a loss of precious identity. Italians might know Latin – indeed almost none of the chief exponents of Latin poetry and drama in this period were from Rome or its neighborhood – but to a considerable extent they remained loyal to their local language, culture, and laws. Non-Romans had as much access to the culture of Greece as Romans. It is outside Rome that we find magnificent architectural complexes that combine temples with theaters, such as those at Praeneste, Tibur, and at Pietrabbondante in Samnium (see figures 15 and 16).

The City

A fourth problem was the city of Rome itself.[17] The wealth that poured into Rome in the period of Mediterranean expansion financed an increase in both public and private building. Numerous new temples were dedicated, though mostly of a modest size compared with those of Augustus' time – for example the republican temples of the Largo Argentina site in the Campus Martius and the temples by the Tiber, that of Portunus (figure 5) and the round temple probably dedicated to Hercules. The Appian and "Old Anio" aqueducts of 312 and 272 BC were supplemented in the second century by the Marcian in 144–140 and the "Warm Water (Tepula)" in 126–125, almost doubling the water provision. Outside the Servian wall, southwest of the Aventine an Emporium was constructed in 174 for the reception of the goods brought up the Tiber from Ostia, whose centre-piece was the Porticus Aemilia which served as an enormous warehouse. Round the Forum Romanum, basilicas were constructed with associated *tabernae* (shops) which allowed commerce to proceed under cover (most legal business, however, still took place in the traditional way in the open air of the forum). The *taberna*, it has been argued, was indeed the characteristic of Rome from the later Republic onwards. Wealth created a demand for the variety of luxury trades, mainly served by the slaves and freedmen of rich families. The

Figure 5   The second-century BC temple, probably of Portunus, by the east bank
of the Tiber in the area of the port of Rome.

tabernae would have been found not only in public spaces, but on the
ground floor of private houses and apartment blocks.

Building was facilitated by the invention of *caementicium*, a form of
concrete, which was originally shuttered by a lining of irregular pieces of
tufa smoothed on the outside (*opus incertum*); this lining was to be
replaced in the first century by pyramidal pieces pointing into the concrete,
which from the outside gave an impression of a network of interlocking
diamonds (*opus reticulatum*). The building usually identified with the
Porticus Aemilia, but more probably a military shipyard (*navalia*) of *c.*140
BC, is probably the oldest surviving example of construction in *caementicium*, where concrete barrel-vaults were used to support the roof.[18] The
invention meant in general that large and complex edifices could be erected
more quickly and cheaply. Even with the shuttering, the concrete was not
beautiful, but this could be remedied by an outer shell of ornamental stone,
such as the easily available *lapis Tiburtina* (travertine) from the quarries
between Rome and Tivoli. We should not think, however, that all Rome
yet resembled the remains visible today of the city that was rebuilt after
the Neronian fire. Most private building was still in mud-brick and the
tenements where the poor lived in the Subura or on the Aventine were

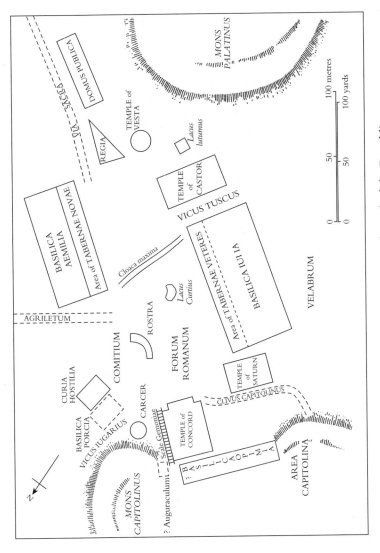

Map 3 The Forum Romanum at the end of the Republic

flimsily constructed, easily liable to fire and collapse; nor was there town-planning outside the monumental center (see chapter 4 below).

Rome was thus generating a huge service industry devoted to construction, luxury trades, the port, and transport within the city, much of which was not easily accessible to wheeled transport (see chapter 5 note 5 for the street widths prescribed in the Twelve Tables) so that loads had to be carried by animals or human beings. If much of the specialized work in the city was done by the slaves and freedmen of powerful families, who would have operated commercially, subject to the authority of their masters or patrons, the use of slaves for manual labor other than personal or domestic service to their masters was not economically rational because of the risk of death or injury. Here free labor was essential, and Rome was an obvious magnet for those seeking employment. We can only make guesses about the total population of Rome about 150 BC (the author's is in the region of 300,000, including slaves). As with the cities of early modern Europe, the unhealthy living conditions of the poor would have rendered Rome a net consumer of human beings – in addition to poor housing and fire there were outbreaks of disease and the peril of Tiber flooding, not remedied until later in Augustus' reign – and we must imagine a steady flow of people into the city from Italy and abroad. Many of them would have been transient; on the other hand there were probably by now the beginnings of the foreign communities which were a later feature of the city.[19] An ever-increasing element in the population was freedmen and their descendants, mainly liberated from the households of great families and remaining under their patronage. Such a population was potentially volatile, if living conditions were bad, and especially, like the peoples of Paris and London in the eighteenth century, if basic food was in short supply. The city was already dependent on regular imports from Sicily, but in an emergency might have to look further afield. Probably about 130 BC an inscription from Thessaly shows a Roman aedile purchasing 450,000 *modii* of grain (enough to feed 45,000 families for two months).[20] He was operating in the spring or early summer when, in the period before the new harvest, grain would in any year be at its scarcest and most expensive.

The Reforming Demagogues[21]

The politics of the later half of the second century were characterized by legislation proposed in the plebeian assembly by tribunes who were called *populares* (populist), because they appealed directly to the plebeian assembly without prior agreement with the senate and claimed to be promoting the welfare of the common people. In 139 and 137 there were laws introducing for the first time secret voting on tablets in the assemblies for elections and non-capital trials. Then in 133 Tiberius Sempronius Gracchus, a noble from a plebeian family, proposed a law to reform the management of public land (a previous attempt in 140 had been abandoned after opposition): the existing limits on agricultural holdings and the grazing of animals were to be enforced with some relaxation for those with children, and the land so recovered was to be redistributed to the poor. Faced with resistance from the wealthy, he avoided discussion in the senate but tried to legislate directly through the assembly – a procedure not illegal, but unusual and provocative to his opponents, who encouraged another tribune, Marcus Octavius, to veto the bill. Tiberius' reaction was to persuade the assembly to depose this tribune, on the ground that he no longer represented the plebs, and so to pass the bill. When obstructed in implementing it, he proposed to use the revenues from the kingdom of Pergamum in Asia Minor, which had been left to Rome by the will of the last Attalid king.

Tiberius Gracchus set up a land commission to carry out his proposals and then stood for an abnormal second tribunate with a new radical program. Opposition to this was even fiercer, violence broke out, and during the elections he was murdered on the Capitol by a mob of senators and their henchmen led by Scipio Nasica, the pontifex maximus. Tiberius' supporters were then treated as conspirators against the *res publica* by a special tribunal set up under the consuls of 132. His land legislation was put into effect nonetheless, though there was opposition from Italians who found themselves losing land they had formerly been able to occupy by default. As for Pergamum, the Romans decided to accept the legacy and make it a province, but could only do so after putting down a nationalist rebellion led by Aristonicus, a bastard of the royal family, who had among his supporters a large number of runaway slaves.

In 125, amid unrest among the Latins, the consul Marcus Fulvius Flaccus proposed a bill which offered Roman citizenship to any Latin and Italian community who wanted it or the protection of *provocatio*, if they preferred to retain their independence. The citizenship provision would have allowed the allies to obtain land on the same terms as other Romans. This bill seems never to have reached a vote, and in the same year a tribune, Iunius Pennus, passed a law which expelled non-Romans from residence at Rome. There was unrest among the Latins and the apparently prosperous colony of Fregellae revolted and suffered complete destruction as a reprisal. Tiberius' younger brother Gaius unsuccessfully opposed Pennus' law, but in 123 he became tribune himself and in this year and the following he was directly or indirectly the inspiration for a larger quantity of reforming legislation than can be ascribed to any other politician during the Republic.

Some measures sprang from his brother's work and the reaction to it. He strengthened the *provocatio* law by forbidding the capital condemnation of Roman citizens without authorization from the assembly, such as had occurred in 132, and providing for the prosecution of the offending magistrates. A new agrarian law revised the regulations for land distribution and ordered the founding of new colonies; it was supplemented by a measure promoting the building of new roads. For the city of Rome Gaius introduced the sale of grain at a low price throughout the year (this was made possible by the construction of granaries where grain bought cheaply after the harvest could be stored). The province created from Pergamum, called "Asia," was reorganized and received a new system of taxation: this was farmed out for collection to partnerships (*societates*) of wealthy non-senators belonging to the order of "equestrians" (*equites*), those qualified to serve in the cavalry; in Africa there was to be land distribution and a colony on the site of Carthage. As for the allies, the jury-court, introduced in 149 to enable the prosecution of magistrates for theft and improper exactions from them (*quaestio de repetundis*), was reformed in early 122: there was to be a large jury, again of "equestrians"; the allies were allowed to bring prosecutions themselves, and, apart from the, now penal, double damages paid to the injured parties, the chief prosecutor, if successful, was rewarded with Roman citizenship or other privileges. The likelihood of a Roman senator being condemned was greatly increased. Moreover, this court became a model for jury-courts dealing with other crimes in the late Republic. We also hear of reforms of the allocation of consular provinces, indirect taxation, and the terms of military service.

In 122 Gaius was also involved with the founding of his new colony, called Iunonia, on the site of Carthage, amid sinister rumors arising from Scipio's curse on the site. However, in the city, with Fulvius Flaccus as a colleague, he went on to propose a more modest measure about the extension of Roman citizenship: only the Latins, the Romans' kith and kin, were to have full citizenship; the Italians were to have some sort of voting rights. There was strong opposition to this bill too, especially from a third tribune, Livius Drusus, who proposed rival measures, and it never became law. The next year, when Gaius was out of office, a proposal was made to repeal his African law; he resisted this and there was violence. The consul Opimius obtained an emergency decree (the so-called "last" decree) from the senate, urging him to defend the *res publica*, and on this basis recruited a militia to suppress Gaius and his supporters. Fulvius Flaccus was killed in the fighting, Gaius committed suicide, and many of his supporters were brought before a tribunal and executed on the consul's orders. The African law was repealed, but only in relation to the town of Iunonia: the settlers were allowed their landholdings. There was later some modification to the grain law, perhaps to the price demanded for the grain, and to the status of the land assigned by the Gracchan agrarian commission in Italy. The rest of the legislation remained in place. Thus Gaius' opponents punished him for his demagogy but took most of his reforms on board. One long-term effect of these was to make the "equestrians" outside the senate into a political factor. The previous importance of those who were undertakers of public contracts was increased by the immensely lucrative farming of the taxes of Asia. On the other hand, the presence of "equestrians" on the jury-courts made it unwise for senators to disregard their interests.

The Age of Marius[22]

After Gaius Gracchus' death politics were once again dominated by the majority of office-holders and former office-holders in the senate, who were called – or called themselves – the "good men" (*boni*) or "supporters of the best" (*optimates*), and by their leaders (*principes*) in particular. However, this dominance was called into question once again by military failure. In Africa the Numidian kingdom had passed to Masinissa's son Micipsa and on his death in 117 was shared between two sons, Hiempsal and Adherbal, and his bastard son Jugurtha. Jugurtha had acquired useful military experience while serving with the Romans, and at the same time friends among their aristocracy. Relying on this, he eliminated by war and assassination his two rivals, but with Adherbal he killed a number of Italian businessmen and must have appeared a potential threat to the Romans now settled in Africa.

Jugurtha frustrated Rome's first declaration of war in 111 by a quick surrender and exploiting his connections at Rome, but his corrupt practices were blatant and led to a special tribunal of investigation, the war being meanwhile renewed. The Romans made slow progress against Jugurtha's mobile forces and this gave an opportunity to Gaius Marius, a man from the local aristocracy of Arpinum (an originally Volscian town granted Roman citizenship in 188), who had pursued a senatorial career as far as the praetorship and was now serving as an officer under Quintus Metellus. Somewhat unfairly, he denounced his superior's strategy and, returning to Rome, stood successfully for the consulship in spite of being a "new man." Once elected, he obtained the command in Africa by a plebiscite and in 107 took out there a new army composed of Roman and Italian volunteers, both experienced veterans and propertyless men who were not regularly recruited into the Roman legions. He had success in eastern Numidia but failed to pin down Jugurtha, until in 105 the latter was betrayed by the neighboring king of Mauretania to Marius' quaestor, Lucius Sulla. Within a few months Marius was back again in Italy, elected consul for 104 and commissioned to defeat the Germanic peoples who were threatening Rome from the north, the Cimbri and Teutoni.

Rome's subjection of Cisalpine Gaul (including Venetia and Istria at the head of the Adriatic) had entailed defending these areas against incursions from the north. From 125 to 121, moreover, Rome had campaigned beyond the Alps in what is now southern France, originally to defend its ally Massilia against that city's Gallic neighbors but ultimately to bring the region as far north as Toulouse and Vienne in the Rhône valley under its own control (see ch. 1 above for the creation of the *via Domitia* and Narbonne). Its troops then suffered a series of military defeats there at the hands of Celtic and Germanic peoples in 113, 109, 107, and, most disastrously, in 105 at Arausio (Orange). Marius introduced military reforms in the legions in the interest of simplicity, flexibility, and mobility off the battlefield. It was no longer a matter of defeating an elaborately organized Hellenistic or Carthaginian army but resisting a mass onslaught of a barbarian tribe. Allies were summoned from Italy and abroad, the latter especially important for cavalry and light-armed troops. Marius was elected to an extraordinary series of successive consulships while the threat lasted. This led to the defeat of the Teutoni at Aquae Sextiae (Aix-en-Provence) in 102. The following year an even greater incursion by the Cimbri into the Po valley was repulsed by a Roman victory at Vercellae. Marius was then elected to a sixth consulship in 100 perhaps as a precaution, in case the threat was not over, perhaps to supervise the resettlement of Cisalpine Gaul.

Meanwhile there had been a revival of *popularis* activity. Major priesthoods were opened to a form of election by assembly. The tribunal to investigate the Jugurtha scandal in 109 was followed by a series of trials of commanders for corruption or incompetence. Eventually, probably in 103, Lucius Appuleius Saturninus introduced a new permanent court on the model of the Gracchan *quaestio de repetundis* to punish the "infringement of the majesty of the Roman people" (*de maiestate*), a charge which could be used against any form of political misbehavior. A law passed by the consul of 106 allowed senators to join the "equestrians" on the juries of the *quaestio de repetundis*, but in 101 they were removed again in a reform of that court by Gaius Servilius Glaucia. Saturninus had assisted Marius in 103 by passing an agrarian bill which provided for the settlement of demobilized soldiers in Africa; in 100 he was tribune once again and Glaucia was praetor. They embarked on a legislative program which recalled that of Gaius Gracchus. There was agrarian legislation on behalf of the veterans of the Cimbric wars, many of whom would have been recruited from the landless: they were to be settled in the provinces or on territory in northern Italy from which the Cimbri had been expelled. A new law made grain available to the urban plebs at a lower price. We also find intervention in foreign and provincial policy, including measures against piracy in the eastern Mediterranean. Some of the legislation was forced through by violence and in defiance of bad omens which would normally have led to the dissolution of the assembly.

Marius' enemy, Metellus Numidicus, was the most conspicuous opponent of the legislators, but was driven into exile by the threat of prosecution. However, at the end of the year, Glaucia sought illegally to be elected directly to the consulship. More violence broke out and Marius was charged by the senate to restore order by a decree similar to that passed against Gaius Gracchus in 121. He formed a militia; Glaucia, Saturninus, and their followers, under siege on the Capitoline hill, surrendered and were temporarily detained in the senate-house, but the mob pelted them to death with tiles from the roof. The fate of the legislation of 100 is uncertain. Some of it was certainly ignored without any formal repeal. Two years later a bill was passed permitting the senate to declare invalid legislation when improper procedure had been used in its ratification, but this does not seem to have been applied retrospectively. How far Marius' soldiers actually received land must remain uncertain. Historians have charged Marius and Saturninus with bringing the army into politics, but this is only true up to a point. The army as a whole was not yet professional: many men were only recruited because of the German emergency. As for Marius, he clearly had no intention at this time of using his soldiers to make a coup d'état. Civil war was first to emerge from a conflict between Rome and her Italian allies.

The War of the Allies[23]

For 30 years after the death of Gaius Gracchus the Italian allies were largely ignored by Roman politicians: only Saturninus seems to have tried to reward non-Roman soldiers with land, although in this period Latin and Italian troops continued to be vital in fighting Rome's wars. However, suspicion about the usurpation of Roman citizenship by non-Romans led to legislation in 95 which offended the Italian elites. It is likely that this provoked them into concerting plans for a possible secession. First, however, Marcus Livius Drusus, a son of the man who had opposed Gaius Gracchus and a friend of leading Italians, attempted to incorporate a citizenship measure into a programme of legislation, when tribune in 91. There were to be new land distributions, a new grain law, an enlargement of the senate and the return of senatorial jurors to the criminal courts, and finally the grant of Roman citizenship to all the Latins and Italian allies. Thus *popularis* methods were to be used to unify Italy under the authority of the senate and, in particular, of Livius Drusus himself and his friends. At Rome he met opposition from the knights and some suspicious senators; outside, he had massive support from certain regions of Italy, but Etruscans were against him, perhaps because their landholdings would become subject to Roman agrarian laws. Drusus' legislation seems to have been ratified in the assembly, but the tribune was accused of tacking the measures together in order to get the whole program ratified in a package, and the senate subsequently declared the laws invalid. Drusus himself was mysteriously assassinated in the atrium of his own house toward the end of the year, and within a few months a Roman magistrate was killed when he stumbled on Italian war preparations at Asculum in Picenum.

The rebellion then broke out. The Romans removed all restrictions on recruiting and enlisted help from allies abroad. Both Marius and Sulla were appointed commanders under the consuls. The criminal courts were suspended apart from a tribunal set up to investigate those alleged to have conspired with the Italians. The Latins remained loyal to Rome, except for one colony (Venusia), and so did the majority of the Etruscans and Umbrians. The remaining allies in peninsular Italy formed a confederation, such as had never existed among them before: they founded at Corfinium a capital with political institutions, called Italica, and issued a federal coinage with legends in Oscan (VITELLIV= ITALIA) and patriotic iconography, such as the bull of Italy trampling on the wolf of Rome. The allied armies failed to invade Latium and threaten Rome, but in Campania Oscan cities such as Pompeii joined the revolt. In 90 the Romans managed to penetrate through central Italy to the Adriatic and the war split into two main fronts, one in the north in Picenum, the other in Campania and western Samnium. Enormous demands were being made on the Roman treasury, demonstrated by the massive coin issues of 90, and military progress was slow. The Romans, therefore, made the major concession of conferring Roman citizenship, through a law passed by the consul Lucius Caesar, on the Latins and allies south of the river Po, who had not taken up arms or had laid them down swiftly. This kept Etruria and Umbria for the most part out of the war.

The main issue of the war was decided in 89. In the south Sulla recovered most of Campania and a number of towns in Samnium, while Cosconius was successful in Apulia. In the north the Marsi were defeated, and at the end of the year the consul Gnaeus Pompeius Strabo captured the stronghold of Asculum. There remained to be subdued pockets of resistance in Campania and Samnium and the whole of Lucania in the southwest. Further laws had been passed making making citizenship available to those who abandoned the Italian cause, but their impact on the Roman assemblies was reduced by confining new citizens to eight or 10 voting districts (*tribus*) to be added to the existing 35. If the consequences for most Italians were calamitous, those for the Romans were also bad. Their casualties had been high; the *res publica* was bankrupt and so were many individuals: a praetor of 89, who had been making decrees in favor of debtors, was lynched by creditors. In this unstable situation Roman dominance of the eastern Mediterranean was threatened as it had not been for a century (and much of her income from there was lost) because of a power that she had underestimated, Mithridates VI, king of Pontus. This in due course helped to precipitate a new crisis in Italy.

Mithridates and the Civil War[24]

Mithridates and his ancestors were Iranian, claiming descent from the Achaemenid kings of Persia, but used the Greek language and were of a mixed culture. The founder of the dynasty had seized a kingdom in northeastern Asia Minor, called Pontus after the Black Sea, amid the struggles between the successors of Alexander the Great at the end of the fourth century BC. The kingdom was rich in agriculture, timber, silver, and base metals. Over more than two centuries the kings had expanded their borders and developed alliances around the shores of the Black Sea, including the Crimea. When Roman power reached Asia, they became Rome's friends: Mithridates V helped against Aristonicus' revolt. His son, Mithridates VI, after vigorously developing Pontic influence in Asia Minor and the Black Sea, in about 100 BC placed his own son on the throne of his southern neighbor Cappadocia, which bordered on the province that the Romans had just created in order to campaign against the pirates in Cilicia. Sulla, as governor there in about 96, replaced this son with a Roman nominee, but Mithridates deposed that king in turn and a few years later installed his own nominee on the throne of Bithynia. In this same period the new power in Iran, the Parthians, took Mesopotamia from the Seleucid kingdom of Syria and extended their authority to the northern Euphrates.

Roman envoys to Bithynia managed to persuade Mithridates to accept the Roman choices for both Cappadocia and Bithynia but then over-reached themselves by encouraging the king of Bithynia to invade Pontus. This provoked Mithridates in 89 into retaliatory invasions first into Bithynia, then, when it was obvious that there was little to resist him, into the Roman province of Asia. From there in 88 he sent a force by land into Macedonia and a naval force (he was allied to the pirates) through the islands of the Aegean to Greece: Athens was brought over to his side by pro-Pontic tyrants and his name appeared on their coinage. He had even made contact with the Italian insurgents, but too late to affect the course of the War of the Allies.

When the news of Mithridates' advance first reached Rome in late 89, Sulla, as one of the consuls elected for 88, was assigned the war against him, but this command was also coveted by Marius, who was allegedly obsessed with a seventh consulship. Marius made a political alliance with the tribune Publius Sulpicius, who was trying to legislate for a fairer distribution of Italian votes. Sulpicius only succeeded by using violence, forcing the consul Sulla to retire to his army which was still besieging Nola in Campania. Sulpicius then legislated to remove the army and the Mithridatic command from Sulla and give it to Marius. However, when Marius' officers arrived, Sulla appealed to the loyalty of his troops and their fear for their future under Marius, and the officers were stoned to death. Sulla then led his army on Rome. He no doubt alleged that he was doing his duty as consul by restoring freedom and order in the capital, but the action of bringing serving legions into the city was without precedent. It started the first Roman civil war. Sulla's soldiers no doubt hoped for a glorious and profitable campaign against Mithridates and any scruples against killing fellow countrymen would have been weakened in their fight with their Italian allies.

The city had no organized defense force and fell to Sulla amid improvised resistance from the plebs; Marius, Sulpicius, and their leading supporters fled. Sulla put a price on their heads, and introduced constitutional reforms that would have increased the size of the senate, given it a veto over legislation, and abolished assemblies based on the *tribus*, especially the plebeian assembly (*concilium plebis*), in favor of the military assembly (*comitia centuriata*), which was stratified according to wealth. These reactionary measures did not survive long. When Sulla at last went out to Greece with his army, some Samnites had still not laid down their arms. One of the consuls of 87, Lucius Cornelius Cinna, fell out with his colleague, Gnaeus Octavius, because he sought to reintroduce Sulpicius' legislation about the Italians. Cinna imitated Sulla by using the troops still besieging Nola to march on Rome. Marius, who had fled to Africa, now returned on Cinna's invitation, and assembled an army from his veterans in Etruria. On the other side Octavius summoned assistance from Metellus Pius in Samnium and Pompeius Strabo, who had taken back the army in Picenum, after he had instigated his troops to kill his official successor Pompeius Rufus, Sulla's consular colleague.

Rome was besieged; Strabo brought his forces but died himself in a plague; Metellus Pius was distracted by his Samnite opponents. Eventually, Octavius decided to surrender Rome to Cinna and Marius, after Cinna had offered liberty to the slaves in the city. Cinna had promised clemency, but in spite of this senators and equestrians who had supported Sulla were killed or forced to commit suicide at Marius' instigation, while the newly liberated slaves took advantage of their position to loot and kill their former masters, until they themselves were killed on Cinna's orders. Sulla was declared a public enemy; Marius was elected to a seventh consulship but died within a few days of entering office in 86. In the following three years, the "reign of Cinna," the consulship was almost monopolized by him and Gnaeus Papirius Carbo, but in other respects peaceful republican government returned. Peace was made with those Samnites still in arms by means of an offer of citizenship, and the war with the allies in the south was brought to an end. Sulpicius' legislation about the Italians was not revived, however, until 84 and no great effort was made formally to enrol allies as citizens. The financial problem occasioned by the lack of liquidity (in such times money tended literally to go to ground, as is shown by the many coin hoards that have been discovered) was remedied by a massive remission of debts.

The Success of Sulla[25]

An army was sent from Rome to Macedonia in 86 under the replacement consul L. Valerius Flaccus, who subsequently crossed the Bosphorus into Asia Minor. Sulla had already marched into central Greece in 87, where he besieged Athens and its port, Piraeus. Athens fell to him on March 1, 86 and Piraeus soon afterwards. He subsequently performed his greatest military feat by two successive victories over Pontic armies in Boeotia at Chaeronea and Orchomenos in spite of being outnumbered. He then advanced to the Hellespont (Dardanelles), where he was joined by a fleet collected by Lucius Lucullus. Flaccus had meanwhile been murdered by mutinous troops incited by his deputy Flavius Fimbria. The latter, however, had successfully pursued a policy of liberating cities from Mithridates, who was by now unpopular on account of some brutal repression. Sulla exploited this to offer terms to Mithridates in 85. The latter was to surrender any territory acquired in this war and evacuate Galatia, Paphlagonia, and Cappadocia, but retain his own kingdom and Black Sea empire. Furthermore, he was to hand over to Sulla 70 warships, grain, and an indemnity in cash. This enabled Sulla to turn on Fimbria, defeat him, and force him to suicide. The cities in Asia which had tried to resist Mithridates were rewarded with privileges; the remainder were subjected to huge fines and forced to give Sulla's soldiers a subsidized vacation.

In 84 Sulla and his army were back in Greece seeking to negotiate a return home. Cinna was assassinated by mutinous soldiers, but negotiations failed. Sulla, therefore, invaded Italy in 83. He advanced from Brindisi to Campania, where the consular army that opposed him was persuaded to desert. A number of leading men who had fled from the Marians abroad now returned, while Strabo's son Gnaeus Pompeius (Pompey) joined Sulla with a force from Picenum. The following year Sulla forced the Marians to evacuate Rome: Marius' son, now consul, was besieged in Praeneste, but the main center of Marian resistance was in Etruria. Eventually, a large levy of Samnites and Lucanians marched on Rome to rescue the younger Marius, but they were defeated amid great bloodshed at the battle of the Colline Gate (November 1, 82). Praeneste fell, Marian resistance collapsed throughout Italy, and its leaders were executed, some after taking refuge in the provinces: the chief exception was Quintus Sertorius who took refuge in Spain.

At Rome Sulla first legitimized his own position by organizing his election as dictator for re-establishing constitutional government, and legitimized the liquidation of his opponents and their assets by means of proscriptions (the term means publication of names). Constitutional reform followed. The number of quaestors and praetors was increased; so was the size of the senate which was henceforth to be recruited from former quaestors; senators were to have a monopoly of jury service on the criminal tribunals (*quaestiones perpetuae*). The statutes governing these courts were revised and the rules affecting provincial governors were made stricter. Above all, the tribunes were stripped of their powers to legislate and to conduct criminal prosecutions before an assembly and were forbidden to proceed to higher offices. The balance of the constitution was thus changed in favor of the aristocracy and those who represented it. The granting of citizenship to the Italians was not revoked, but certain communities who had favored the Marians were deprived of their rights and, in general, formal registration of new citizens proceeded slowly. In the city the grain subsidy was abolished. Outside, land confiscated from Sulla's opponents, especially in Etruria and Campania, was used to settle his demobilized soldiers: thus Oscan Pompeii became a Sullan colony. Sulla moved from the dictatorship to the consulship in 80. The next year he was once again a private citizen, only to die early in 78. His partisans, however, now dominated both the senatorial order and the equestrians and had enriched themselves through looting and the proscriptions. Land became concentrated in fewer hands. Even the slaves Sulla had liberated became a significant body in the city population.

The Aftermath of Sulla[26]

Less than 30 years were to separate Sulla's death from an even more wide-ranging civil war: indeed some years had to pass before the conflict between Sullans and Marians was finally extinguished. While discontent over Italian inequality was on the way to being satisfied, the land seizures in Italy had redistributed the problem of agrarian poverty, rather than solving it, and in the city the emasculation of the tribunes did nothing for stability. However, an equal, if not greater, force for change was to be the demands made, and opportunities afforded, by empire. The expansion of Roman rule was a tempting route by which to secure the resources which could be used for the placation of the discontented at home and the advancement of the career of the successful commander.

Sulla was not yet dead when the consul of 78, a Marcus Lepidus, proposed the rescinding of Sulla's land confiscations and the restoration of the supply of cheap grain in the city. He was sent to crush a rising in Etruria but put himself at the head of the rebels. When he marched on Rome the following year, he was defeated by his former colleague Quintus Catulus with the aid of Pompey, who also suppressed the Marian insurgents in Cisalpine Gaul. Pompey, now in his late twenties, had recovered Sicily and Africa for Sulla in 82, but was too young to become a quaestor or senator, let alone a regular military commander. He was, nevertheless, sent first to put down a Gallic rebellion in the Transalpine province and then to assist Quintus Metellus Pius in Spain against Sertorius. The latter had temporarily taken refuge in Morocco but by 80 had re-established himself in Lusitania (Portugal), whence his authority spread into Andalucia and over much of the Iberian peninsula. He created out of the existing Roman settlers and the Marian refugees a microcosm of the Roman Republic, but at the same time raised many Spaniards to Roman status by education and military training. For most of the decade Metellus and Pompey made little impression on his power: indeed they were compelled to winter their armies outside the peninsula.

In the east the Romans had some military success in central Asia Minor, but refused to settle their relationship with Mithridates by a formal treaty. The latter, therefore, when Nicomedes IV of Bithynia died in 75 and left his kingdom to Rome, once more invaded Bithynia and the province of Asia. A year later the consuls Lucius Lucullus and Marcus Cotta were sent against him amid a scandal over provincial appointments (they allegedly depended on the mistress of a power-broker, Publius Cethegus). Mithridates still had an alliance with the pirates, especially those based in Cilicia and Crete, and even used their ships for diplomatic contact with Sertorius in Spain.

The pirates preyed on Rome's merchant shipping, especially the grain trade, thus threatening the food supply at Rome and causing the plebs to riot. In response, a law was passed in 75, restoring to the tribunes the right to pursue higher office, and in 73 cheap grain distributions were reintroduced for part of the city population. However, the commander specially commissioned in 74 to defeat the pirates, a Marcus Antonius, was ineffective. Violence between the slave gangs of the landowners in Italy had become common, but in 73 there was the only major Italian slave revolt, when a group of gladiators, led by Spartacus, Oenomaus, and Crixus, broke out of their training school at Capua and obtained widespread support from not only slave but free herdsmen on the big estates in southern Italy. They were victorious over several regular Roman armies before being finally defeated by Marcus Crassus in 71; those who survived the battle were ruthlessly executed.

In Spain Metellus and Pompey eventually restored the control of the government in Rome, after Sertorius was murdered by leading Romans in 73, allegedly for sacrificing military efficiency to luxurious living; his second-in-command, Perperna, could not match his skills. In the east Mithridates was originally able to control the approaches to the Black Sea with his fleet, but could not securely establish himself by land in western Bithynia. Lucullus and Cotta eventually drove Mithridates out of Bithynia and were victorious by sea. An invasion of Pontus itself followed in 71 and Mithridates was defeated at Cabeira and fled eastwards into Armenia. Lucullus was now in a position to reorganize Asia Minor in Rome's interest, but he had ambitions to advance Roman authority further.

When Pompey returned to Italy he stood for the consulship of 70 in conjunction with Crassus, in spite of the fact that he was not legally qualified to do so. Moreover, the pair did so (unusually) with a program: they proposed to restore full powers to the tribunate and put an end to the corruption in the courts, where the juries were exclusively senators. Even leading partisans of Sulla supported the restoration of tribunician power because of the corruption of the aristocracy. A flagrant example of this was Gaius Verres. His ascent through the magistracies had involved embezzlement, theft, and bribery, most strikingly in his recent three-year governorship of Sicily, where he had expected to extract enough money to bribe a senatorial jury, while retaining ample funds for advancing his future career. Pompey was exempted from the laws regarding eligibility for office, and he and Crassus were duly elected in an assembly which included many of their own demobilized soldiers. A consular law gave the tribunes back their former authority and later in the year jury service was entrusted to panels drawn from not only senators but equestrians and other wealthy men. Meanwhile, Verres was condemned by one of the last purely senatorial juries after a well-organized prosecution conducted by Marcus Tullius Cicero. He came, like Marius, from Arpinum and, after an education in Greek as well as Latin, had trained to be an advocate, beginning his practice under Sulla's dictatorship. After showing himself adept in both private and criminal cases, he was now also pursuing a senatorial career and knew Sicily through his quaestorship there in 75.

The Late Republic and the Dynasts[27]

With peace in Italy and Sertorius eliminated, the wars of the eighties at last seemed to have been put to rest. Censors were elected for the first time for 15 years and formally enrolled a great number of Italians; they also expelled from the senate 64 unworthy men. The tribunes first became policy-makers again in 67. Mithridates had taken refuge with Tigranes of Armenia, a Parthian vassal, who had also taken over the remnant of the Seleucid Syrian kingdom in the eighties. Lucullus used this as an excuse for an invasion of Armenia and even planned to invade Parthia. However, Mithridates returned to Pontus and inflicted defeats on the subordinates that Lucullus had left to defend it, while Lucullus himself was hampered by a mutinous army. The provinces of Asia Minor were successively transferred to other commanders by the senate, and in 67 the tribune Aulus Gabinius transferred Pontus itself to the consul Acilius Glabrio. More significantly, he sought to end the depredations of the pirates through a bill creating an enormous military and naval command for three years throughout the Mediterranean. The general was to have 15 lieutenants, at least 270 ships, 20 legions, 4000 cavalry, and the right to use public money wherever it was stored in the empire. The bill was passed in face of determined senatorial opposition, and the command was conferred on Pompey. It was supported by a young patrician senator, whose aunt had been married to Marius – Gaius Iulius Caesar. In the same year Gabinius and his colleague Cornelius introduced bills to restrict corrupt practices by magistrates and senators (Cornelius' measure about electoral bribery was blocked but replaced by a less drastic statute proposed by the consul).

The vast resources put at Pompey's disposal had immediate results. The pirates were eliminated from western waters within weeks and in three months from the Mediterranean as a whole. Pompey's forces then turned to besiege their strongholds in Crete and Cilicia. Meanwhile neither Glabrio nor Lucullus, whose weakened army had returned from Armenia, could defeat Mithridates. In consequence, a tribune of 66, Gaius Manilius, backed by some ex-consuls and by Cicero (now praetor), passed a law transferring the command in Cilicia and Bithynia and the Mithridatic war to Pompey under similar terms to the Gabinian law; Pompey was given in addition the authority to undertake new wars and make alliances. Pompey rapidly defeated Mithridates at Dasteira in Pontus, and the king fled by land through the Caucasus to the Crimea. Tigranes surrendered to Pompey without a fight and was allowed to keep Armenia, but not his Syrian gains. Pompey then campaigned in the Caucasus, and the peoples of the Iberi and Albani there became Roman allies. Territory beyond the Euphrates was for the most part accepted as Parthian, but Pompey intervened in Judaea to install his own nominee, Hyrcanus, as high priest, and a Roman army entered northern (Nabataean) Arabia.

In 63 Mithridates was finally either killed or forced to commit suicide by his son Pharnaces, who promptly surrendered his kingdom to Pompey. Pompey's mission was now over. He had been already reorganizing Roman rule in the east. When he returned home in 62, he left behind four provinces under direct Roman rule – Asia, Bithynia-Pontus, Cilicia, and Syria – with a large number of territories ruled by kings and dynasts, such as Galatia, Cappadocia, Judaea, and the city-states of Apamea and Emesa. These were attached to the provinces and often intertwined with provincial territory. Their rulers became Pompey's clients and were sometimes literally in his debt for their positions.

In Rome meanwhile there had been in 65 an unsuccessful proposal, backed by Crassus and involving Caesar, to intervene in Egypt. This had been left to Rome by the will of Ptolemy Alexander in the eighties but was still in the hands of a king, Ptolemy the new Dionysus, known as the Flute-Player (Auletes). Crassus was also thought to be in the background when the tribunes elected for 63 proposed the first major agrarian bill for some time, which sought to purchase land for distribution in Italy by selling public land in Italy and the provinces. Cicero had by then achieved his ambition of election to the consulship and led the opposition to the bill. Like most senators, he was in any case by instinct opposed to the public redistribution of land, but he was able to exploit suspicion of the powers of the proposed commission and the potential for corruption in sales and purchases. Among his defeated competitors in the consular election was Catiline (Lucius Sergius Catilina), a patrician and former henchman of Sulla, who was notorious for luxurious living and corruption and had been fortunate to be acquitted of extortion in his province of Africa in 66.

Catiline had probably been expected to assist Rullus' agrarian bill. When he stood again for the consulship later in 63, with a proposal for cancellation of debts, he was supported by discontented settlers and dispossessed peasants from Etruria. His candidature failed once again, and in late November his supporters in Etruria broke out in rebellion. Catiline himself was forced to leave the city by Cicero after coming under suspicion of planning a coup d'état through information provided by Crassus, among others. Catiline's supporters in the city continued to plot, but their leaders were arrested and, after an investigation by the senate, executed (December 5) – a measure of dubious legality, as Caesar protested in the final senate debate. The rebellion in Etruria was crushed early the following year, as were a number of other pockets of agrarian unrest; minor conspirators were prosecuted in the regular courts. The conspiracy exposed the persisting rural unrest in Italy, and the problem of debt, which affected in different ways both hard-pressed peasants and aristo-crats overspending in the pursuit of power, prestige, and pleasure.

An attempt to bring back Pompey swiftly from the east to deal with Catiline was blocked. When he did return in late 62, this was eclipsed as a news story by a scandal involving sex and religion. A young patri-cian, Publius Clodius, was accused of sacrilege for surreptitiously attend-ing in drag an all-female ceremony in honor of the Good Goddess (*Bona Dea*), held in the house of Caesar, who was then praetor. Clodius was acquitted in 61 amid allegations that the jury had been bribed, after Cicero had given evidence against him. Public religion was an important part of the political fabric (see chapter 6), so both the alleged offense and the acquittal were treated by conservatively minded members of the elite as tantamount to political subversion. Meanwhile Pompey took nine to 10 months to prepare the most elaborate triumphal procession and ceremony there had ever been. However, he met opposition, especially from Marcus Cato, a descendant of the censor and a relative of Lucullus, over the details of his elaborate settlement in the east, where graft must have been apparent. Nor could he get a bill through to provide distribu-tions of land for his demobilized soldiers. Cato also opposed an attempt by the equestrian tax-collectors to obtain a remission of what they had bid for the taxes of Asia but had been unable to collect through the exhaustion of the province.

Caesar's political importance had been growing. He had been elected pontifex maximus in 63 and so suffered some embarrassment from his wife's participation in the Bona Dea ceremony; after his praetorship in 62 he was a successful commander in Further Spain. He returned to be elected consul for 59, but, before he entered office, he concerted a coali-tion with Pompey and Crassus (Cicero was asked to join but refused). With their support, Caesar first passed an agrarian bill to purchase land for the demobilized soldiers, using them to force it through by violence in face of obstruction by tribunes and the announcement of evil omens. A proposal in the senate to have this declared invalid failed, and Caesar with the aid of the tribune Vatinius enacted further measures: Pompey's Asiatic settlement was ratified; the tax-collectors of Asia received their remission; the king of Egypt received formal recognition in return for a huge bribe; a further agrarian bill provided for the redistribution of public land in Campania to the plebs of Rome; and Caesar himself was given a five-year command in Cisalpine Gaul and Illyricum (the Dalmatian coast). Furthermore, Pompey received Caesar's only daughter in mar-riage to seal their political alliance, while Clodius was transformed into a plebeian so that he could stand for the tribunate.

On Pompey's proposal the senate added Transalpine Gaul (the province then covered roughly Provence and the Languedoc) to Caesar's command. Roman rule there was threatened first by a migration of the Helvetii from their Alpine home and secondly by the Swabian chief Ariovistus, who had extended his power west of the Rhine and was threatening Rome's allies the Aedui in what is now Burgundy. Caesar was provided with a magnificent opportunity to obtain wealth and glory. He defeated both the Helvetii and Ariovistus in 58 and in subsequent years used the pretext of new Gallic alliances to lead his army northward and westward, extending Roman power to the Atlantic, the Channel, and the Rhine. This was to culminate in punitive expeditions across the Rhine in 56 and into Britain in 55 and 54.

Pompey seemed to have achieved a primacy for himself at Rome, but Clodius, elected tribune for 58, used the support he had been cultivating among the urban plebs to make himself temporarily master of the city. He restored freedom of assembly to the *collegia*, the urban associations based on trade, domicile, and religious cult, and exploited them systematically for violence. Cato in 62 had extended cheap grain distributions to the whole free population of Rome; Clodius now abolished the charge. Other laws of his placed limits on the use of religious obstruction against legislation, changed the allocation of provinces in the interest of the consuls, Gabinius and Lucius Piso, and set in motion the annexation of Cyprus (left to Rome by its final Egyptian ruler, Auletes' brother). This last task was entrusted to Cato, who had a reputation for incorruptibility and was thus conveniently removed from Rome. Clodius had not forgotten Cicero's evidence in 61 or his treatment of the Catilinarians and passed a law exiling anyone who had executed a Roman citizen without trial. Cicero, under threat from Clodius' gangs, eventually withdrew from Rome, and Clodius passed a second bill forcing him to live outside Italy and confiscating his properties (his Palatine house was to become a shrine to Liberty).

Pompey had done nothing to help Cicero, in spite of earlier promises. Clodius now reduced Pompey's stature further by terrorizing him into self-incarceration in his own house. Even after he left office in December 58, Clodius controlled the streets until Milo and Sestius mobilized gangs of professional fighters in Cicero's interest. Pompey finally lent his authority to Cicero's recall in summer 57 at a time when Clodius' credit was damaged by a bad harvest and high corn prices. On Cicero's return the consuls created a new post for Pompey in charge of the corn supply, but Clodius systematically undermined his popularity with the urban plebs. In spring 56 Caesar's political enemies were planning to replace him in Transalpine Gaul. In consequence, the three dynasts held a summit at Luca (modern Lucca) , in which it was agreed that all three should have provincial commands and armies. Caesar's command was to be extended for five years; Pompey and Crassus were to become consuls again in 55 and then to govern respectively the Spanish provinces and Syria for five years. Elected consuls through a mixture of political chicanery and violence, they duly put into effect this distribution of military power (between them the three now controlled upward of 20 legions). Pompey, moreover, was permitted to govern Spain in his absence through deputies (*legati*).

After his invasions of Britain Caesar was occupied from 54 to 51 by a series of Gallic revolts. Crassus had a project for extending Pompey's conquests in the east by an invasion of Mesopotamia, now Parthian territory. He and his army, however, was cut to pieces by the cavalry and mounted archers of King Orodes on the plain of Carrhae in 53. Pompey mostly remained in his villa on the fringe of the city of Rome. Violence and corruption continued to dominate politics, until in January 52 Milo's gang murdered Clodius on the Appian Way. Pompey was then granted what he had been seeking to secure for a number of years – a commission to restore order at Rome (for a time he was elected sole consul). Milo and others were condemned by a special court for violence; others for electoral bribery. For the future, provincial commands were not to be given to those holding city magistracies, in order to leave the men open for prosecution. The exception was Pompey himself, who continued to command his legions in 51.

The death of Crassus in 53 and that of Pompey's wife Julia, the daughter of Caesar, in 54 had transformed the trio of dynasts into a mutually suspicious couple. Pompey wished to retain his prime position in Roman politics without the need for the corrupt methods he had used before; Caesar, with the glory of his Gallic victories and with enormous quantities of Gallic gold and silver at his disposal, wanted a triumphant return home, a second consulship, and then perhaps a further command in Parthia. He did not want to be in Rome as a private citizen in case his enemies should prosecute him over the violence or corruption he had been party to in the past. He therefore, obtained from the tribunes of 52, with Pompey's support, a statute that permitted to him to stand for the consulship in his absence and so return to the city as a magistrate immune from prosecution. After his own consulship, however, Pompey feared that, if Caesar did become consul a second time, new popular measures would destroy the order he had established, and in this he was supported by most leading members of the conservative aristocracy. In consequence from mid-51 there was pressure on Caesar to give up his army and return home without the guarantee of a second consulship. Caesar offered to reduce his command and army to a minimum, but eventually the senate voted on January 5, 49 that he should leave his provinces and his army should be disbanded by a fixed date. Two tribunes vetoed this but under the threat of an emergency decree they left the city. When Caesar heard the news he led a small force across the river Rubicon, which divided his Cisalpine province from Italy.

Civil War, Dictatorship, and more Civil War[28]

Our story has now reached a point less than 30 years from the Indian embassy. For the first 20 years of this period, as Tacitus (*Annals* 3.28) was to point out, there was civil conflict somewhere in the Roman empire, or at least the threat of it: traditional morality and the rule of law went for nothing. The forms of the Republic, it is true, continued to exist, and on occasion, especially in the aftermath of Caesar's assassination, gave the illusion of freedom, but they were manipulated by those with armies under their command. One sign of this was the insignificance of the tribunes, who in this period lost their independence. It is clear that the enormous military power required to defend and control the Roman empire had come to overawe both the original city-state and its now immensely enlarged territory, Italy. That had not necessarily entailed military rule: much was contingent and circumstantial in the origins of the civil wars. The soldiers as a whole were not mercenaries without loyalty to their fellow citizens, and their commanders needed to gain their support by political persuasion.

Conflict would not have occurred without discord and vast ambitions among the governing class. The great men, on the other hand, were not masters of their situation but dependent on those who fought for them. In particular, the rural population of Italy, which supplied the legions, looked for adequate land distribution as a reward for their services, and this required controversial legislation at Rome. The city population, for its part, which inevitably had regular and direct contact with the political process, also wished to improve its social and economic condition and was devoted to anyone, such as Clodius, who offered to provide this. It was an ungovernable Rome which provoked Pompey's third consulship of 52 and the introduction of legions into city politics, and it was Pompey's subsequent military presence near the city, which provided a military challenge to Caesar and his Gallic legions. There were solutions:

one unchallengeable military commander, regular provision of land for the soldiers, and the subjection of city politics and the city population to the needs of the empire. The sacrifice of republican tradition, however, was for a long time unacceptable: it was perhaps only the exhaustion of opposition that allowed all changes to be achieved.

In 49 BC the senate commissioned Pompey to defend the *res publica* against Caesar, but with his inadequate forces he abandoned first Rome, then Italy, and sailed to Greece. Negotiations that were attempted broke down through mutual distrust. Caesar seized Rome and the treasury and turned first to pacify Pompeian supporters in Massilia (Marseilles) and Spain. Meanwhile his lieutenant Curio seized Sicily but was unsuccessful in Africa. Caesar crossed the Adriatic with some difficulty in the winter of 49–48 and almost met disaster besieging Pompey's forces at Dyrrachium (Durazzo) in Albania. He retreated to Thessaly, pursued by Pompey, but in a pitched battle at Pharsalus (August 7, 48) the quality of his battle-hardened Gallic legions proved too much for the Pompeians. Looking for new sources of support, Pompey fled first to Asia and then to Egypt, but was murdered there by a former Roman soldier now serving the Egyptian royal house before Caesar could arrive in pursuit. Pompey's family and supporters fled either to the African province or Spain.

Caesar was detained in Egypt by his support for Cleopatra against her brother the king and by other problems in the east, but finally returned to Italy in the autumn of 47. After Pharsalus he began to hold a series of dictatorships which in theory were for re-establishing constitutional government but in practice were occupied to a great extent by further campaigning against Pompeian forces: he spent some eight months in 47–46 on an African campaign and a similar period in 46–5 on one in Spain against Pompey's sons. In Italy he introduced a number of measures, many promoted by a cabinet of advisers in his absence, most of which were reactions to immediate problems. Money was raised from confiscation of the property of his enemies. He settled veterans in Italy and abroad, especially in Spain and southern Transalpine Gaul; in the city he abolished most of the *collegia*, on which Clodius had based his power, reduced the numbers eligible for free grain with the aid of a new form of registration, and settled many of the urban plebs abroad. There were measures to relieve debt and introduce a form of voluntary bankruptcy. Penalties in the criminal tribunals were made more severe. The inadequacy of the Roman lunar calendar, caused by the failure to insert intercalary months, was remedied by a solar calendar of 365 days. However, apart from an increase in the numbers of praetors, aediles, and quaestors and an experiment with a new hierarchy of city magistracies while he was away in Spain, there was no attempt to restructure the Republic. It soon became apparent that the only significant change would be his permanent tenure of the dictatorship.

In early 44 Caesar had been made *dictator perpetuus*, but was planning to leave for the east for a campaign against the Dacians and Parthians, having held in advance the elections for the chief magistracies for the next two years, the most powerful positions being left in the hands of loyal partisans like Mark Antony and Lepidus. In the year since his defeat of Pompey's eldest son in Spain he had been heaped with honors, some of which suggested monarchy, others divinity. His statues were placed among those of the gods in temples and public displays at festivals and on floats at the games. Notoriously, he had been offered a diadem by Mark Antony at the festival of the Wolfmen (*Luperci*) in February and the presence of Cleopatra and her young son led to rumors of his planning a Hellenistic kingdom in the east. This was the background to his murder (March 15, 44) by a group of senators, numbering originally about 20, led by Marcus Brutus, Gaius Cassius, and Decimus Brutus. They seem to have thought that political freedom would never return, if Caesar was allowed to leave the city (where he had dismissed his bodyguard) and surrounded himself once more with devoted legionaries. However, they had no policy for what was to follow: indeed it is hard to see what policy they could have sensibly formed.

On Caesar's death there were two remnants of Pompeian resistance: Pompey's younger son Sextus, who was operating as a guerilla leader in Spain, and Caecilius Bassus, an adventurer who had begun a rebellion with one legion in Syria. There were over 30 legions spread round the Roman empire, whose primary sympathies would naturally be Caesarian. The city population, for whom Caesar continued to show his patronage in his will, were for the most part hostile to the assassins. In Italy, the leading men of many country towns, whether *colonia* or *municipium*, had largely favored Caesar since 49 BC. Money and sources of bullion were mainly in Caesarian hands. The conspirators were indeed granted (for the time being) an amnesty, but at the price of allowing the senior consul Mark Antony discretion to put into effect any plans that he found in Caesar's papers.

Two conspirators, Decimus Brutus and Trebonius, were allowed to go to their provincial governorships under Caesar's arrangements. Marcus Brutus and Cassius were hounded out of exercising their city praetorships and eventually left Italy also, in theory with public commissions relating to the corn supply in the east, in practice to foment military rebellion. The leading Caesarians' control of Rome and the west would have been unshaken, had Caesar not left an heir, who was to provide a rival focus of loyalty. This was the man who, as Augustus, was later to be the acknowledged ruler of the Roman world.

Gaius Octavius was the great-nephew of the dictator through his sister Julia, born in 63, the year of Cicero's consulship. His father came from the *municipium* of Velitrae (Velletri) and had pursued a senatorial career as far as the praetorship. Caesar, who had no surviving legitimate children of his own, had made him his chief heir, while dictator, and was planning to take him on his eastern expedition. Octavius inherited in theory two-thirds of Caesar's wealth and his legal personality, becoming the head of his family, eventually by a form of adoption, and being responsible for the payment of legacies and debts. After the legal formalities he became Gaius Iulius Caesar Octavianus (he is usually known in modern works as Octavian). He called himself, however, Caesar and eventually was to exploit the rumors inspired by the appearance of a comet after the dictator's death to consecrate his adoptive father formally and to create for himself a title, *imperator Caesar divi filius*, "Caesar the commander, son of the divine." As Caesar's heir, he was the natural patron of the dictator's innumerable dependants, in particular soldiers, both serving and discharged, and he quickly gave himself a high profile in the city, supporting the games created in honor of Caesar and his family. Mark Antony made it difficult for him to get hold of all of Caesar's money, but there were wealthy partisans of Caesar to help fund his expenditure. Octavian made a cause out of avenging Caesar; Antony also took a harder line against the conspirators and began to behave in a more authoritarian fashion himself. In consequence, in the words of Augustus' later official biography, "at the age of 19 I recruited an army on my personal initiative and at personal expense, through which I forcibly liberated the *res publica* which was oppressed by the domination of factional power."[29] The expense was considerable: he was offering 500 silver *denarii* a man, more than twice an ordinary soldier's annual pay.

After Octavian had made an abortive march on Rome and successfully suborned the loyalty of two of Antony's legions, Mark Antony retired before the end of his consulship to Cisalpine Gaul, which he planned to take over from Decimus Brutus. The following year (43 BC) Antony's Caesarian opponents made an improbable and impermanent alliance against Antony with certain of the conspirators. The consuls, Aulus Hirtius and Gaius Vibius Pansa, supported by a legitimized Octavian (given the right to command, though a private citizen), led armies to

Cisalpine Gaul to relieve Decimus Brutus, who was being besieged by
Antony. Meanwhile in the east, when Marcus Brutus illegally seized
control of Macedonia and its legions from Antony's brother, this was
approved by the senate, as was eventually a similar coup by Cassius in
Syria.

Cicero was the conspirators' chief representative at Rome and the
"Philippic" speeches against Antony and his faction were his oratorical
swansong. However, after Antony had been twice defeated at Mutina at
the cost of the lives of the two consuls and many men on both sides,
political logic reasserted itself. Caesar's heir and avenger would not
cooperate with Caesar's assassin, Decimus Brutus, with the result that
Antony escaped to Transalpine Gaul, where he brought over first Lepidus
and then other Caesarian generals, Plancus and Pollio, to his side. A
powerful factor was the soldiers themselves and their officers, who, after
the carnage at Mutina, could not see why good Caesarians should be
killing one another. Octavian for his part, with an army whose demands
for money and land could not be satisfied by a resourceless senate, chose
to march on Rome and got himself elected consul a month before his
twentieth birthday. Immediately a law was passed providing for special
prosecutions of the conspirators against Caesar. Three months later
negotiations between the Caesarians near Bononia led to the formation
by statute of a triumvirate for re-establishing constitutional government
(November 27, 43), originally to last five years. This was in effect a triple
dictatorship, whereby Antony, Octavian, and Lepidus were to defeat the
conspirators and the republicans with them, satisfy their soldiers with
land, and to control public administration, as Caesar had done, for the
foreseeable future.

There are two main intertwining stories in triumviral history: first
the elimination of opposition to the Caesarians, secondly the rivalry
between the Caesarian leaders themselves. The triumvirate began with
proscriptions, like Sulla, designed as much to seize assets in money
and land, as to kill people. Moreover, 18 cities in Italy were marked
down for the future settlement of the soldiers who were to march
under Antony and Octavian to the east against Brutus and Cassius.
The latter had imitated Pompey's strategy in mobilizing the east, partly
through charisma but also through ruthless exactions from provincials
of money to pay their armies. One of Brutus' coin issues had a reverse
recalling the assassination – the cap of liberty between two daggers
and the legend "EID. MAR."[30] Antony and Octavian crossed the
Adriatic only to be cut off from Italy by fleets loyal to the conspirators. However, when the armies confronted one another on a plain in

Macedonia beside the great road to the east, the *via Egnatia*, Cassius and Brutus allowed themselves to be provoked into pitched battle. The first battle was indecisive but led to Cassius' suicide; the second was a Caesarian victory (October 23, 42). The site, near the town which Alexander the Great's father had created to serve the nearby mine-workings, was later celebrated by the foundation of the Roman colony of Philippi.

The cause of the Republic was now lost. Antony, to whom administration of the east was assigned, took over the allegiance of the republican fleets, except that of Sextus Pompey who had established himself in Sicily. The latter's stranglehold over Rome's corn supply was a threat to Octavian, whose task it was to settle the demobilized troops and restore peace to Italy. The seizure of land for distribution provoked a rebellion, aided by Antony's brother Lucius, who was consul, and Antony's wife Fulvia. The rebel base, Perusia, was besieged (sling-shots survive from this siege with obscene messages directed at Octavian, Fulvia, and Lucius Antonius). When the city fell, Octavian took vengeance on the prisoners-of –war. The dissidence among the Caesarians in the west led to the return of Antony to Italy in 40. While in the east he had had his first liaison with Cleopatra, who bore him twins, a boy and girl, and he would have no doubt derived satisfaction from the attempted destabilization of Octavian, whether he had authorized it or not. It seemed that he would settle matters by arms, but, when he landed at Brundisium, the Caesarian soldiers refused to fight one another and forced a reconciliation, which was cemented by the marriage of Antony to Octavian's sister Octavia.

Lepidus, who had first administered Italy in 43–42 and then Spain, was assigned Africa, where he may have begun the refoundation of Carthage as a Roman colony, a project planned by the dictator (see figure 4b). The rest of the west was left to Octavian, though the command of Sextus Pompey in Sicily, Sardinia, and Corsica was recognized by agreement (he was also offered, but never in fact received, the Peloponnese). Meanwhile in the east Quintus Labienus, a supporter of Brutus and Cassius, fled to Parthia and returned in a unique fashion. He shared the command of Parthian forces with their prince Pacorus and led his men as far as the Aegean, farther west than any other Parthian army ever marched. He struck Roman silver *denarii* with his head and the legend, Q. LABIENUS PARTHICUS IMP(erator), on the obverse and Parthian iconography on the reverse.[31] However, the Parthian armies were twice defeated by Antony's deputy Ventidius Bassus, a man who as an Italian boy had been led in a triumph after the War of the Allies.

Figure 6   The harbor at Cape Misenum developed by Marcus Agrippa for the war against Sextus Pompey, looking south towards the bay of Naples.

Antony returned to the East with his new wife in late 39. For a time they were based in Athens, where the couple received divine honors. The marriage produced two daughters but no son. Antony supervised the reorganization of Asia Minor after the Parthian retreat, creating a number of dependent monarchies for men he trusted. Before long he needed to return to Italy. The term of the triumvirate ended at the beginning of 37. Octavian was now, unsurprisingly, at war with Sextus Pompey; there had been friction over Sextus' control of the corn supply and one of the latter's subordinates had defected, bringing with him control of Sardinia and Corsica. A new agreement between the two triumvirs (Lepidus was not consulted) was eventually reached at Tarentum for the triumvirate to continue a further five years. Antony left Octavian ships to make up for his losses in two naval defeats, while Octavian promised Antony legionaries for an anticipated Parthian campaign; they were never to be sent.

In 36, after the creation of a new naval base at Cumae and Misenum by Octavian's admiral Marcus Agrippa (figure 6), a full-scale invasion of Sicily was mounted with Lepidus' cooperation. At sea Sextus defeated Octavian but lost to Agrippa. More important, the invasion forces got ashore. Sextus was soon confined to the northeastern tip of the island. He was finally defeated at sea by Agrippa at Naulochus (September 3, 36) and fled with a few ships to the east, where he tried to cause trouble for Antony but eventually was captured and killed. On land Lepidus seized Messina and tried to negotiate for himself a greater command, but the loyalty of his troops was unreliable and they put themselves in Octavian's hands. Lepidus was stripped of his membership of the triumvirate and military command, though not of the post of pontifex maximus that he had acquired after Caesar's death. He was to live almost invisibly until 12 BC. Three dynasts had become two.

Octavian exploited the victory by claiming the civil wars were now ended (no Pompeians were left in arms in the west). To lend substance to his claim, he demobilized some troops, took measures to end the general breakdown of law and order in Italy, and encouraged a semblance of republican government. In his *Res Gestae* (25.1) he did not refer to Sextus by name but described the operation as a suppression of piracy and stated that he returned about 30,000 slaves to their masters for punishment.

In the same year Antony had taken over Caesar's great project for an invasion of Parthia, hoping to exploit any confusion at the beginning of the reign of Phraates (IV), son of Orodes. His attempt to do the unexpected by entering from the North – through Armenia into Media Atropatene – proved delusory. Once the Parthians had reacted, his ally, Artavasdes of Armenia, deserted him, and he had a difficult retreat through inhospitable terrain in winter. He had earlier resumed his relationship with Cleopatra. So, with a conflict on the horizon, he was already handing a considerable propaganda advantage to Octavian. However, he concentrated his energies on a further expedition to the east; Artavasdes of Armenia was brought back in chains to Alexandria in 34 and the Parthian border continued to be his military focus. At the same time, apparently uncaring of the effect that this would have in Italy, he behaved simultaneously as a Roman supreme magistrate and the consort of the Egyptian queen, becoming Dionysus (Osiris) to her Isis, recognizing her eldest son as Ptolemy Caesar, and, in a notorious ceremony at Alexandria, assigning territories in the east to him and to Cleopatra's other children whom he himself had fathered.

The insults to Octavian and his sister gave rise to a war of words, including a defensive pamplet by Antony, "On his own Drunkenness," but Octavian's underlying purpose was clear – to portray Antony as someone in league with an alien and a potential enemy of Rome.

Meanwhile, he gained more military experience and credibility by a campaign in Illyricum in 34. In 32 the 10 years of the triumvirate theoretically came to an end; neither triumvir resigned. Instead the pro-Antonian consuls, Sosius and Domitius Ahenobarbus, used their position to denounce Octavian's behavior. He responded by entering the senate with an armed guard, and the consuls fled. For the rest of the year Octavian continued to behave as if he were triumvir without asserting the title. He opened and read in the senate an alleged copy of Antony's will, which contained a recognition of Caesarion as Caesar's son and large bequests to him and to Cleopatra's other children: Antony himself was to be buried beside her in Alexandria. On this basis Octavian obtained a declaration of war against Cleopatra; Antony's name was not mentioned. Neither Antony's nor Cleopatra's name was to appear on the subsequent celebratory coinage[32] or in the *Res Gestae* (27.1).

Octavian then engineered an oath of loyalty from Italy and the western provinces, granting exemption to those under Antony's patronage, if they wished to use it. In his own version, they "demanded him as their leader in the war which he won at Actium."[33] He acquired a more constitutional legitimacy by being elected consul for 31 BC. For his part Antony swore to his troops that he would fight to the end without negotiation and within two months of his victory would return his powers to the senate and people. In the meantime the majority of his Roman silver *denarii* continued to display him as triumvir, while on other Roman and Greek issues he appeared on the obverse with Cleopatra on the reverse, suggesting an alternative life, once he had given up office at Rome.

In spite of the great forces assembled on either side the campaign was something of an anticlimax. An invasion of Italy with Cleopatra's support would have been politically disastrous as well as militarily problematic. So Antony chose to defend his frontier, the western coast of Greece. However, both Agrippa and Octavian landed forces and Antony was soon confined to his base at Actium on the Ambraciot gulf (modern Preveza). He had suffered minor defeats at sea; he had lost control of the north side of the gulf; his sea-borne corn supplies were cut off; to his rear Corinth and Patras were now in the hands of his opponents. He chose to sail out (September 2, 31), apparently to fight, but in fact to retreat after a comparatively brief battle (perhaps his plan from the beginning). In the event he had ceded victory not only in the battle, but in the war.

In the next eleven months Octavian was able to win over the eastern provinces and kingdoms until only Egypt remained, under attack both from Cyrenaica and the east. There was some attempt to negotiate, but Antony was defeated in a major engagement, and on August 1, 30 Octavian entered Alexandria. That day Antony committed suicide in a painful but spectacular fashion; Cleopatra followed suit even more sensationally nine days later when in Octavian's custody. Egypt was now subjected to the power of the Roman people, and Caesar (Octavian) both succeeded to the throne of the Ptolemies and pharaohs and at Rome was the only dynast left in power.

4

The Emperor and His People

The New Regime

> After Antony was killed, even the Julian party had only one leader left, Caesar. He laid aside the title of triumvir and paraded himself as consul and content with the tribunician right to protect the plebs. Once he had seduced the army through bounties, the populace through the corn supply, and everyone through the delight of peace, he gradually advanced his power, drawing to himself the functions of senate, magistrates, and laws, with no opposition, since the most militant had fallen on the battlefield or through proscription, while the remainder, in proportion to their readiness for servility, were being advanced through wealth and high office and, because they prospered under the new dispensation, preferred the security of the status quo to the dangers of the past.

So wrote Rome's greatest historian, Tacitus (*Annals* 1.2) on the general progess of Augustus' reign. Elsewhere he marks out the political turning point: "finally in his sixth consulship (28 BC) Caesar Augustus, unchallenged in his power, abolished his enactments during the triumvirate and granted us the laws which gave us peace and a prince (*princeps*)" (*Annals* 3.28). The ensuing regime was not called a monarchy (*regnum*), anathema for Romans since the last king was expelled in 509, but a "principate." Augustus' action has been strikingly illustrated by a unique gold coin, recently acquired by the British Museum: its obverse has Augustus' head and title in 28 BC, "Imperator Caesar son of the divine (i.e. Julius Caesar), consul for the sixth time," and its reverse shows the emperor seated, taking a scroll from a box, with the legend "He restored laws and justice to the Roman people."[1]

The years of war and arbitrary authority were set aside, but stability and justice were to be assured by Augustus' continuing leadership. In his official autobiography the emperor was to state that in his sixth and seventh consulships (28 and 27 BC), when in control of everything with universal consent, he transferred public affairs (*res publica*) from his power to the direction of the senate and people. In return for this he was given the name "Augustus"; his doorposts were wreathed with laurel (the emblem of victory: in fact coins show his doors with laurel trees growing on either side); a crown of oak-leaves, awarded for saving the lives of fellow citizens, was placed on the lintel, and a golden shield was placed in the senate-house, commemorating his manly virtue, clemency, justice, and piety. A marble copy of this shield has been found at Arles (Arelate) in Provence.[2] Subsequently, continues the autobiography, "I was supreme in authority but had no more power than the others who were my colleagues in each of my magistracies" (*RG* 34.1–3).

This first claim about the transfer of power was fraudulent, the final claim disingenuous. It is not the aim of this book to discuss all the detail of Augustus' constitutional arrangements, to which the work of Werner Eck[3] provides a useful introduction, nor to follow the twists of politics, which led Augustus to redefine not only his constitutional powers but the function he conceived that he had to fulfill.[4] The essentials, however, give the lie to the autobiography. The emperor, it is true, was officially, when consul, only one of the two consuls at Rome, but his continuous run of nine consulships from 31 to 23 BC inclusive was hardly republican. Moreover, his tribunician power, whose protective element had been granted in 30 BC and was to be amplified in 23 by the political elements, was equivalent to the power of the whole college of tribunes, since the ordinary magistrates were not his colleagues. When later he received colleagues in this special power – first Agrippa, then his stepson Tiberius – these were members of his family. In 27 BC, while consul, he was assigned a gigantic package of territories to govern, in which the bulk of the legionary troops were stationed: the Gallic and Spanish provinces, Syria with Cilicia Pedias (in the plain), Cyprus, and Egypt. For most of these he appointed deputies of praetorian rank (*legati pro praetore*) to carry out day-to-day government; in Egypt there was, exceptionally, an equestrian prefect. From the middle of 23 BC when, on demitting the consulship, he was granted an overarching "greater" proconsular power, he was the superior not only to his own deputies but to any governor anywhere (Agrippa was eventually given equal power to any governor anywhere; otherwise only Tiberius at the end of the reign shared Augustus' exceptional proconsular power). Moreover, this power remained with the emperor when he entered the city of Rome and from 19 BC was amplified by active consular power there.

Theoretically, returning the direction of public affairs (*res publica*) to senate and people was the restoration of republican government, even if it was only superficially the old Republic, and the contrast between appearance and reality created tensions and friction. Why did Augustus bother? In this way he might avoid assassination by "honorable men"; he could use the lawyers on his side; he could check the infinite demands on his patronage from those who had helped him (or claimed to have done) in the civil wars; above all, he could avoid the question "Why not restore the Republic?" The Republic was, after all, the only constitution that Rome had had in the last 500 years and the foundation of its greatness. However, not only present government but past history was to be subsumed in the dominance of Augustus and his family.

This was certainly the vision of Rome's allies, who saw Augustus as the one figure of universal power left, both before and after the official abolition of the triumvirate. In 29 BC a spokesman of the fishermen from the tiny Greek island of Gyaros came to Corinth in order to ask Augustus directly for a remission of tribute. About three years later Chaeremon of Tralles in Asia Minor went not to Rome, but to Augustus in northern Spain, to seek help for the rebuilding of his city.[5] By this time there were temples in Asia Minor dedicated, not only to Rome and the Divine Julius at Nicaea and Ephesus, but to Rome and Augustus himself at Nicomedia and Pergamum: the cult of Rome and Augustus followed shortly at Ephesus.[6] In Egypt the situation was even more extreme: Augustus had become the successor to the pharaohs and Ptolemies. He was represented on Egyptian temples in the same way as the former rulers, including Cleopatra. Already in 30 BC the lamplighters in the village of Oxyrhynchos were taking an oath by Caesar the god, son of god, and the emperor was subsequently termed god in an apparently automatic fashion – as in the lease of a red cow called Thayris at the Fayum village of Socnopaiou Nesos in 26 BC.[7] In due course the honors and cult were to spread both geographically to the west (though there the cult of the living was avoided) and dynastically to his wife and other members of his family.[8]

The Emperor's Family and Friends

The family had always been the core of the life of a Roman aristocrat: a man derived reputation (*fama*) from his ancestors – primarily the agnatic ascendants in the male line, but cognates through his female relatives were also important – and he sought to transmit the glory of his own achievements to his descendants. Thus families could claim to be *nobiles*, well-known. This was illustrated above all in the funerals of the aristocracy, where hired mourners in the cortège put on the death-masks (*imagines*) of the ancestors of the recently deceased and the panegyric (*laudatio*) was as much, if not more, about them as about the man or woman on the bier.[9] More generally, the family was the basis of society and law: the senior male (*paterfamilias*) had "paternal power" (*patria potestas*), over his sons, unless he emancipated them, his daughters, unless married according to the form that transferred power (*manus*) to the husband, and over his wife, if power had been transferred to him on marriage. This had a legal advantage, in that those in "paternal power" could be regarded as the agents of the *paterfamilias*, if acting with his consent. The slaves of the household were obviously subject and could be likewise used as agents; even the freedmen and freedwomen (*liberti/ ae*), were part of the household and, although not in the power of their former master, owed him devotion and were regarded as extensions of his legal personality. The family was thus central not only to the operations of the aristocracy in their political and military life, but to all Romans in their business activities: indeed most Roman business firms were families.[10]

In spite of Julius Caesar's reputation for sexual activity, we know of only two daughters by his three Roman wives (other children may have died in infancy), and allegedly one son by Cleopatra, Ptolemy Caesar. It was thus that Caesar's great-nephew, his sister's grandson Gaius Octavius, came to be adopted and become Caesar Octavianus, later the emperor Augustus. He had married during the triumvirate Scribonia, the sister of the father-in-law of Sextus Pompey, by whom he had a daughter, Julia, and then, after two hasty divorces, Livia Drusilla, the former wife of Tiberius Claudius Nero, a senator of republican sympathies. Livia brought him two stepsons, Tiberius and Drusus, the latter in her womb, the former to be eventually Augustus' successor. Augustus' full sister Octavia was married to an elderly senator, Gaius Marcellus, before her ill-starred marriage to Mark Antony, and from these had a son, Marcus Marcellus, two daughters called Marcella, and two daughters called Antonia. Thus, although the emperor had only one natural offspring, his own family was to become part of a nexus of aristocratic alliances.

Marcus Marcellus married Julia at the time when Augustus had become seriously ill in 23 BC. However, it was not clear that Augustus intended him to be his chief heir; more probably that position would have fallen to Agrippa (perhaps with the condition that he should be adopted into the Julian family).[11] Since the principate was not a monarchy, it could not be officially inherited: at best the will would have indicated the most appropriate person to fill Augustus' place, should a fully republican regime not be restored. Augustus without doubt already had dynastic ambitions. A symbol of this was the huge mausoleum built in 28 BC, whose remains are still to be seen by the Tiber in the Campus Martius, and which was part of a public park.[12] However, in 23 BC the principate was not yet secure enough to be declared openly a monarchy. As it was, Augustus, thanks to cold baths, survived the illness and, putting aside the thought of restoring the republic,[13] reformed his constitutional position; Marcellus for his part died of the same disease and his ashes were the first to occupy the mausoleum. Agrippa then married Julia and produced a large family, whose eldest boys, Gaius and Lucius, were adopted by their grandfather as his sons and Julii. Augustus' stepsons, Tiberius and Drusus, were also advanced in their careers and their families became part of the dynasty. When Agrippa died in 12 BC, the stepsons became Augustus' colleagues in his administration, while his adopted sons were not old enough to share in it. The story of the subsequent dynastic tensions and quarrels is a long one, best left to be read elsewhere.[14] The point to be stressed here is that, even if Augustus had been prepared to see the Republic return on his death, it would have been important to find an appropriate heir for his immense wealth and patronage over people of all ranks, especially the armed services. Moreover, the members of his family were among his most important advisers and the most trusted executives of imperial policy.[15]

The heads of aristocratic families traditionally consulted a group of advisers (*consilium*),drawn from both the family and outside, before taking important decisions, such as over a marriage, the punishment of a delinquent member of the family, political policy, or the making and breaking of political alliances. Two notable tribunes, Tiberius Gracchus in 133 BC and Marcus Livius Drusus in 91, had each among their advisers two of the most senior senators of the time: Gracchus had Appius Claudius Pulcher and Publius Licinius Crassus Mucianus; Drusus had Marcus Aemilius Scaurus and Lucius Licinius Crassus. A striking characteristic of the two greatest dynasts of the late Republic, however, is the importance of advisers who were neither from the family nor senators, nor even in some cases Italians. Pompey used Theophanes of Mytilene and Lucius Cornelius Balbus, who was originally from Gades (Cadiz). Caesar also used Balbus and the equestrians Oppius, Matius, and Rabirius Postumus; in 46–45 BC, when Caesar left Rome to fight Pompey's sons in Spain, these men effectively ran Rome.[16]

As Caesar's heir, Augustus had taken over some of his advisers, such as Balbus and Matius, but he also collected friends of his own: Agrippa, his chief general; Statilius Taurus and Valerius Messala Corvinus, also successful commanders; the equestrian Gaius Maecenas, patron of Virgil and Horace; the poet Cornelius Gallus, the first prefect of Egypt, but brought to ruin by what was held to be excessive ambition;[17] C. Proculeius, another equestrian; and the descendant of the historian, Sallustius Crispus. Augustus also provided for the appointment every six months of a formal council, which was in effect a sub-committee of the senate, including ordinary senators drawn by lot.[18] However, councils of family and friends must have been more frequent and overall more significant. Regrettably, but understandably, we know next to nothing about what went on in them. Secrecy, as the historian Dio Cassius pointed out (53.19.2), became the defining feature of the principate, and much of its business was among the "secrets of the household, the counsels of friends."[19] However, a torn papyrus gives us a glimpse of a reception in 12 AD of Alexandrian ambassadors in the Roman library of the temple of Apollo on the Palatine. The Alexandrians are probably arguing for the restoration of their political institutions. Present with Augustus is a council composed largely from a later generation of advisers: Tiberius, the latter's son Drusus, Messala Corvinus, a certain Masonius, Aulus Avidius Urgulanius, and others whose names are lost.[20]

We clearly have the embryo of a monarchic court under Augustus, but, as yet, it seems to be an embryo. One reason for caution about its extent is the lack of a suitable physical basis for it. The great palace still visible on the Palatine was largely a creation of Domitian (81–96 AD) after preliminary work by Augustus' Julio-Claudian successors. Augustus himself bought up two republican houses in the northwest angle of the Palatine, the so-called "House of Livia" and the "House of Augustus." The eastern rooms of the latter were used for the foundations of a temple to Apollo, which was directly accessible by a ramp from the house itself and whose portico was to be frequently the venue for senate meetings. On the east side of the piazza surrounding the temple were the Roman and Greek libraries (see above).[21] The domestic quarters of the houses, however, were little more than the home of a late-Republican noble.

Nevertheless, Augustus had a large corps of freedmen and slaves. Many indeed operated independently far from Rome. Direct attestation of these persons is comparatively rare. Their predecessors who served Julius Caesar appear in a letter of Cicero describing how he entertained Caesar with dinner on December 19, 45 BC.[22] Caesar was traveling through Campania with 3,000 soldiers and a civilian staff over 20 strong. The latter Cicero entertained in three *triclinia* (dining rooms), separating the more presentable freedmen from those less presentable and the slaves. One slave manumitted by Caesar, Licinus, was later Augustus' freedman and became a financial agent (*procurator*) in Gaul, where he used the Celtic lunar calendar as an excuse to extract 13 months of taxation each year.[23] The wealth and importance that even a slave could attain in imperial service is exemplified by a funerary dedication to a cashier of Tiberius' at the Gallic treasury from a staff of 16 slaves who were his dependants.[24] In a papyrus letter probably of the Augustan period one Suneros gives his friend Chios news received from the royal cashier of the Egyptian village of Oxyrhynchus about the corrupt practices of a certain Epaphraes: "You mustn't allow the man to ruin you; excessive kindness is the greatest disaster for men. The man who makes such a big profit from such a small sum wants to cut his master to pieces." The address shows that Chios, the "master," was in fact an imperial slave.[25]

Members of Augustus' staff at Rome – like the freedmen secretaries Polybius and Hilarion, who helped to write out his will, and those who provided the statistics in the brief guide to the empire (*breviarium*) he left behind[26] – will have been lodged near Augustus' house. There must have been also a base on the Palatine for Augustus' bodyguard. The praetorian cohorts, who derived their origin from the headquarters staff of the commander of a legion, were in effect Augustus' regiments of guards; they were intended to protect Rome and the emperor from a major attack and for the most part billeted outside the city at this time.[27] However, for more intimate security he employed another inheritance from Julius Caesar, his German bodyguards.[28] The tradition continued in the family, and names of those who served later emperors are to be found on funerary inscriptions outside Rome.[29]

Populus Romanus

We can at best make a hazardous conjecture about the totality of the persons the emperor ruled. One figure offered is 54 million.[30] On the other hand, we have figures for Roman citizens, because from early times the Romans counted them and their property, in order to determine qualifications for service in the army, to establish numbers of those liable for taxation, and to assign those counted to their appropriate position in the *comitia centuriata*, the assembly of military centuries.[31] Originally, this census probably did no more than assess and distinguish cavalry, infantry, and those males incapable of providing arms and only liable for military service in an emergency, the "proletarians" or "the men counted by head alone." Then grades were devised for the infantry, which marked off those armed more heavily from light-armed skirmishers. By 200 BC the assembly contained 18 centuries of cavalry, five "classes" of infantry centuries – of which 70 centuries were in the first, wealthiest class and 100 in the remaining four – four or five centuries of military attendants, and one century for the proletarians. In the next 100 years distinctions in military equipment became an anachronism and the elaborate organization was only important for political purposes. A century was originally 100 men, but as the population of Rome expanded, the centuries of the assembly became simply its constituent units without any precise numerical significance. For political purposes the *comitia centuriata* was biased in favor of age and wealth. It was retained by Augustus and his successors for one of its traditional functions, that of choosing the senior magistrates, the consuls and praetors. The outcomes of these elections came to be increasingly managed during the course of the reign, so that procedure was primarily ceremonial. Thus it was that, when Augustus' adopted sons died young, a law of 5 AD introduced a special pre-election in the assembly by newly formed centuries of senators and equestrians.[32]

Under the Republic the census was held approximately every five years. Every citizen was required, on pain of losing his property and liberty, to register with the censors under oath his age and property, with the names of his father, wife, and children.[33] The so-called "Altar of Domitius Ahenobarbus," an ensemble of sculptured reliefs of late-Republican date, represents, it has been argued, the registration and the sacrifice that formed part of the concluding purification rite.[34] It was possible for absentees to get another to register them, and by the late Republic this seems to have been happening automatically: Cicero is found trying to prevent Atticus being registered in his absence in order to give him a chance to make his own declaration.[35] In addition we find on a bronze inscription from Heraclea in Lucania regulations from the period after the War of the Allies, whereby the appropriate local magistrate in each community in Italy was required to conduct a census at the same time as that at Rome and to convey the documents with the results to the censors there.[36] Augustus conducted three formal censuses himself – in 28 BC, 8 BC, and 14 AD (*RG* 8.2–4) – and a further one was concluded by elected censors in 22 BC. However, we also see evidence of provision for continuous registration and assessment. Senators and equestrians were reviewed by separate commissions.[37] From the time of the law of Aelius and Sentius in 4 AD Roman fathers had to declare their children at birth,[38] and men or women their illegitimate children.[39]

Augustus records totals of Roman citizens registered which range from 4,063,000 in 28 BC to 4,937,000 in 14 AD.[40] This far exceeds the last figure for the Republic (70 BC) of 900,000 (or 910,000). The grant of Roman citizenship to most of the Italian allies after the War of the Allies would have vastly increased the citizen population (figures from the second century BC do not exceed 400,000), and we must conclude that the census of 70 BC was considerably incomplete. Nevertheless, it is hard to explain the climb from less than a million to over four million by better registration, combined with natural increase, especially in a period that included almost 20 years of civil war. The view originally held by K.- J. Beloch that, while the Republican figures represent Roman adult males, the Augustan figures represent all Roman men, women, and children has been convincingly challenged recently, but, although all women and children do not seem to have been counted, it remains highly unlikely that the Augustan figures represent only adult males.[41] The emperor also informs us about the population of the capital by declaring the numbers of members of the Roman plebs who received free grain from him – never less than 250,000, and on one occasion in 5 BC 320,000 (*RG* 15.1–2). These included boys.[42] We may consequently infer a citizen population of Rome and its neighborhood of *c.* 700,000, which would have been swelled by slaves and visiting foreigners, producing perhaps a total population of about one million.[43]

Senators and Equestrians

Roman society was structured not only by the "classes" of the military assembly but also by ranks or orders (*ordines*). The upper ranks, however, were not closed but accessible to those born to a lower station. The civil wars and the patronage of Julius Caesar and the triumvirs had granted certain men an accelerated ascent and to some extent confused the boundaries between these ranks. Nevertheless, when the wars ended, it was one of Augustus' policies to restore the hierarchy and its definitions. The supreme order was that of senators, no longer an enclave of the patricians, as when the kings were expelled, but a body which during the Republic had become less hereditary and more an aristocracy of talent in so far as it was drawn from former magistrates, who had acquired their magistracy by popular election. Since Sulla's time election to the quaestorship had brought automatic membership of the senate, though this could be lost by criminal or disgraceful behavior. Reviewing the order, as was his duty as censor in 28 BC, Augustus cut down a senate, filled with the placemen of the triumvirs and numbering over 1,000, to its traditional level, presumably that envisaged by Sulla of about 600.[44] Entry was to be still through the quaestorship, but the minimum age for this office was reduced from 30 to 25.[45]

There had been earlier no specific property qualification for senatorial status, except the low one of 400, 000 sesterces which qualified a man for the equestrian order of cavalrymen, the wider circle of the elite. *De facto* a senator would have needed more than this to pursue public office. Augustus introduced a qualification of one million sesterces.[46] In this way he reinforced the pre-eminence of the order. Moreover, he stressed its original hereditary character by granting the sons of senators the tunic with the broad stripe and the right to attend senate meetings before they were 25 (the time between their coming of age at about 16 and their entry to the senate was occupied by military service and certain minor magistracies).[47] At the very end of his official autobiography, *Res Gestae* (App.4), he remarks on the innumerable amounts he had spent on senators whose property he had increased to the appropriate level; clearly poverty was not absolutely prejudicial to membership, but imperial patronage was often critical.

The poet Ovid (Publius Ovidius Naso) was by heredity a cavalryman, born in 43 BC.[48] Both he and his brother were also granted the broad-striped tunic, presumably through Augustus' patronage in about 27 BC, as an earnest of future senatorial membership, meanwhile forming part of the squadrons of cavalry who rode in the annual parade.[49] Ovid's brother died, and, though he had held the minor magistracy of *triumvir capitalis* and was on the verge of senatorial membership, Ovid then dropped out of politics, to pursue equestrian duties in the courts and to write the poetry that had been distracting him from his duties.[50] By contrast many others attained equestrian rank through military service and used it to pursue public careers. The development of this order under Augustus was one of the most interesting features of the period.

The equestrian order was originally the source of cavalry for the Roman army.[51] In 225 BC, when the number of Roman and Campanian infantry counted in the census was 250,000, the cavalry were 23,000, roughly 9 percent of the total military manpower.[52] A select number of cavalry were granted a horse at public expense, an institution that seems to have been abolished before 100 BC. The last clear evidence for Roman cavalry fighting in units is in the history of the Jugurthine war.[53] However, when conscripted in the late Republic, they arrived with their horses. In 52 BC Caesar gave the horses of his military tribunes, Roman cavalry, and Roman reservists to his German cavalry, who were poorly mounted.[54]

The property qualification of 400,000 sesterces seems to have been already in effect in the middle Republic.[55] Hence the order roughly represented the majority of the wealthy upper class, subject to the requirement of good character and respectable birth: neither freed slaves nor their immediate descendants would have normally qualified. The status, which might in effect become hereditary, as with Ovid and Cicero's friend Atticus, was a source of pride to all its holders, as it separated them from the common plebs.[56]

The poet Horace (Quintus Horatius Flaccus) was one exception to the rules, holding the equestrian post of military tribune under Brutus in time of civil war, although son of a freedman, but then apparently failing to maintain equestrian status.[57] Another freedman's son, the unsavory Vedius Pollio, who fed his disobedient slaves to lampreys, seems to have acquired and kept equestrian rank through his services to Augustus.[58] Meanwhile, a freedman of Cotta Maximus was granted the equestrian census by his patron, and his son M. Aurelius Cottanus served Augustus as a military tribune.[59] It was only in 23 AD that a decree of the senate laid down that the gold ring, one of the insignia of the order, could only be worn by those who not only had 400,000 sesterces, but whose father and grandfather had also been freeborn and who had been permitted by the rules of Augustus' law about the theater to sit in the first 14 rows assigned to equestrians. Nevertheless, this regulation too was disregarded.[60]

In the late Republic, largely because they were made judges in the criminal courts, equestrians acquired a political importance (see ch. 3 above). Certain of them, moreover, especially those who bid for the state contracts in construction and tax-collection, had special interests to defend that might divide them from senators, who were not permitted direct involvement in such contracts. However, to describe them as a business class is to assign them an identity that is deceptive. From one point of view their interests were those of any landed class and in this respect shared with senators; from another, individuals differed considerably in their pursuits.[61] Cicero's friend Atticus prided himself on neither bidding for public contracts nor acting as financial guarantor for them. Similarly, he kept away from the law courts, neither prosecuting in public cases nor suing in his own interest in private suits; his frequent residence abroad would have disqualified him from jury service. Finally, he refused any offer of joining the staff of a provincial governor.[62] He is taken by Varro as the leading representative of the raisers of livestock in Epirus[63] – a highly profitable business, which would have advanced his status without the need for further economic pursuits.

In his speech advocating Pompey's command against Mithridates Cicero treated the tax-collectors (*publicani*) as the cream of the equestrians and distinguished them from the other businessmen in Asia.[64] Certainly, a contractor for tax-collection and his partners needed both property of their own and friends who would stand surety, in order to provide security for the vast sums involved in five-year contracts, each one amounting to tens of millions of sesterces per annum. Gnaeus Plancius, a senator who rose to the rank of aedile and was defended by Cicero in court, was the son of a leading member of the Asiatic tax-collectors. Another client, the mercurial Marcus Caelius Rufus, who reached the praetorship, was the son of a man who may have been a tax-collector in Asia and whose family certainly had wide-ranging business interests from property in Italy to estates in Africa and trading in Egypt.[65] Senators were forbidden any significant investment in shipping,[66] but the view that they could not own property abroad is mistaken:[67] it was simply that the restrictions on their leaving Italy meant that they had to manage this through agents or indeed equestrian partners. However, leading equestrians would have been as wealthy as senators were and less constrained in what they did.

Many other wealthy equestrians appear in the literature surrounding the career of Cicero.[68] Iulius Calidus was rated the most elegant poet in the period immediately after the deaths of Lucretius and Catullus. He had great estates in Africa and was in due course put on the proscription lists by Antony's aide-de-camp Publius Volumnius Eutrapelus on this account. He was also associated with Publius Cuspius, who was for a time the chief agent of the African tax-company.[69] Another man, originally equestrian, with business in Africa was Lucius Aelius Lamia. As a knight he led protests on behalf of Cicero in 58, being banned from the city for his pains, and was spokesman for the Syrian tax-collectors in 54,[70] but after Caesar's dictatorship he pursued a senatorial career, which led his family to consular status under the Principate. A client of Cicero's, Gaius Rabirius (formerly Curtius) Postumus, is known to have shipped goods from Egypt, where at one point he was appointed as a royal administrator, and appears on amphora stamps from Germany, south Italy, and Sicily.[71]

A number of Cicero's friends, who by wealth at least should have been of equestrian rank, came from Puteoli (Pozzuoli), the most important sea-port on the west coast of Italy, before the emperor Claudius built a new harbor at Ostia. Marcus Cluvius is found to have been owed money by five cities in the province of Asia.[72] Gaius Vestorius – uncultured, but a good businessman and property-manager – introduced to Puteoli the manufacture of blue pigment according to an Egyptian formula.[73] Gaius Avianius Flaccus had a public contract to ship grain to Puteoli from Sicily, while a relative in Sicyon organized the production there of Greek statues for sale abroad.[74]

Ovid claims that he was not made a cavalryman by the whirlwind of military service.[75] Many must have attained this status through the civil wars. Horace, as we have seen, was made an equestrian officer by Marcus Brutus. Among the less visible friends of the emperor, Vedius Pollio, of freedman descent, acquired this status through his services. Marcus Mindius Marcellus from Velitrae (Velletri) perhaps possessed this status through inheritance before he became prefect of the fleet during Octavian's war with Sextus Pompey.[76] The same may be true of the officer Marcus Lucilius Paetus, who was commemorated by a large circular mausoleum beside the old *via Salaria*.[77] However, another plausible example of a new equestrian is Gaius Cartilius Poplicola, who was honored with a monumental tomb at public expense outside the sea-gate at Ostia, which had a frieze with triremes' rams and scenes of fighting (figure 7); he was the chief magistrate of the colony, both absent and present, eight times, an honor that would have involved considerable expense on his part.[78]

Later, under the military organization established by Augustus, it was possible to pass from the rank of centurion to the equestrian ranks of tribune of the soldiers or prefect of a cohort or wing of cavalry.[79] Moreover, there was the possibility of an administrative career after military service – as one of the emperor's financial agents (*procurator*), as the commander in a minor province, and ultimately, for a few, as one of the prefects of the corn supply (*annona*), of Rome's city watch (*vigiles*), of the praetorian guard, or of Egypt. The most notorious figure of Tiberius' reign was L. Aelius Seianus from Volsinii in Etruria, his prefect of the guard. He had previously shared this task with his father L. Seius Strabo, who in 15–16 AD went on to become prefect of Egypt.[80] When Seianus fell in 31 AD he was replaced by Quintus Naevius Cordus Sutorius Macro, who is commemorated at Alba Fucens in the Apennines by the dedication of the amphitheater constructed according to Tiberius' will (see figure 19).[81] Military service, however, may have been a preliminary to a private career. Horace's friend Iccius left his philosophical studies to join an expedition to Arabia under Aelius Gallus in 25–24 BC, but later is found as a managing agent (*procurator*) for the estates of Agrippa in Sicily.[82]

Figure 7 The tomb of Gaius Cartilius Poplicola outside the Sea Gate at Ostia, built at public expense about 20 BC in return for his services to the town. The surviving part of the frieze shows (left) an officer and line of infantrymen and (right) the prow of a trireme with an armed warrior being grappled by another figure.

Plebeians, Freedmen, and Slaves

Society was further stratified below the level of the equestrians. A special class were those who attended on the magistrates (*apparitores*): lictors, who were the physical instruments and protectors of the senior magistrates; *viatores*, the messengers and attendants of all magistrates; heralds (*praecones*); above all, scribes, who were their secretaries and record-keepers.[83] These were all free men, but were in their turn assisted by public slaves. When the number of quaestors was raised to 20 by Sulla, he also made elaborate arrangements for the appointment and allocation of further attendants for them.[84] These were organized into *decuriae*, divisions associated with the various magistracies.[85] Horace, we are told, purchased the post of quaestorian scribe, after being pardoned for fighting at Philippi.[86] In the National Museum at Rome there is an elegant funerary altar of Quintus Fulvius Priscus, a scribe of the aediles, displaying a relief depicting him at his work with other members of his college, and also one of Quintus Natronius Rusticus, a scribe of the quaestors.[87] We even find a "master," i.e. guild principal, of the "poet scribes" or "poets and scribes": the term is ambiguous.[88] We know, however, that the addressee of one of Horace's verse epistles, Celsus Albinovanus, combined, as Horace had done, the pursuit of poetry with the profession of scribe, in which capacity he accompanied Augustus' stepson Tiberius on his expedition to Armenia.[89]

Free birth was also an important distinction. The plebeians of non-servile origin regrettably lie for the most part below the historian's horizon. Even in funerary commemoration they are greatly outnumbered by freedmen and their families: in the microcosm provided by inscriptions of the later Republic they make up about one in three, sinking to about one in four in most of the Italian epigraphy of the Principate.[90] Furthermore, under the Principate the majority of the free betray an ultimate servile descent by their nomenclature.[91] In the non-funerary prosopography provided by the later tablets relating to Pompeii, Puteoli, and Herculaneum, the vast majority of the free are either freedmen or freedwomen themselves or, as it appears by their names, ultimately of slave descent.[92] There are probable distorting factors: the evidence comes largely from towns and cities, above all Rome, where we would expect a greater number of freed slaves. Moreover, the freed urban slaves frequently belonged to funeral societies, which could defray the cost of a memorial for their ashes. In general, those freed would be likely to feel a pride and a more urgent need to commemorate their relatives and be commemorated themselves. We find at Rome the occasional modest memorial to a free person, of an apparently free family – Marcus Pullius Laetus, from the Frentani people in the Abruzzo, enfranchised after the Social War, or the trader in the cattle market (Forum Boarium) at Rome, Quintus Brutius.[93] Generally, however, the majority of the freeborn poor belong to those who have no memorial, their ashes in pots covered with tiles and earth (*a cappucina*) or unmarked amphorae, such as have been found in an area next to freedmen's tombs at the port of Rome or in the Vatican necropolises.[94]

The poor freeborn man became a figure of satire. Umbricius, freeborn but unable to perform what was now expected of a client, was later set up as an example by Juvenal in a denunciation of city life.[95] An epistle of Horace, the aim of which is to show that you cannot make a country-mouse out of a town-mouse, centers on the story of the great orator Philippus (consul in 91 BC) and a man of slender means, an auctioneer of cheap goods, Vulteius Mena, whom Philippus found at the end of the day sitting in an empty barber's stall, cleaning his own nails with a knife. Mena is free and apparently has no effective patron of his own, though his last name betrays the ultimate slave origin of his family. Philippus makes him his client by having him to dinner, leading him into a cycle of morning visits and evening dinners at Philippus' house, and ultimately tempting him to become a farmer through a part gift, part loan of the purchase price of the property. The enterprise fails, and Mena is relieved to return to his former life.[96] The less satisfactory the livelihood of such men, the more important was their pursuit of patronage, especially as those born free were not tied to a specific patron. This was part of the political system, so long as there was some freedom in popular elections. Horace pictures a member of a voting district, invited to dinner, carrying his cap and slippers under his arm-pit.[97] The memorandum on election-eering addressed to Cicero mentions both the "hard-working city folk," presumably freeborn, and the freedmen who are to be found in the forum and might help him. They would constitute a major part of the morning callers of a candidate and of those who formed a cortège when he went down to the forum.[98]

The manumission of slaves was much more common at Rome than in the Greek world and brought with it Roman citizenship. Originally, it seems that freed slaves were only enrolled by the censors in one of the four city voting districts (*tribus*). Then Appius Claudius, the censor of 312 BC, allowed them to join one of the more prestigious rural districts, but this decision was reversed by the censors of 169–168, and the original restriction remained in force till the end of the Republic. Leading Romans in that period were reluctant to see the influence of freedmen on elections and legislation spread too widely.[99] Traditionally, manumission took place either through a formal process before a higher magistrate, or through a declaration by the master at the census, or by the provisions of a will.[100] However, in the later Republic a less formal process was used among a group of friends of the master or mistress which granted them freedom without manumission. This was a kind of precarious freedom under legal protection. It meant that the property of all those so freed and the children of every woman were regarded as still belonging to their former master or mistress.[101] The procedure, nevertheless, must have contributed to the increasing number of freed slaves in the citizen body. Although a stigma still attached to the son of a properly manumitted freedman, like Horace, and his descendants, they might, as we have seen, even achieve equestrian status. It was only in 23 AD that a rule was established requiring three generations of free birth for those classified as knights.[102]

Augustus, we are told, disliked the pollution of the citizen body by foreign and slave blood: seeing the audience at one of his public speeches in grey cloaks (the equivalent of "hoodies") he cried out, quoting Virgil, "Look at the Romans, the race in togas who are masters of the world."[103] The Fufian Caninian law of 2 BC limited the proportion of the slave household that could be manumitted in a single will; the Aelian Sentian law of 4 AD added further restrictions depending on the age of the manumittor, the age of the slave, and the proof of a just cause before a council of assessors in formal legal procedure.[104] It seems to have been thought impossible to forbid informal liberation of slaves: instead the Iunian law assigned to those who received freedom in this way a defined status, inferior to that of citizen, called Iunian Latinity. They were unable to inherit or make wills, their property reverting to their former master or mistress. Publicly, they could not vote or stand for office. However, there was an escape route. If a man married and had by a Roman or a Latin woman a child who lived for a year, he achieved citizenship for himself and the child. A woman achieved the same through marriage and a child, but only with a Latin husband.

Manumission and its complexities led to curious personal histories. On a funerary monument from near Caserta, Pontia Rhodope, a freedwoman, commemorates her son Quintus Pontius Paullinus, who had also been freed but died aged 12.[105] Like his mother he took his name from his former master Q. Pontius Rufus, but she proudly states that he was the (illegitimate) son of Gaius Sosius, a man at least of the family of the consul of 32 BC – Mark Antony's admiral, but subsequently accepted into the Augustan aristocracy – if not that C. Sosius himself. Perhaps Sosius had asked for the manumission of mother and child. Another inscription, found in the Campus Martius at Rome but now lost, commemorates a family of freed slaves, three of whose male members were either record-keepers (*scribae librarii*) or messengers (*viatores*) for magistrates.[106] Both Gaius Proculeius Heracleo and Proculeia Stibas must have been slaves of C. Proculeius, the equestrian friend of Augustus. They had a child in slavery, but she was not liberated by Proculeius; instead Culicina, the "little mosquito," became first a slave and then the freedwoman of the empress Livia. Once freed herself, she had two successive *viatores* (messengers) as husbands, Calpetanus Cryphius and Fabius Cytisus, the latter once the slave of Quintus Fabius Maximus Africanus, the consul of 10 BC. The former gave her a son, named Calpetanus Livianus, who went on to become the senior centurion in a legion (*primus pilus*), marrying a free woman Plasidiena Agrestina. It was she who set up the monument to the family, including Cytisus' brother, who had also probably changed hands as a slave, being called Lucius Nymphidius Philomelus.

The most intriguing microhistory, however, belongs to a later period, a lower level of society, and a provincial town. A group of tablets from the Casa del Bicentenario at Herculaneum documents a lawsuit in the reign of Vespasian, brought by a young woman called Petronia Iusta, who was free, but confessedly illegitimate ("daughter of Spurius"), and had been brought up by foster-parents, Petronius Stephanus and Calatoria Themis. Iusta's mother, a freedwoman called Petronia Vitalis, was apparently dead, but Iusta was seeking to prove that she herself was actually born free, after her mother had been manumitted. This would have allowed her to escape the status of Iunian Latin with its restrictions on marriage. Her foster-parents contested this, claiming that she was their freedwoman. Sadly, we neither know the result of the case nor the identity of her natural father, a role for which there were at least three candidates. What the case does document, however, is how the liberated slaves of a household could go on living in close proximity, in this case in what was probably once the family home of the original master.[107]

Their potentiality for liberation made even slaves significant members of Roman society. So did their contribution to Roman administration, industry, and commerce. At the summit of this were the slaves of the emperor, as we have seen, who enjoyed more wealth and power than many free men. Some worked in the public sector; others did what the slaves of any wealthy man might do, make money for themselves and their master.[108] Imperial slaves were only an extreme example of the important role that slaves performed more generally. A reason for this was the restricted notion of agency in Roman law. If a free man, not in the "power" (*potestas*) of another, as a man's son might be, was appointed an agent (*procurator*) by mandate, this did not create a liability between the principal and any third party that he, the agent, was authorized to deal with or vice versa: the mandatee agent was liable to the principal, while the third party and the mandatee were mutually liable. However, this was no longer true if the agent was a slave, a so-called *institor*, who could bind his master with any undertaking he made, providing that he was acting on the master's instructions, and similarly could create a liability of a third party to his master, so that the latter could sue on a contract. By the late Republic this capacity of a slave *institor* had been extended by legal interpretation to a freedman in the same situation.[109]

Slaves were active in trades and professions. A man called L. Manneius, freedman of Quintus, a doctor who cured by giving wine, was by birth Menekrates, son of Demetrius, of Tralles in Asia. He must have obtained his Roman citizenship after having first become a slave, perhaps using this as an underground method of obtaining Roman citizenship.[110] In 54 BC a freedman of Cicero's enemy Gabinius, his official secretary (*accensus*) Antiochus Gabinius, was condemned under the Papian law for acquiring Roman citizenship illegally. He is said to have been formerly a painter from the studio of Sopolis and presumably was thought to have posed fraudulently as a slave in order to be manumitted later.[111] The freedman goldworker from the Sacred Way at Rome, Marcus Caedicius Eros, probably started business as a slave, gaining liberation after he prospered.[112] In the dedications made by certain guilds from Rome to Fortuna Primigineia at Praeneste – cart-drivers, cooks, butchers, basket-makers, and others – slaves are found together with the freedmen.[113]

Like freedmen, slaves might travel as agents for their master. Both Gaius Numidius Eros and Lysa, the slave of Publius Annius Plocamus, inscribed their names by the road that led from the Nile to the Red Sea; Epaphroditus, the slave of Novius, a perfume-seller from the Sacred Way, is found on the island of Ithaca.[114] Cicero commended to Appuleius, the acting quaestor of Asia, a slave of the equestrian Lucius Egnatius, named Anchialus, on business for his master in the province "with the same energy as if I were commending my own business."[115] Slaves, like freedmen, acted as couriers for the elite.[116] Quintus Cicero's slave Statius may have been still his slave, when first appointed as his governor's secretary (*accensus*): his brother Marcus was enraged that the man had been getting above himself.[117]

There was always, however, the other side to slavery. A slave was a chattel, without the protections available to free men, to be treated by masters or mistresses as they liked, and to be sold or otherwise disposed of at their discretion or that of their creditors. The tablets relating to Pompeii, Puteoli, and Herculaneum illustrate both the business activity of slaves and at the same time how, if their master was in financial trouble, they could be put up for auction like an animal or a piece of furniture.[118] Punishment was also severe. We are told that Augustus combined severity with affability and clemency towards his slaves and freedmen. When a slave expressed exceedingly disrespectful thoughts about him, he did no more than fetter him. A freedman who was found to have had sex with married women was forced to commit suicide; a slave secretary who received bribes had his legs broken; the slave attendants of his son Gaius, who used the occasion of the latter's illness and death to be highhanded and exploit the provincials, were thrown into a river with weights round their necks.[119] We possess a fragment of a bronze tablet from Puteoli, plausibly dated to the Augustan period, displaying the terms of the town's contract with the municipal undertaker and executioner.

> The contractor shall execute punishment according to their wishes for anyone who wishes punishment to be executed privately on a slave or slave-woman. If the person wishes the slave taken to the cross on a hurdle, the contractor is obliged to provide posts, fetters, ropes for the floggers, and floggers. And whoever shall execute punishment is obliged to pay for each of the operatives who carry the hurdle, and for each of the floggers, and likewise for the executioner, 4 sesterces.[120]

For a public execution by magistrate, the contractor had to provide crosses, nails, pitch, wax, and candles *gratis*, also operatives dressed in red, if the body was to be dragged off with a hook.

During the Principate measures were introduced by a number of emperors to control the treatment and punishment of slaves. If they committed a criminal offense, they were to be tried like free men – a senate decree of Tiberius' reign. Those exposed on the Tiber island (figure 8) because they were ill were to become free and Iunian Latins if they recovered – a decree of Claudius. First Domitian, then Hadrian, banned castration of slaves, and the latter both forbad the killing of a slave without the support of a public judgment and restricted cruelty and torture, while Antoninus Pius ruled that the killing of a slave should be treated as homicide. However, rulings from the later Empire suggest that there was then some retreat from the more liberal attitudes of the second century AD.[121]

Figure 8 The bridge (seen from the south) originally constructed by Lucius Fabricius, a curator of roads, in 62 BC which connected the Tiber island and its healing sanctuary of Aesculapius with the Campus Martius.

The Status of Women

In a society composed of families, each of which was in the power of a male *paterfamilias*, women were inevitably in an inferior position to men in private life. In public life the traditional ethos of the Republic, like that of other ancient cities, was that full citizenship was for those who fought to defend the community (the adult males), and this was expressed in the centuriate assembly created by the classification of the censors. Nevertheless, the exploitation of certain facets of Roman law had created by Augustus' time a certain amount of independence in private matters for women, of which they – especially, but not exclusively, the wealthy and members of the elite – made full use, when free from male intervention.

Much depended on marriage and the form it took. An unmarried woman would, on the death of her father and the dissolution of paternal power (*patria potestas*), become *sui iuris*, legally independent. So would a married woman in her husband's power on his death. According to the law of the Republic, all independent women, except the privileged Vestal Virgins, were required to have a guardian (*tutor*) to approve legal transactions, and originally he was either the man designated by the father or husband in his will or, in case of intestacy, the closest member of the agnatic family. However, both a husband and a father could allow a woman choice of guardian in their wills.[122] Moreover, by the end of the Republic a number of women, owing to their own or their father's preference, married "without the hand" and so remained in their fathers' power. This meant that they were likely to become independent sooner than if they were in the power of a comparatively young husband. Finally, Augustus in his marriage legislation granted to women with three children not only independence but freedom from the need to have a guardian.[123]

The extent that women engaged in business transactions later is shown by a decree of Claudius' reign, the *senatus consultum Velleianum*, which forbad women to undertake another's liability.[124] The decree presented itself as a generous move to exempt women from being induced to rescue a husband or other connection from debt, but underwriting others might also have had a financial *quid pro quo* in the shape of a property concession or a business partnership. In high society women are found owning property designed to yield profits. Cicero's client Aulus Caecina had married a wealthy widow, Caesennia, who had sought to get ownership of a number of contiguous estates in Etruria.[125] The emperor Nero's aunt owned fishponds at her Baian villa and warehouses at Puteoli.[126] At the other end of society Gavia Philumena from the Aventine hill was involved in business with a slave goldsmith Cucuma and a freedman of a different family,[127] while Atistia, the wife of the baker Vergilius Eurysaces whose famous oven-shaped tomb stands outside the Porta Maggiore at Rome, probably worked in the family firm; she was commemorated on a travertine slab, inserted into the facade of the tomb, representing a bread-basket.[128]

Few professions, however, except the oldest one, were open to them. In the Republic the two women perhaps best known to us outside the aristocracy are prostitutes: Faecenia Hispala, who informed on the Bacchanalian conspiracy, and Manilia, who stopped an aedile visiting her by force.[129] However, the stage was a route to fame. "You ask about Arbuscula," Cicero wrote to Atticus, "She went down really well." Once, when hissed off the stage, the mime-actress remarked, "It is enough if the knights applaud me."[130] One actress who never fulfilled her promise is commemorated at Rome by a long epitaph, for the most part in verse.

Eucharis, freedwoman of Licinia, was an artist, "taught almost by the Muses' hand," who "gave beauty with her dancing to the shows of the nobles" and was "the first to act on the Greek stage," but died aged 14.[131] Education could also add charm to a society woman: Sempronia, on the fringe of the Catilinarian conspiracy and responsible for outrageous actions typical of a man, was learned in Greek and Latin literature and could play an instrument and dance more elegantly than was required of a good woman.[132] Nevertheless, a more typical example of a Roman woman is also found on a verse epitaph: Claudia loved her husband, gave birth to two children, one of whom had died, talked pleasantly, and looked nice when she walked. She looked after her house and worked wool.[133] For her this last achievement was probably a contribution to the self-sufficiency of the home. Augustus himself was known for ordinarily wearing only clothes made by his wife, sister, or other female members of his family;[134] for poorer families the extra income from selling garments would have been important.

The primary task of a married aristocratic woman was to look after her household. This might lead her into politics. The long and complex panegyric set up in Augustus' reign by a husband to his wife – originally but probably incorrectly identified with Turia, the wife of Quintus Lucretius Vespillo – is a commemoration of her utter loyalty to his and her parents' families.[135] After her parents had been assassinated, she defended the interests of her husband and herself in a dispute over her father's will; she also defended a family home against the troops used by Milo in his uprising against Caesar in 48 BC. Although her husband was a Republican, she secured his pardon, after petitioning Lepidus at the expense of her own physical maltreatment and later securing Octavian's support also. She even urged her husband to divorce her and keep her on as a housekeeper, when their childlessness made them vulnerable to Augustus' marriage legislation. All of this was directed at preserving her husband, his and her families, and their property.

The daughter of the great orator Q. Hortensius, Hortensia, made a name for herself under the triumvirate by actually making a public speech in her father's style deploring a heavy property tax on wealthy women.[136] There was a role not only for wives, but for matriarchs. We find Servilia, the mother of Marcus Brutus, twice presiding over family councils in the period after Caesar's murder – in early June 44 and late July 43. In the first, with Brutus and Cassius present, she silenced Cicero when he was in full oratorical flight; in the second Cicero describes her presiding in the same terms as a magistrate presiding over the senate.[137] As for Augustus' own wife, her influence was widely acknowledged: her great grandson, the emperor Caligula, referred to her as Ulysses in a dress. In particular she was praised for urging her husband to spare Gnaeus Cornelius Cinna, who had been denounced for conspiracy.[138]

More regularly under the Republic, the wife of a magistrate or senator sent abroad as commander, officer, or diplomat, had to look after the family and its property while he was away. Cicero's brother Quintus served as governor in Asia from 61 to early 58 BC; the year following he joined Caesar as a legionary commander in Gaul, where he stayed until 52; then he was away for about 18 months accompanying his brother Marcus during the latter's governorship in Cilicia. Shortly after this the civil war broke out. It is not surprising that his wife Pomponia became used to being the effective head of the household and, during his time in Italy in early 51, took it hard when Quintus and his freedman Statius organized a lunch party at one of their farms without consulting her first. "I am just a guest here," she said and retired to her room.[139] Under the Principate, it became customary, following the example of members of the imperial family, for wives to accompany their husbands when they went out to the provinces as commanders. The behavior of Germanicus' wife, the elder Agrippina, and Plancina, the wife of Gnaeus Piso, aroused suspicions, and in AD 21 there was a vigorous debate in the senate about the desirability of wives accompanying commanders.[140] The consensus was that there was no harm in the practice in time of peace and that it removed temptation from both husbands and wives, especially "the weaker sex" exposed to the vices of the city.

The Coherence of Society

Mention has been made already of the vertical links that held Roman society together. Patron–client relations between rich and poor continued to be important under the emperors. In particular, Tacitus remarked about the families of the nobility under the Julio-Claudian emperors that "even then it was permitted to cultivate the plebs, the allies, and foreign kings and be cultivated by them: the more brilliant a family was in its riches, domestic architecture, and furnishings, the more illustrious it was regarded through its name and clients."[141] However, such display aroused jealousy and suspicion among emperors which proved calamitous to the families. In fact, even under Augustus the patronage of the imperial family was dominant. The emperor distributed grain and money to the plebs, and bought land for his veteran soldiers.[142] Under the Republic a further vertical bond was that of the voting divisions (*tribus*), where the richer members handed out money to their poorer associates. Augustus carefully gave 1,000 sesterces every election to each member of the Fabian and Scaptian divisions, to which he belonged. In return, we find all 35 divisions of the urban plebs contributing money for dedications to members of the imperial family.[143]

Horizontal ties among the Roman plebs in the Republic were created by a multiplicity of organizations termed by the Romans "colleges" (*collegia*). Some of the most ancient of these were guilds of trades or professions, such as those of scribes, musicians, and wood- and metal-workers. Similarly well established were associations connected with districts within the city (*vici*) and settlements outside (*pagi*). These characteristics might easily overlap, given the tendency in cities for trades to concentrate in particular quarters. Moreover all would have been associated with a presiding deity or deities. In the last years of the Republic the growing city population spawned an increasing number of these associations, which were exploited for electoral bribery and violence, pre-eminently by Publius Clodius. In consequence, they were largely suppressed, only the most ancient and respectable surviving.[144] However, Augustus gave new authority to the "masters" (*magistri*) in the city districts, giving them charge of religious cults of divinities associated with the local trades and, linked with them,the cult of his *genius*, the divine spirit of his family.[145] Later in the Principate we find, as well as those associated with a trade, licensed "colleges" in the form of funerary clubs of the poor, each with its own divinity.[146]

With the final defeat of the Italian rebels in 82 BC, Italy became Roman and Rome became Italian. In Virgil's great epic of the Augustan period the word "Italia" is dominant and the Italic peoples are treated with respect, even when they are enemies of the hero. It took time for the Italian peoples to be enfranchised, for their local constitutions to be adapted to a Roman pattern, and for their societies to receive Roman private law.[147] Some of their leaders, especially no doubt those who had prudently chosen Sulla's side, such as Gaius Aelius Staienus and Gaius Fidiculanius Falcula, became senators in the late Republic. The turbulence of the later civil wars elevated many other Italians to the highest Roman ranks through their services to the faction leaders. Julius Caesar granted men like Titus Statilius Taurus, Gaius Calvisius Sabinus, Gaius Fuficius Fango, and Marcus Cusinius magistracies and places in the senate;[148] Marcus Vipsanius Agrippa and Quintus Salvidienus Rufus were prominent among the early supporters of his heir. Later, in Augustus' reign we find, for example, Quintus Propertius Postumus, Gnaeus Pullius Pollio, Quintus Varius Geminus, who claimed to be the first Paelignian senator (it might have been Ovid), and Gaius Pontius Paelignus honored at Transpadane Brixia (Brescia) on the edge of the Alps.[149]

It is clear from the writings of Cicero, Horace, and Sextus Propertius that men from Italy retained a loyalty to their place of birth. How far they retained a local identity, and how far they were perceived to retain one, is more difficult to assess. Catullus' poem about the dental hygiene of Egnatius, a Roman from Spain, lists various local identities – urban, Sabine, Tiburtine, fat Umbrian, obese Etruscan, swarthy and long-toothed Lanuvine, and Transpadane – an indication at least of stereo-types.[150] On the other hand, there is a variety of evidence for the disappearance of the different local Italian cultures and their assimilation into a single Roman one.[151]

The two important Italic languages that survived the War of the Allies– Etruscan and Oscan – effectively disappear from written texts by Tiberius' time, though learned men, like the emperor Claudius, knew Etruscan. In the memorials to great men of the past created at Tarquinii under the Principate their exploits, for example the expedition to Sicily in the fifth century BC of Velthur Spurinna, are recorded in Latin – not Etruscan.[152] The Greek language survived at Neapolis, Velia, and Greek cities in the far south of Italy, but this reflects the fact that it was still the dominant language of Sicily and the east Mediteranean. Some rural shrines in Italy declined; local funerary traditions died out and were replaced by others derived from the city of Rome. A uniform type of civic architecture developed. Above all, the various local religious calen-dars became matters of antiquarian interest in face of the systematic diffusion of the Julian calendar with its Roman festivals, not least those associated with the imperial family.[153] An outstanding example of a new calendar is the Fasti of Praeneste, the work of the grammarian Verrius Flaccus.[154] Much of the other "Romanization" may be ascribed to the deaths of so many Italians in their rebellion against Rome and the civil wars, and to the subsequent forcible settlement of veteran soldiers under Caesar, the triumvirs, and Augustus. Many of these veterans were of course Italian – for Horace a typical Roman soldier is Marsian or Apulian[155] – but their military service would have constrained them to speak and act like Romans.

Some of the inhabitants of Italy were Roman citizens of non-Italic origin. A few had obtained the citizenship as an honor in return for military or other services to the Romans. The advisers of Pompey, Pompeius Theophanes from Mytilene and Cornelius Balbus from Gades, are examples from the late Republic, likewise at least one of the Spanish cavalrymen enfranchised on the field of battle by his father Gnaeus

Pompeius Strabo at Asculum in November 89 BC: Arranes, son of Arbiscar, or his son, appears later as Publius Otacilius Arranes, a magistrate of Casinum (Monte Cassino).[156] The practice of regularly granting citizenship to the foreign auxiliary soldiers of Rome at the end of their service began by the reign of Claudius. In Augustus' time it had been established that foreigners who acquired Roman citizenship could remain active in their own communities and retain a local citizenship there.[157] Citizenship grants did not therefore entail necessarily new immigration into Italy. On the other hand, ambitious provincials might come to Rome to pursue a political career. Already in the reigns of Tiberius and Gaius men from Gallia Narbonnensis (Provence) – Domitius Afer from Nîmes (Nemausus) and Valerius Asiaticus from Vienne (Vienna) – became consuls and were renowned for their oratory.[158] Iulius Graecinus from Fréjus (Forum Iulii), the father of Iulius Agricola who became governor of Britain and father-in-law to the historian Tacitus, reached only the praetorship before falling foul of the emperor Gaius.[159]

The city of Rome had been acquiring a non-Italic population since the third century BC. Some of them were slaves, a number of whom became freedmen and freedwomen; others were visiting or resident foreigners. The paucity of evidence makes quantification impossible; at best we can notice a few pointers. In 59 BC, when Cicero defended Valerius Flaccus on an extortion charge resulting from his governorship in Asia, the Jews already formed an organized group who would form a claque at events in the Forum in which they had an interest.[160] Perhaps earlier still is a grave-marker of three freedmen, two of whom have Semitic *cognomina* (final names) – Marcus Aronius Zabina and Publius Caesonius Aciba.[161] By Tiberius' reign a Jewish community is attested settled in Trastevere; they were eager to proselytize, according to Horace.[162] A stone of the Republican era has a freedman surnamed "Surus," the Syrian, and this is also the surname of Publilius, a famous writer of mimes in the late Republic, and of the freedman principal of the guild of poet scribes in the Augustan age.[163] Greek surnames among freedmen are abundant: in many cases this may result from a fashion among their former owners, but the origin of any such fashion must lie in the original massive importation of slaves from the Greek world.

The turbulent history of the city in the late Republic had among its causes the swelling population of the plebs, living in poor accommodation and threatened with fire, flood, and food shortages. Multi-ethnicity was probably only a minor problem by comparison. However, we would be wrong to rule it out entirely: it was certainly a perceived problem among the authorities, not merely for a satirist such as Juvenal.[164] When

Agrippa was despatched in 21 BC to bring the rioting at Rome under control, one of his actions was to forbid the performance of Egyptian rites, that is those of Isis and Sarapis, within a mile of the religious boundary of the city; in this he was following a tradition of similar actions taken in the late Republic and by Augustus himself.[165] The association of foreign religious rites with political subversion goes back to the repression of the Bacchanals in 186 BC. Augustus expelled slaves, gladiators, and foreigners in a year of food shortage.[166] In 19 AD, a year where corn was in short supply and there were protests among the plebs, the senate decreed that not only Egyptian and Jewish rites should be banned from the city, but that 4,000 Jewish freedmen should be conscripted as soldiers and sent to Sardinia.[167] It was in this tradition that Nero placed responsibility for the great fire of Rome on another oriental sect, the Christians.[168]

For Roman citizens their most important identity was that they were Roman citizens. A domicile or origin outside Rome, whether in Italy or overseas, supplied another. For those of foreign origin who lived in Rome or Italy, religion might provide a third. These further identities tended to be a source of suspicion and contempt among those who felt themselves Roman through and through. Catiline sneered at Cicero, who was from the originally Volscian municipality of Arpinum, as an immigrant in the city of Rome; in the work of Tacitus, himself probably of provincial origin, Tiberius' prefect of the guard Seianus, a man from Tuscan Volsinii (Orvieto), is said to be committing "municipal adultery" with the princess Livia Iulia.[169] The best hope of avoiding prejudice was to become as Roman as possible, not merely in citizenship, but in culture. At the end of the first century AD Statius addressed a lyric poem to the young equestrian from Leptis Magna in Africa, Septimius Severus, whose descendants were ultimately to become Roman emperors: "Neither your accent, your dress, nor your way of thinking is Carthaginian; it is Italian, Italian. The foster-children who can give glory to Libya are from the city and the squadrons of Romans."[170]

5

Town and Country

The City of Rome

Rome's imperial success under the Republic had changed the city of Rome, but not in any wholesale or coherent fashion, and this reflected the fact that Rome remained in essence the city-state that had emerged from the rule of the kings about 500 BC and re-invented itself after the Gallic sack in the early fourth century. Its focus, the Forum Romanum (see figures 1 and 2) – with the extension of the small assembly area (*comitium*) – was still in the last century BC the location for much of the political activity, for legal business, commerce, public events, and simply people meeting people. Here it was that Philippus met Vulteius Mena and Horace had his unpleasant encounter with the bore, which was only broken up when the latter was seized by a man who was bringing a legal action against him there. A lawyer conducting a case in the Forum might see a funeral passing behind the court: indeed the Rostra were used for the funeral panegyrics of great men and women.[1] Even gladiatorial shows continued to be held in the Forum up to Augustus' reign: the shafts surviving in the pre-Augustan pavement have been interpreted as a means to allow fighters to emerge from the subterranean galleries.[2]

After the construction of the fourth-century BC Servian wall the Republican city had developed in a haphazard way. Temples under the Republic were on the whole more conspicuous for their number than their grandeur. Some of the finest were ancient foundations, such as that of Capitoline Jupiter, inherited from the kings, and the temples of Saturn and Castor in the Forum. The others were frequently the product of financial windfalls, especially those deriving from military victories, being thus an expression of the competitive pursuit of glory by the aristocracy: examples are the temple to Honor and Virtue by the Capena gate, dedicated or rededicated by Marcus Marcellus after the capture of Syracuse in 211 BC, or that to the Good Fortune of this Day, vowed by

0   500 m

Parks and gardens

QUIRINAL

VIMINAL

ESQUILINE

Campus Martius

26

25
24

20   22
19   21
18   16
15   17   14
23   13
11   10   9
8

12

29

Tiber

4   5
1   FORUM   2
3
6

22   27

28

PALATINE

CAELIAN

AVENTINE

Defense wall said to
be of Servius Tullius

Rome's sacred boundary
(pomerium) from the
time of Augustus

1 Temple of Jupiter Capitolinus	16 Theater of Balbus
2 Basilica Aemilia	17 Circus Flaminius
3 Basilica Iulia	18 Theater and portico of Pompey
4 Forum of Caesar	19 Baths of Agrippa
5 Forum of Augustus	20 Pantheon
6 Temple of Apollo	21 Saepta Iulia
7 Circus Maximus	22 Subura district
8 Sublician bridge	23 Amphitheater of Statilius Taurus
9 Aemilian bridge	24 Horologium of Augustus
10 Cestian bridge	25 Altar of Peace
11 Fabrician bridge	26 Mausoleum of Augustus
12 Bridge of Agrippa	27 Portico of Livia
13 Theater of Marcellus	28 Market of Livia
14 Portico of Octavia	29 Naumachia of Augustus
15 Portico of Philippus	

Map 4   Rome in the age of Augustus

Catulus before the battle against the invading Germans at Vercellae in 101 – the latter plausibly identified with the round temple in what is now the Largo Argentina.[3] In general it is far from clear what procedure was involved in the selection of a temple site, whether this was a matter of exploiting an existing sacred area or one that had been publicly confiscated, or, alternatively, finding a suitable site that could be purchased. However, we find that by the late Republic acquisitions were made as part of a wider architectural scheme. Opimius' temple to Concord on the Capitoline slope, celebrating his suppression of Gaius Gracchus, was linked with a new Basilica Opimia, perhaps the building usually called now "Tabularium" (Record Office) (see figure 2) after an element with this name added to it.[4] Pompey's temple to Venus Victrix was part of his theater complex in the Campus Martius. Julius Caesar purchased a large site to create his forum with the temple of Venus Genetrix as its chief feature. Augustus' temple of Apollo on the Palatine may have been an afterthought after his initial purchase of houses, but the temple of Mars Ultor (the Avenger) was surely planned as part of his Forum (see figure 9) and resulted from the acquisition of a large part of the district called Subura.

There were a few Republican building regulations, some going back to the time of the Twelve Tables – but no town-planning. This deficiency was ascribed to the haste to rebuild after the Gallic firing of the city.[5] By the late Republic the outcome was a jungle of tall buildings both on the hills and in the valleys, built out of unfired brick and timber to accommodate the poor. These were unwisely permitted even to clutter the banks of the Tiber, making more difficult any measures to control flooding.[6] Private houses of the elite were to be found not only on the northeast slope of the Palatine hill by the Sacred Way, as they were in the regal period (though a late-Republican owner like Cicero had apparently no appreciation of the historical significance of his site), but also elsewhere on the Palatine: the "House of the Griffins" goes back to the second century BC.[7] Other such houses were on the Capitoline, the eastern hills of the city, and the Velia, the saddle that joined the Palatine to the Esquiline. The Subura, the low-lying area between the hills to the northeast of the Forum, was chiefly for the plebs, as was the Aventine hill.

In the area immediately outside the Servian wall were the residences of the dead; in Greek and Roman culture interment within the city was only allowed for a few heroic figures. Tombs were to be found especially, but not exclusively, along the roads leading from Rome (see figure 18). As the city expanded beyond the Servian wall, it enveloped many of them: Republican tomb monuments are to be found within the third-century AD Aurelianic wall, for example the tombs of the Scipios and the Sempronii. The Servian wall ran along the north slope of the Capitoline hill, leaving the whole of the Field of Mars (Campus Martius) outside the original city proper. This was the rendezvous of the army at the time of a levy and of the military assembly (comitia centuriata) meeting in the Pens (Saepta); it became later the center of the medieval and modern town. The southern part of this area gradually became occupied by public buildings during the Republic and Augustan period. A series of temples were built in the Flaminian circus, immediately north-west of the Capitoline hill, and a further group to the north of this in what is now the Largo Argentina. West of these, Pompey constructed his stone theater, completed in 55 BC, and the temple of Venus Victrix. This was followed by the theater of Balbus to the east of the Largo and in the Circus Flaminius the theater Augustus raised in memory of Marcellus. To the north of these monuments permanent Saepta were constructed in concrete and stone by Agrippa and, adjacent to them, the temple called Pantheon, the ancestor of the still-surviving Hadrianic Pantheon; yet further north was the park with the solar meridian (horolo-gium), Augustus' mausoleum,[8] and, to the east, the Altar of Peace, decreed as a thanksgiving for Augustus' return from Gaul in 13 BC.[9]

More generally, the city spread outside the Servian wall. By Augustus' time the powers of a tribune of the plebs reached as far as the first mile-stone beyond the old walls. A particular feature was the garden villas (horti) of the elite. That of the luxurious Lucullus, who had fought Mithridates in the east, was on the Pincio, Pompey's in the Campus, Caesar's across the Tiber. The Horti Sallustiani were just outside the Colline gate on the Quirinal, while the old burial ground of the poor on the Esquiline was leveled and purified in order to become the location of Maecenas' gardens.[10] This allowed their owners the space and relative tranquillity that was not to be found in the crowded center of the city, where prices in a fashionable district were huge. Cicero paid Crassus 3,500,000 sesterces for his Palatine house, but at least one price three times that amount is recorded.[11]

By contrast to the developments elsewhere, building in the area of the Forum Romanum itself seems to have been controlled, as was essential when a rectangular space roughly 400 by 100 meters, including its adjoining buildings, was the center of so much public and private activity. As we have seen, there was redevelopment in the late fourth century BC: the "meeting-place" (comitium), with the associated Rostra and senate house (curia), was remodeled, and the "New Shops" (tabernae *novae*) on the northeast flank of the Forum were created facing the "Old Shops" on the southwest flank. The shops seem to have been structures within porticoes, above which balconies (*maeniana*) were created projecting over the Forum, providing simultanously an observation platform and shade for those below.[12] In the second century BC these porticoes were replaced by the first basilicas, the Aemilia, Fulvia, and Sempronia, in which a covered columned hall was flanked by a portico facing the Forum with, as before, shops at ground level and a balcony above;[13] there was also the Basilica Porcia flanking the senate house. By this time any private houses adjoining the Forum, such as that of Scipio Africanus,[14] were replaced by public buildings. In the late Republic two major new basilicas were begun, the Basilica of Aemilius Paulus on the northeast side and the Basilica of Julius Caesar to the southwest. The senate house was rebuilt first by Sulla, then by his son Faustus, and subsequently by Caesar; it was then marginally relocated to align with Caesar's new forum. Caesar also created new Rostra along the short northwest side of the Forum.[15]

Under Augustus, the Forum Romanum became dominated by monuments of the imperial family. After Paulus' Basilica (completed in 34 BC) burnt down, it was rebuilt with an added portico on the Forum side dedicated in the names of Gaius and Lucius, Augustus' adopted sons. It faced the Basilica Iulia which almost filled the other long side. On the other diagonal, Caesar's Rostra, extended by Augustus (see figure 2), faced the temple to the Divine Julius with its altar at the southeast end of the Forum. At that end also were Augustus' triumphal arch and the temple of Castor, rebuilt by Augustus' stepson Tiberius (see figure 1).[16] At the same time, however, the centrality of the Forum Romanum in Roman life was diluted by the creation first of Caesar's Forum with the temple to Venus the Progenitor (*Genetrix*), and secondly of Augustus' own, stretching through the Subura into the valley between the Quirinal and Esquiline hills, with its center the temple to Mars Ultor, vowed on the field of Philippi (figure 9). The temple and its adjacent porticoes were a monument to the Julian family, including its divine ancestors Mars and Venus, and to the great men of the Republic.[17] Moreover, this Augustan Forum was to become the seat of the urban praetor and thus another focus of forensic life under the Principate,[18] while the business of the Forum Romanum moved largely indoors into the basilicas and its pavement became filled with statues.

The center of Rome and the Campus Martius were thus remodeled, but much of the city, especially the homes of the poor, remained what they had been in the late Republic. Augustus and Agrippa did improve

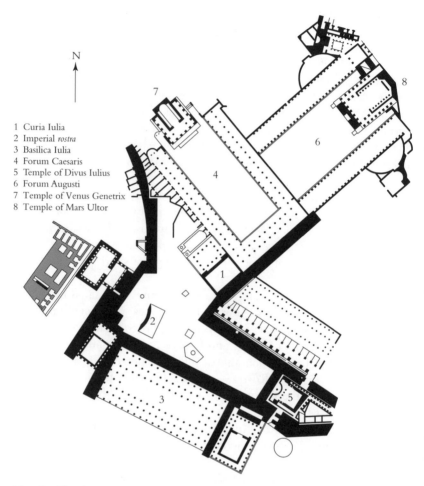

N

1 Curia Iulia
2 Imperial *rostra*
3 Basilica Iulia
4 Forum Caesaris
5 Temple of Divus Iulius
6 Forum Augusti
7 Temple of Venus Genetrix
8 Temple of Mars Ultor

Map 5   The Augustan Forum Romanum, the Forum of Julius Caesar, and the Forum of Augustus

living conditions generally by clearing and raising the Tiber banks, by constructing three new aqueducts (one of which, the Aqua Virgo, still brings water into the city), and improving the sewerage of Rome, including the main drain (*cloaca maxima*) which ran through the Subura and under the Forum Romanum to the river.[19] Under the Republic we hear of privately owned baths at Rome – as sites of skulduggery: Sextus Roscius' father was murdered outside the Pallacine baths in the Campus, and Caelius was alleged to have used the Senian baths to obtain poison

Figure 9   The northeast end of the Forum of Augustus with the temple of Mars Ultor, vowed on the battlefield of Philippi in 42 BC and inaugurated in 2 BC. The retaining wall behind it shielded it from the Viminal hill and the district of the Subura.

for a murder.[20] Such places were probably on the scale of those found in country towns like Pompeii.[21] Agrippa's baths in the Campus Martius, left to the people of Rome in his will, were the first of the great bath-houses of the Principate. Here entry was free: Augustus financed this from the proceeds from other property left for that purpose.[22] However, it was only the great fire in 64 AD which permitted the general recon-struction of the city with broader throroughfares and apartment blocks fronted by shops, constructed in concrete shuttered by fired brick: their remains can be seen on the ground and are represented on the fragments of the great marble plan of Rome of *c.* 200 AD.[23]

Public Business – the Administration of the City

If we leave aside religion, which will be considered in the next chapter, the workings of civil society were determined by three main factors: politics and administration, the law, and money. To consider the first, the Republic was constituted of three elements, the assemblies, the senate, and the magistrates. Formal assemblies were necessary for elections and votes on legislation or public trials; the majority of these (the military assembly being the exception) originally took place in the Forum or on the Capitol, but by the late Republic all elections were held in the Campus Martius. Informal assemblies were held by magistrates in the Forum, where they and other men of standing discussed future legislation and other problems before any who chose to attend; they were also used simply to circulate information about public affairs or, like certain ministerial speeches and broadcasts nowadays, to reassure the public and repress discontent. Virgil famously compared Neptune calming a storm to a distinguished man calming a riot with a speech.[24] Some of Augustus' measures were enacted by laws passed in an assembly, such as those about marriage and adultery; elections for the magistracies were still held, although subject to increasing control by the emperor. However, the importance of assemblies in determining policy and the choice of those who were to hold high office gradually dwindled. As for Augustus himself, where we find him addressing the people of Rome, it is as Virgil's orator, responding to agitation about the price of wine or his failure to pay a cash subsidy that he had promised.[25]

The senate remained under Augustus the central deliberative body in the community and, because of the distinction of its members, the repository of authority. We have already seen how Augustus sought to control its membership and enhance its status. Much policy, however, was now decided, whether by the allotted council or the imperial family and friends, behind the closed doors of a room in one of the imperial residences. Under the Republic a senator, if not indisposed or away on public business, was expected for most of the year to be available for meetings at short notice, since in an emergency there was no other appropriate body to discuss and resolve on policy. Now that this function was taken over by the emperor and his advisers, the remaining business was normally less urgent and frequently routine. As a remedy for absenteeism, the emperor allowed the less fit senators to retire but retain their status as a sinecure. Moreover, he limited regular meetings to the kalends and ides of each month, e.g. January 1 and 13, reduced the required quorums for certain measures, and allotted a restricted number of senators to serve in the months of September and October, unhealthy months in Rome.[26]

Nevertheless, the senate, especially if it met in the Julian senate house or another location accessible to the general public such as the Saepta,[27] provided an imposing spectacle of the great men of Rome formally discussing and approving a measure. Furthermore, here the emperor could be seen among the peers of whom he was the chief (*princeps*), in meetings over which not he, but one of the consuls, presided. He was thus embedded in the *senatus populusque Romanus*, the traditional designation of political authority. The Republican senate had been essentially an advisory council, even if some of its decrees established general norms. By the end of Augustus' reign the senate's decisions had the force of law.[28]

We must not forget, however, the third element of the constitution – the magistrates. Traditionally the Republic had given free rein to its executives in their limited periods of office. They were expected to use their discretion and do what they thought was best, subject to censure or punishment after they had demitted their posts.[29] The two consuls were officially the supreme authority in Rome and Italy and presidents of the senate, working now in conjunction with the emperor when he was present. Ovid in one of his letters from the Black Sea to Pomponius Graecinus, supplementary (*suffectus*) consul under Tiberius in 16 AD, describes the rituals and tasks awaiting his friend: the procession at his inauguration, his speech of thanks to the emperor, his dispensing of justice, letting of tax-contracts, proposal of measures in the senate, and conduct of religious sacrifices, especially those on behalf of the imperial house.[30] By the end of Augustus' reign more than one pair of consuls was elected a year, in order to share the honor as widely as possible, and the *suffectus* consul or consuls would replace the original holders of office later in the year. Those in office on January 1 continued to give their names to the year (there was as yet no agreed era based on a date for the founding of the city). Below the consuls there were the praetors, 12 in number at the end of the reign. Two of these were given charge of the public treasury in the temple of Saturn (figs. 1 and 2),[31] two performed jurisdiction over civil lawsuits, as before, and the rest continued to preside over criminal courts. They also managed all the festivals, including the "Roman games" and the "games of Ceres," formerly the business of the aediles.[32]

The aediles, six in number since Julius Caesar's dictatorship, traditionally looked after the fabric of the city and the life led there. Many of their functions were reallocated during Augustus' reign to special boards of ex-magistrates or prefects from the equestrian order.[33] There were "curators of waters" to look after the aqueducts and curators of the banks and bed of the Tiber;[34] two former praetors were in charge of the distribution of grain, and its importation became the business of a prefect of the corn supply (*annona*).[35] When the *vigiles*, a paramilitary body charged with the prevention and extinction of fires, were created in 6 AD, a prefect was placed in command (up to this time the aediles retained charge of a slave fire-brigade). The chief tasks that remained for the aediles were the supervision of sales and markets and the cleansing of the streets.[36]

The political powers of the tribunes of the plebs, whether to legislate, prosecute, or veto, fell largely into disuse under the Principate, except when exercised by the emperor himself (we find a few instances of tribunes effecting or attempting vetoes in the Senate).[37] How far they continued to afford protection to the ordinary citizen is uncertain, though they were among the magistrates to whom in 7 BC supervision of the new regions of the city was given.[38] Deprived of its authority, the office lost its attraction: we know that at one election that there were not enough candidates to fill the vacancies.[39] Quaestors no longer managed the treasury; they would have continued as assistants to the consuls and to the emperor in the city, reading speeches for him in the senate.[40] Others had posts in Italy,[41] but the majority, as before, were assistants to provincial governors.

The minor magistrates became a college of 20, some of them equestrians who would not progress to being senators.[42] Among them, the three moneyers (*tres viri monetales*) still put their names on the bronze coinage issued at Rome (gold and silver coinage was issued by the emperor in the provinces); the 10 "judges of civil suits" (*decemviri stlitibus iudicandis*) became presidents of the court of 100 men, which traditionally dealt with inheritance disputes; a board of four looked after the city streets, while the three "capital" magistrates (*tres viri capitales*) continued to supervise the prison and executions. Ovid was first a *triumvir capitalis* and later a *decemvir stlitibus iudicandis*.[43] The *tres viri capitales* in time seem to have lost their general functions relating to public security. Some duties fell to the prefect of the fire-watch (*vigiles*) in 6 AD. However, even more significant was the entrusting of routine security in the city to a new imperial appointee, the prefect of the city (*praefectus urbi*). He was in due course given control of a gendarmerie, those cohorts of the praetorian guard known as "urban." The presence of these and the *vigiles* meant that there was for the first time in Rome a limited form of policing. Moreover, in 7 BC the city was divided into 14 regions, each under one of the praetors, aediles, or tribunes, selected by lot; within the regions each ward was subject to one or more of the new "masters of the wards (*vici*)."[44] The best documentation of wards in their appropriate regions is a later dedication to Hadrian.[45]

Thus the society of the city of Rome became more structured under a pyramid of officials, all ultimately subordinate to the consuls and the emperor. Perhaps the best modern analogy is that of a corporation, in which the emperor resembles a chief executive, who holds his position until death or resignation and meanwhile has members of his family in subordinate executive positions and on the board, i.e. in the senate. The presidency of that board, the consulship, rotates and its incumbents tend to owe their position to the chief executive. The primary aim of all officials is the smooth running of the corporation. As Tacitus put it, "relatively few matters were handled by force, so that the rest might have peace."[46]

Law and Society

In the century before Augustus those criminal cases which the Romans then regarded as matters of public interest were handled by jury courts presided over by a magistrate or other appointee (see chapter 3 above). These courts continued under the Principate (how long and to what extent is a matter of debate). However, some criminal cases involving the elite came to be heard in the senate, while other cases were investigated by the emperor. In time perhaps the majority of criminal cases were submitted either to him or to the subordinate officials to whom he delegated their hearing, such as the prefect of the city. Moreover, whereas the trials under the Republic were a public matter, heard in the open in the Forum Romanum, criminal justice was now moved indoors and sometimes behind closed doors. Its location was now a basilica, a space in one of the emperor's residences, or the headquarters of the imperial official.[47]

Prosecution under the Republic had always been a matter of private initiative, though humbler citizens could seek legal assistance and even advocacy from a patron. In time advocacy became a profession and clients frequently sought skilled orators to represent them, not the wealthy men on whose patronage they were regularly dependent.[48] Many crimes only came to light through the activities of informers, who either reported to magistrates or put their information at the disposal of an orator who made a practice of accusation.[49] The situation did not change with the appointment of a prefect of the city under Augustus or with the creation of the *vigiles*. Curiously, the only description that we have of detective work in the early Principate involved an emperor himself. A praetor, when denounced for murder, alleged that his wife had thrown herself from an upper story of their house while he was asleep, but Tiberius visited the bedroom and found traces suggesting that she had struggled and been pushed.[50] There was no public detective force.

However, it came to be regarded as sufficient, both when crimes involved the elite and were tried in the senate, as here, and when they involved ordinary citizens and slaves, for information to be laid before the emperor or other magistrate; it was not necessary to undertake a prosecution formally, as in the regular criminal tribunals (*quaestiones perpetuae*).

Civil actions over private matters traditionally had two stages: first, the preliminary submission of the issue to the urban or the "peregrine" praetor (the latter deriving his name from his original responsibility for foreigners, *peregrini*), secondly the actual hearing by one judge or a small panel. These two praetors performed jurisdiction, that is, they decided whether the complaint submitted was justiciable under the law. If so, they appointed a judge or judges, instructing them in most cases with a formula, which defined the issue to be decided and gave the magistrate's authority to the verdict and the form in which a condemnation or acquittal was to be made. The urban praetor's tribunal was in the meeting-place (*comitium*) by the senate house from the time of the Twelve Tables until the second century BC, but moved into the Forum Romanum in the late Republic; at least we know that litigants met at the well (*puteal*) of Libo,[51] which has been variously located, either near the eastern end of the "New Shops" or in the southwest corner of the Forum near the Palatine.[52] By the time of Nero's reign the tribunal had moved again– into the Forum of Augustus (see figure 9). Cases may have been actually heard by the judge or judges in public, but not necessarily: some were certainly heard in private houses.[53]

Roman private law had become much more flexible since the Twelve Tables in the fifth century BC, where actions depended on the precise performance of ritual actions and recitation of ritual language. Praetors were permitted to adapt the traditional actions created by early Republican laws or invent new ones to remedy wrongs. Even before this, a Republican law provided for actions on contracts made by solemn verbal promise (*sponsio*) before witnesses, and this became a regular basis of business agreements, including those before a marriage.[54] By the late Republic it had become customary to record these on writing tablets; account books and receipts could also be produced as evidence for financial liability.[55] However, as we have already noticed, the law recognized agency only to a limited extent – hence the importance of family, freedmen, and slaves.[56] The law relating to partnership, moreover – that is, company law – was rudimentary and the subject of debate in the late Republic. Partnership was inferred to exist when there was activity in common, whether or not there was a written agreement, and, in default of any understanding to the contrary, it was assumed that all partners had equal shares, whatever financial contribution they had made initially to the partnership. An existing partnership was automatically terminated on the death of one of its members or when any of them chose to sue for its dissolution; an exception was made for the companies of tax-collectors, because it was in the public interest that their existence should be continuous for the length of any contract they had with the authorities of the Roman people.[57]

To judge from the juristic literature, the most important part of civil law related to wills and inheritance (Books 28 to 38 of Justinian's *Digest* and sections elsewhere) – a field made more complex by Augustus' introduction both of inheritance tax and, as a penalty for failure to meet the requirements of his marriage legislation, of the forfeiture of rights to inherit.[58] This reflects the fact that inheritance was the most important mode of transfer of capital in times of peace, when there was no question of proscriptions or confiscations. The central feature of inheritance was the institution of an heir, who would take over the legal personality of the deceased, acquiring his assets, or at least some of them, but also his obligations. The law of intestacy still privileged the agnatic family (ascendants in the male line), but those who made wills had considerable freedom, except that legacies were not permitted to burden the estate of the heir or heirs disproportionately. Augustus' reforms were conservative: he was content that property should remain with the families who possessed it, but if the family did not reproduce itself adequately, however, he wanted the money for his own or the public treasury. This helped to pay for the armed services and the civilian posts which were among the chief routes for social mobility, and to provide food for those who for the most part would never inherit or bequeath any significant amount.

Business and Money

Although some taxes were paid in kind and barter between individual citizens or allies was probably common, Roman administration and commerce were generally monetized. We have seen (chapter 2 above) how the Romans moved from using weighed bronze as a general medium of exchange, first to a bimetallic silver and bronze coinage where coins of both metals were originally of full value (though the weight-standard of the bronze gradually declined), and then to another largely bimetallic coinage, based on the silver *denarius*, where the bronze coins were fiduciary: the *as*, once a pound of bronze, came to weigh an *uncia* (ounce), one twelfth of a pound. The *denarius*, a little over four grams of silver, was at first worth ten *asses*; a smaller silver coin, the *sestertius*, equal to two and a half (the "third half") *asses*, was a quarter of the *denarius*. There were other denominations of silver (*quinarius* and *victoriatus*) and various fractions of the bronze *as*. The *sestertius* became the normal unit of accounting for the Romans, though Greek writers tended to translate sums into *denarii* to provide a rough equation with their own silver *drachmai*. A *denarius* every three days was the pay of the ordinary soldier from *c.* 150 BC until Caesar's pro-consulship in Gaul, when it doubled.[59]

Shortly after 150 BC, probably in response to increased demand for silver, the Romans upvalued the *denarius* and *sestertius* to 16 and four *asses* respectively and these equivalences remained in force during the Principate, as long as the system lasted. However, silver *sestertii* disappear after the eighties BC, while the obsolete *quinarius* (half a *denarius*) was revived. Gold was briefly minted in the crisis of the second Punic war and by Sulla, but although the Romans had access to gold in Spain from the late third century BC, they did not mint it regularly until the gold mines of western Gaul were in their possession after Caesar's conquests. The *denarius* coinage had been a response to the exigencies of the second Punic war, and in general subsequent coin issues tended to fluctuate in proportion to the need for military expenditure.[60] Peaks of production are in the years of the war with the Italian allies and the later civil wars. When gold coins (*aurei*), worth 25 *denarii*, were produced by Julius Caesar and the military dynasts that followed him, it became easier to transport the huge sums required to pay the warring armies and to satisfy the increased expectations of the soldiers. The Brescello (*Brixellum*) hoard, buried in or shortly after 38 BC, contained 80,000 *aurei*.[61]

Augustus took charge of gold and silver minting, above all at Lugdunum (Lyon) in Gaul. He continued to mint *aurei* and, in silver, *denarii*, but *sestertii* were now issued as the most valuable bronze coins. During the Republic moneyers had used the reverse (tails) of coins to celebrate their ancestors and the latter's exploits, occasionally their own careers. Julius Caesar was the first Roman to have his head on a Roman coin, like a Hellenistic monarch; the triumvirs, Sextus Pompey, Quintus Labienus, and even Marcus Brutus followed his example. Under Augustus the emperor's head was regularly, but not universally, on the obverse, while the reverses were used to celebrate his achievements, his family, and his honors.

In the New Testament the silver coin with which taxes are paid is a *denarius* with the head of the emperor.[62] Previously, under the Republic, *denarii* of Roman weight-standard had circulated in Spain, but with local types and legends, while in the east a number of silver coinages continued to be minted by Rome's allies, which were accepted by the Romans – in Macedonia, Athens, and the Pergamene kingdom in Asia Minor.[63] These also reached the Roman treasury as tax or booty. Macedonian and Pergamene silver coins were actually issued by Roman magistrates during the Republic in their own names. Pergamene coins – called *cistophoroi* because they portrayed on the obverse a mystic box (*cista*) with a serpent emerging – were still being issued by Mark Antony before Actium and by Augustus at the outset of the Principate. However, henceforward the *denarius* became the universal provincial silver coinage, except in Egypt. Here debased silver coins, resembling those of the Ptolemies but commemorating the Roman rulers, were minted at Alexandria from Tiberius' reign onward.[64] Allied communities were still permitted to mint their own bronze.

Although a city would have a secure room or rooms in which to deposit its cash, private citizens, as far as we can judge, were not so well provided. Money unwanted at the time was often put in the ground, and the death or forgetfulness of its owners are the cause of the many Roman coin hoards that have been unearthed in more recent times. The wealthy would put out their spare cash in loans either to friends whom they trusted or to others who could provide good security, especially in land. Money was not only awkward to store, it was also awkward to move. Tax money collected in the provinces was frequently left there in strong-boxes (*fisci*) to be used by Roman magistrates when required. The tax-collecting companies had a system whereby money could be deposited in, let us say, Asia, and its equivalent could be drawn at Rome, or vice versa: this seems to have been used by Cicero as governor of Cilicia, when he wished to get cash for his expenses in the east.[65] Nevertheless, there was no general system of transferring credit through bankers, like the bills of exchange available in the Renaissance period.

For Vitruvius the spaces within the porticoes around a forum are for the shops of money-changers (*tabernae argentariae*).[66] These and the businessmen associated with them were among the chief occupants of the Forum Romanum by his time, in particular in the region of the "New Shops," where there were three Janus arches, perhaps four-pillared, such as are found in the forum of Carsulae.[67] They would have shared these spaces with sellers of books[68] and other merchandise. The sellers of produce had been removed from the Forum proper to a nearby market (*macellum*) by the middle Republic, perhaps on the site of the later Temple of Peace of Vespasian,[69] perhaps in the Velabrum.[70]

Augustus constructed a further produce market dedicated to his wife Livia, probably outside the Esquiline gate.[71] It would be wrong to compare the Januses and their shops to the City of London, despite their symbolic value to the poets. The money-changers would receive deposits and make loans, but on a small scale – a potential source of indebtedness to a man like Horace in his earlier years and others of his station.[72] Large loans were made by the elite to the elite in the private deals to which we find cryptic allusions in the letters of Cicero. However, when someone went bankrupt, it would have been here in the Forum that his or her assets would have been auctioned, on the orders of the administrator placed in charge by the creditors after the appropriate legal process.

One important type of public financial transaction would have also taken place in the Forum, the letting of contracts by the censors or consuls. Contracts were let for the undertaking of public works – such as the construction or repair of roads, bridges or temples – and for the collection of taxes, including some provincial taxes. Bids were made by the lifting of hands and the successful bidder was called *manceps* (purchaser). He was backed by partners (*socii*), and was expected to provide guarantors (*praedes*) or real security (*praedia*), which was mortgaged to the treasury against the proper performance of the contract. It is not clear whether a successful bidder for taxes had to provide a deposit, but the absence of positive evidence suggests not. Tax contracts ran for five years, their letting being normally performed under the Republic by the censors. However, if there were no censors in the appropriate year, the task was performed by the consuls, and they effectively took over this function under the Principate. A major contract, such as the collection of transit dues or land taxes from a province, required considerable organization and personnel. Hence the purchaser and his partners built up corporations that were recognized by the law and could probably have been passed on by one purchaser to a subsequent successful bidder.[73] Some of the best evidence for the letting of tax contracts by censors and consuls is in the Neronian dossier engraved at Ephesus regarding the transit dues of Asia.[74]

City Life and Work

The Forum Romanum and the spaces adjacent to it were the center of administration and business of the ruling city of the Mediterranean world. The rest of the city provided services for the great men of Rome and housed most of those who performed the services. There was a great demand for manual labor in construction, dock labor, and transport in the city, where wagons were not allowed to move from dawn to the tenth hour (late afternoon) and hence during those hours objects and persons were carried either by beasts or humans.[75] Such labor was mostly casual and often dangerous: for these reasons it was generally less economic to use slaves and the free poor found employment. When an engineer offered the emperor Vespasian the design of a device for transporting huge stone columns cheaply, he is said to have paid for it generously but not used it, remarking that the engineer should allow him to keep his poor plebs fed.[76] On the other hand, specialized slaves such as chair-carriers were chic – the band of eight given by the Egyptian king to P. Asicius or the Bithynians whom Varus' girl-friend expected Catullus to possess. Later, in Juvenal's time, sedans carried by Liburnian slaves were popular.[77]

While there was no large-scale production of goods at Rome itself, small-scale production of necessities and luxuries flourished. Sadly, for the most part we cannot map it, as we can the activity at Pompeii.[78] There are some indications, however, in inscriptions and scattered literary sources. The sandal-makers clearly congregated in a ward which worshiped Apollo Sandaliarius, perhaps in the Subura, to judge from a memorial to a freedman sandal-maker; the Hall of the Shoe-Makers (*Atrium Sutorium*) was used for the ceremonial cleaning every March 23 of the trumpets used in religious rites.[79] The scythe-makers gave their name to a ward where, in the house of Marcus Porcius Laeca, the Catilinarian conspirators met; we do not know where this was.[80] Luxury trades were to be found in the Sacred Way. Goldsmiths from the Via Sacra dedicated at Praeneste, and they and others connected with their trade appear on funeral monuments, notably two Caedicii, who may be members of the same firm.[81] Merchants of pearls and gems and sellers of perfumes and unguents worked also in the Sacred Way.[82] *Purpurarii*, who dealt with both dyes and cloth are found in the *vicus Iugarius* under the Capitol and the *vicus Tuscus* under the Palatine;[83] wine-sellers in the Velabrum between Forum and river.[84] Some slaves and freedmen would have worked out of shops in the front of their master's or patron's house; others no doubt moved to a quarter where their fellow tradesmen were. The grants of grain or money by the emperor or other patrons could not have sustained the poor by themselves: they needed to work. The building projects of the emperors were one great source of employment; the service of the elite, as it competed in luxury and magnificence, was another.

Much of our knowledge of city life comes from satire, which is revealing but of its nature tendentious. As an alternative, two vignettes are provided here, one of work, the other of pleasure. In the first, Alfenus Varus, the Augustan jurist, is discussing actions for damages under the Aquilian law.[85]

> Mules were pulling two loaded carts on the Capitoline slope. Because the front cart had tilted back, the muleteers were lifting it so that the mules could pull it easily. The higher cart began to go backwards and, when the muleteers between the two carts had got out of the way, the cart behind had been struck by it and slipped backwards, crushing a certain person's slave boy. The master of the boy was asking me whom he should sue. I replied that the law depended on the circumstances. For if the muleteers who had been supporting the front cart had got out of the way of their own accord and for this reason it came about that the mules could not prevent the cart from slipping and were pulled backwards by the load itself, there was no action with the master of the mules, but the men who had been supporting the tilted cart could be sued under the Aquilian law (concerning wrongful loss) … But, if the mules had backed up because they had shied at something, and the muleteers had abandoned the cart for fear that they would be crushed, the men could not be sued but the owner of the mules could be.

The jurist goes on to say that, if the burden was just too much for the front mules, there was no action against either the muleteers of the front cart or the owner of its mules: in any case the owner of the rear mules could not be sued.

The dead boy was a slave and therefore it was his master who had suffered damage perhaps actionable under the Aquilian law, in the same way that the owner of the mules on the rear cart might have sued if they had been hurt. If the muleteers of the front cart could be sued, they must have been free hired laborers, and the passage illustrates how such men obtained employment in the city. We also see the burden placed by the demands of the metropolis on its limited transport system. If the technology is primitive, however, the system of private law is sophisticated.

Sophisticated also is Ovid's manual of seduction, *The Art of Love*. In the first book the poet tackles the primary problem of how to find a lover. Being in Rome is a good start: the city has so many beautiful girls, whatever talent lived anywhere on the globe before. Ovid first advises his pupils simply to take a walk in various places – the shadow of Pompey's theater or the porticoes of Livia on the Oppian, of Octavia in the Circus Flaminius, and of Apollo on the Palatine, and the shrines of Isis and Adonis. There are also the Fora, especially that of Julius Caesar, where Venus from her temple laughs when she sees lawyers in love and lost for words. Better still are the theaters, to which women are devoted, and the Circus, which has the particular advantage that there are no rules about separated seating and you can sit next to your intended mistress: indeed the line-marks require you to press your flank against hers. The identity of the chariot teams is an obvious opening gambit of conversation and you are away.[86] Even for those who were not chasing girls, Augustan Rome had agreeable spaces to walk in and there were so many things to see: the new monuments, such as the Mausoleum and solar meridian (see above), the representation of Agrippa's map of the world in the *porticus Vipsania* completed by Augustus after Agrippa's death,[87] and, from time to time, exotic animals, such as the rhinoceros in the Saepta, the tiger in the theater, and the huge snake at the front of the *comitium* – the last two presumably the gifts of the Indian embassy of 20 BC.[88]

The Towns outside Rome

There was a general pattern which early Rome shared with other Italian towns – a walled circuit, a central public space or spaces for commerce and public life, and one or more acropolises on the higher ground, which were usually the site of major temples. Orthogonal town-planning had developed in the Greek world since the earliest period of colonization, *c.*700 BC and was consequently to be found in the Greek colonies of southern Italy and Sicily. We also see it in some Etruscan foundations.[89] The Romans themselves had a tradition of creating rectilinear military camps centered on a headquarters and parade area. This seems to have influenced the design of the permanent forts which were the first purely Roman colonies, such as the original settlement at Ostia. An early Latin colony, Norba, which is on a plateau site where physical features dictate the plan, shows traces of formal alignment without any rigid organization. However, in 303 BC, when Latin colonies had become an element in Rome's strategy of colonization, Alba Fucens, another plateau site (figure 10), was laid out in a more regular pattern of rectangular subdivisions, with a central forum, organized for voting, and public buildings, surrounded by residential quarters: the two acropolises with their temples lay outside the formal grid. More striking is the effect of Roman reconstruction of the Greek colony at Paestum (Poseidonia) from 273 BC, where the chief Greek religious sites remained intact but the public space to the east of the center of the city was extensively remodeled: the Greek assembly ground was eliminated and instead a forum and associated *comitium* was created.[90]

Figure 10   The colony of Alba Fucens, founded in 304 BC, on the Via Valeria in the central Appennines. The excavated area contained forum, basilica, *comitium*, and markets. Shrines were on the two acropolises, one center right, the other left foreground.

By the end of the Republic a standard pattern had developed for the central area of a town. Vitruvius describes how an oblong forum should be created with basilicas, a senate house, treasury, and prison adjoining it.[91] A major temple, perhaps replicating the cult on the Roman Capitol of Jupiter, Juno, and Minerva, was now to be found in or adjacent to the forum itself. In the Augustan period this system was exported to Roman colonies founded in the provinces, notably in Spain, where the forum of Emporiae (Ampurias) was transformed, and those of Conimbriga, Augusta Emerita, Barcino, Tarraco, and Saguntum were created.[92] The most remarkable provincial forum was that created at the Julian colony at Carthage, where the Romans leveled the top of the Byrsa hill and extended the resulting platform outward on concrete piers, like the deck of an aircraft-carrier, covering the remains of Punic houses destroyed in 146 BC (see figure 4b).[93]

The towns in Italy and the western provinces were given constitutions, which to some extent mirrored that of Rome. There were magistrates elected by assemblies and local senates. The function of the assemblies, however, was limited to these elections, and decision-making, in so far as it was permitted, rested with the senates in each town. Their membership was restricted and previous tenure of a magistracy was a necessary but not a sufficient condition for membership. Eventually, the general pattern of magistracies was that there should be each year two *duumviri* who, like Roman consuls or praetors, were the community leaders and performed jurisdiction, two aediles to supervise the fabric of the city and its services, and two quaestors to handle finance. These communities differed from Rome in that the constitution was incorporated in a single written text, a copy of which was engraved on bronze tablets and posted in a public place; a number of these tablets have been discovered, mostly in Spain.[94]

The Countryside

Most ancient cities were by their nature closely associated with the countryside surrounding them. They were, or had been, military strongholds, and were centers of administration and the provision of public and private services for those who lived and worked on the land. However, the wealth that sustained them derived ultimately from the land. Manufacture in the towns, even if the products were significant enough to be exported, was on a small scale. Large-scale production of items like ceramics and bricks was located in the countryside. Where we nowadays have artificial materials and fabrics created from chemicals in a factory, the ancient Roman world had hides and fleeces from animals, ropes and straps made of leather and grass, pottery made of clay, glass of sand, and basketwork of wicker. Even Roman artillery depended on torsion provided by the twisted entrails of animals. Hence stockbreeding was closely associated with the armaments industry. Rome now imported colored marbles from around the Mediterranean, but major building had depended from the first on the quarrying of local stone – a variety of tufas, and the travertine limestone from Tiburtine territory east of Rome (*lapis Tiburtinus*). Timber production was essential for construction of all kinds, including the manufacture of ships, and for fuel.

A central question in the study of the Roman countryside is the ownership of the land.[95] There are unproved and unprovable modern theories which argue respectively that land was owned originally by extended families or by villages. What is clear is, first, that by the time of the Twelve Tables private ownership by nuclear families was well established, and, secondly, that public land played a large role in the agricultural economy of Rome for most of the Republic. The reason that Rome possessed a great deal of public land over this period was conquest: an important early acquisition was the territory of Veii between Rome and Lake Bracciano.[96] Some of this land acquired in war was handed over to the towns (*coloniae*) that Rome founded, some was distributed as private property, but the rest was kept in public hands and either rented out to individuals or left for exploitation by anyone who so desired, whether for agriculture, pasturage, or other purposes.[97] Much of it thus performed the function that "common land" once had in Britain. Land distribution was facilitated by the development of rectilinear surveying, which yielded grids of squares (*centuriae*), each 200 *iugera* in size, many examples of which are still detectable in the landscape today. The original basic allotment of the poor, the *heredium*, is said to have been a mere 2 *iugera*, roughly half a hectare in size, thus little more than a good-size garden.[98] Those who owned no more could have only survived by exploiting public land. The Judgment of the Minucii about public land in the territory of Genoa in 117 BC has provision for the use of *prata* (meadows) and the collection of wood from common pasture-land.[99] The people of Italy pastured animals on meadows or used the forests to graze domestic pigs; forests were also for hunting and the collection of herbs, fungi, berries, and firewood.[100] Many of the poor were as much hunter-gatherers as cultivators.

By the time of the Gracchan agrarian legislation in the late second century BC allotments made to the poor seem to have increased in size: we find the figure of 30 *iugera* (*c.* 8 hectares).[101] Common pasture-land, however, was still important.[102] There had been, as we have seen, improper appropriation of public land by the wealthy, which the legislators sought to remedy. However, even when the holdings of the wealthy had been restricted, but confirmed as private, and much former public land had been distributed in allotments and was now the property of the poor, there were still a number of categories of public land which were on lease to their occupiers.[103] Other farmers would have been tenants of private owners, their lease perhaps requiring from them not only rent but assistance to their landlord in farming the land he directly managed himself.[104]

The encroachment of the wealthy on public land formed part of a more general phenomenon – the growth of estates resulting from the influx of wealth into Italy from foreign conquest and commerce. Land was the best long-term investment even for those who had not become rich through agriculture. In the long term this was to produce the vast

Figure 11   Settefinestre in Etruria. The view westward from the (originally late-Republican) villa, toward the promontory on which the colony of Cosa stood. In the center, amid the scrub, are the corner-turret and the wall of the formal garden of the villa.

estates (*latifundia*) attested in the early Principate. In the late Republic, on the other hand, the evidence suggests rather an accumulation of separate properties.[105] The excavators at Francolise north of the river Volturnus noted that the proximity of villas in a small area implied that some of the land associated with each would have not been contiguous with the villa site, but distant from it.[106] Many of the elite would have selected properties as much for their amenity as their agricultural yield (figure 11), in particular those at the seaside.[107] Possession of a number of properties also allowed an eminent man, while traveling, to spend as many nights as possible under his own roof(s). The letters of Cicero tell us of his maritime villas at Antium, Astura, Formiae, Baiae, Puteoli, and Pompeii. An interesting example, whose remains still survive, is the villa at Sperlonga (figure 12), built originally in the late second century BC, which the emperor Tiberius seems to have inherited from the Livian side of his family and developed so as to display mythological sculpture in a kind of *son-et-lumière* presentation in caves by the seaside.[108] Massive walls and vaults of another late-Republican villa are to be found at Scauri, southeast of Formiae.[109]

Figure 12   Sperlonga: the villa of the emperor Tiberius. The mouth of the grotto where the statue groups were displayed; in the foreground, walls in *opus incertum* belonging to the earlier Republican villa.

Money was one cause of the development of the Roman villa; another was the improvement of agricultural techniques and management. Modern scholars have created from this a theory of the overthrow of a peasant economy by capitalist production in the second century BC,[110] but it is better to visualize a process that was less drastic and more gradual. Country houses existed even in the regal period (see chapter 2). It is reasonable also to assume that the rich possessed some form of dependent labor from the earliest times, while chattel slaves became available from Rome's early conquests. By the second century BC there was more money in circulation and slaves were plentiful and cheap. In this period Cato the Censor in his work on agriculture advocated a systematic and businesslike approach to the farming of estates. Elsewhere Cato is reported to have advocated stockraising as the most profitable activity for a family farm.[111] His book, however, is primarily concerned with cultivation. Among the forms of cultivation his order of preference is a good vineyard, a watered garden, an osier bed, an olive-yard, a meadow, a grain-field, a wood for timber, a grain-field interspersed with vines on trees, and a wood producing acorns.[112] In what follows he assumes that a farmer will not practice monoculture: the manure from the cattle is to be used to fertilize the plough-land; conversely he advises the planting of elms and poplars on the boundaries of land devoted to olives so that there are leaves for the sheep and cattle to eat.[113] His modules are 100 *iugera* (*c.* 25 hectares) for vineyards and 120 or 240 for olive-yards,[114] thus much larger than the probable size of the plots assigned to the poor in the Gracchan legislation. However, he nowhere talks of a farm as big as 500 *iugera*, the basic quantity of public land that the same legislation permitted the rich to retain.

What Cato is advocating is not a technical revolution –the only real technical innovation he discusses is the olive-press (*trapetum*), where hemispherical stones rotate round an iron pivot in a basin[115] – nor is it production purely for the market. Those who run farms are expected to be largely self-sustaining, selling locally, hiring extra help locally, and receiving help in return for being a good neighbor.[116] The basic labor-force is slave, but free labor is also to be hired, and this implies free laborers living nearby.[117] Although cultivation expected to be profitable, it is a long-term enterprise: it would not have generated speedily the huge returns that more risky enterprises, such as money-lending and tax-collecting, might yield.

Cato assumed that farms were pleasant for the owner to visit, but his instructions for building give no hint of luxury.[118] There were luxury villas in his time: a fragment of a speech he delivered in 152 BC runs "I can say whose villas have been elaborately built and fitted out with citrus-wood, ivory, and Punic pavements."[119] However, these villas seem to have been the exception. The pre-Sullan phases of late-Republican villas[120] were more like Cato's own basic farmhouse or the house of Cicero's father at Arpinum which was only modernized early in the last century BC.[121] However, excavated villas of the late Republic and early Principate are not only equipped with presses and vats for producing wine and oil on a large scale but have elegant living quarters for the visiting owner.[122] These foreshadow the large establishments built for grandees under the rule of the Caesars throughout the empire.

When the antiquarian, M. Terentius Varro, came at the age of 80 (37–36 BC) to write a manual on agriculture addressed to his wife, though he cited Cato on certain points[123] and Saserna,[124] he based the work especially on the voluminous writings of the Carthaginian Mago. These had been translated into Greek with supplements from other Greek writers by a Roman freedman from Utica some 60 years before.[125] Varro, like Cato, assumes a mixed form of agriculture, adapted to the nature of the land. He advises the use of a mixture of slave and free labor, the free being used for the heavier jobs and the less healthy areas.[126] Denouncing the fashion for luxury villas, he points out that a form of building organized to meet the requirements of storage, stabling, and the feeding of the work-force yields more profit.[127] The second book is totally devoted to stockraising. Varro laments the fact that pasturing has taken over former grain land, but admits that he himself had large establishments of sheep in Apulia and horses at Reate in Sabine territory: in fact the sheep wintered in Apulia and were moved north along the drove-roads to summer pasture in the Reate mountains.[128]

The third book illustrates how agriculture had diversified. It concerns the care of livestock close by or in the farmstead: that is, the keeping of bees[129] and the rearing of animals, birds, and fish. What had been a natural way of augmenting the diet of those on the farm had now become a highly profitable industry, which supplied the increasingly diverse constituents of Roman dinners – everything from hare, chicken, ducks, and geese through peacocks, nightingales, and quail, to home-reared boar, snails, dormice, and a variety of fish.[130] It also led to architectural conceits, such as the combined aviary and fishpond that Varro himself created at Cassino, which had a central dining-space, so that guests could eat surrounded on all sides by their future meals.[131] At the Livian villa at Sperlonga, the outdoor dining platform is a masonry island into whose banks small tunnels have been made as homes for the fish which swam in the surrounding moat.

From the beginning Varro stresses the rich agricultural resources of Italy; on the other hand he laments that Romans have become townsmen and that it is imported grain and wine that sustain them.[132] The vast population of Rome certainly could only be adequately supplied by seaborne grain, and the freedmen in its population were unlikely to turn to agriculture. How far estates like those discussed by Varro had supplanted the peasant farmer remains difficult to assess. Indications from field surveys suggest that the patten of settlement varied from region to region.[133]

By the last decades of the Republic the complicated pattern of land occupation which existed in the Gracchan period had been greatly simplified.[134] There were still some important pieces of public land, especially forests, but much of it was now in private ownership, legally or illegally. After Sulla's victory, land confiscated from the vanquished was used to settle veterans, while estates seized from the proscribed passed at auction into the hands of Sulla's henchmen and other survivors of the wars. When the tribune Servilius Rullus sought to make major new settlements in Cicero's consulship (see chapter 3), there was little public land left to exploit and perforce he had to propose the purchase of private land: his bill failed. A later tribune actually proposed to check the validity of tenure of land which had been public up to 133 BC but was now alleged to be in private ownership; this too did not find favor among powerful landowners. The statutes Julius Caesar forced through in 59 provided only for purchase from private landowners and for the distribution of the Campanian land, the chief remaining area of land publicly leased for cultivation. Subsequently, Caesar himself as dictator and the triumvirs found land for their veteran soldiers through the confiscation of land from both their enemies and those who did not oppose them.[135] Augustus in his turn made a point of purchasing the land he required for the same purpose.[136]

A peasantry still existed: indeed some peasants were essential for the wealthier in order to provide part-time labor. Veteran soldiers from the lower ranks would have formed a sizeable part of this class and seem to have had more substantial farms than others settled in the past. Other free men formed professional gangs of harvesters.[137] The Augustan era, nevertheless, was a time when the houses of the rich were becoming grander and their estates bigger. The accumulation of landholdings under the Principate is best illustrated by the later inscribed lists from Veleia and the neighborhood of Beneventum, documenting the wealthy men in Trajan's time who gave their estates as security for the imperial money they were required to dispense for the maintenance of children in their area.[138] One proprietor at Veleia owned as many as 18 farms named after earlier owners. Horace reproaches any wealthy reader for building his seaside villa out over the sea and extending his estates at the expense of clients by illegal removal of boundary-stones.[139] His own, in his view modest, Sabine farm, run by a bailiff with six or seven slaves, embraced five earlier peasant holdings and combined the cultivation of vines and olives with pasturing and the exploitation of woods and fruit-trees.[140]

Where had the previous farmers gone? Civil or foreign wars had perhaps claimed their lives or led to resettlement elsewhere in a military colony. Alternatively, they may have joined the gangs of harvesters mentioned above or sought their fortune abroad, like Virgil's Meliboeus.[141] The attractiveness of migration to the provinces is illustrated later by the fact that even soldiers settled in colonies in Italy frequently preferred to return to the provinces in which they had served, where their status as veterans and Roman citizens would have ensured them a privileged position.[142] Thus the rural population of Italy helped in the long run to create the elite of the Roman empire.

6

Customs, Culture, and Ideas

Religion

In 193 BC a Roman magistrate writing to a Greek city ascribed the current success of the Romans to their piety and the consequent favor of the gods;[1] conversely, Augustan poets attributed moral corruption and the misery of the civil wars to the collapse of piety.[2] It is understandable, therefore, that Cicero's ideal comprehensive law code – something which classical Rome never in reality possessed – begins with regulations about the cult of the gods. He justifies this by arguing that one must persuade citizens that the gods are in control of everything, have concern for men, and take account of those who are pious and impious: this belief is not only true but useful, because it creates respect for oaths and solemn agreements, deters men from crime, and enforces the community of citizens.[3] The word Cicero uses for respect is *religiones*, in the plural because it refers to the restraints which act in each oath and agreement. *Religio*, singular, is later linked with *pietas* as a description of the correct attitude to the gods that should be fostered in a community:[4] it evidently means an attitude of awe and scruple that is manifest in behavior. The religious code that Cicero subsequently enunciates – which is essentially traditional Roman religion, as he understood it – is almost exclusively concerned with priestly duties and ritual, but he does lay down near the end that no impious man should venture to placate the wrath of the gods with gifts.[5] The notion that divine good will cannot automatically be bought is as old as Homer:[6] what Cicero seems to be requiring is not simply belief in the gods, which would be consistent with seeking to manipulate them, but belief that they are concerned with human conduct in general. He does not closely define what sort of behavior stems from piety. However, it is clearly that which accepts the restraints imposed by membership of a family and a community. The bonds arising from religion are links to both gods and human beings.

As among other ancient peoples, religion was not an adjunct to Roman society but a constituent part of it. This is not to say that there were no private forms of religious observance, but Roman authority reserved the right to outlaw or restrict those that it considered subversive to the community, such as those of the Bacchanals, Jews, and worshipers of Isis (see chapter 4 above). Moreover, public religion was under political management. Many ceremonies were performed by magistrates, not priests, while under the Republic major decisions regarding public religious policy were taken by the senate or entrusted to the vote of a popular assembly – for example, the introduction of a new cult or a change in the number of priests in the main colleges. Nevertheless, it was accepted that, in spite of its integration into political life, religion was governed by different principles from those in secular decision-making, which could not be overridden by secular considerations. Legislators indemnified themselves by a clause which nullified any measure included in the statute which was in conflict with sacred law.[7]

The colleges of priests were important, both as bodies and individuals, as interpreters of religious tradition for the benefit of political authority, but in the later Republic their view could only be translated into an executive decision through the senate and/or a magistrate. Priesthoods were held by members of the aristocracy. The main colleges were the pontiffs, augurs, the (ultimately 15-strong) committee concerned with the performance with rites, which had charge of the prophetic books of the Sibyl, and the seven-strong committee for sacred banquets. Membership of these came originally through co-option but in the late Republic through a form of popular election. However, ancient priesthoods connected with a specific cult and the position of "king of religious rites" were still conferred by the chief pontiff (*pontifex maximus*). Priesthoods were held for life and (with a few exceptions) did not preclude the tenure of magistracies or other political and military activities. In the Republican era no person could normally hold more priesthoods than one, and no more than one person from each clan (*gens*) could be a member of the same college at a time. The chief pontiff had authority over priests in general in respect of their priestly duties, with powers to coerce them. He also presided over an antique form of assembly, which dealt with religious matters such as the inauguration of priests, the appointment of Vestal Virgins, and the making of testaments – the last because they transmitted authority over family rituals.[8] He was the one priest whose activities at times resembled the political activities of a magistrate.

It is easy to see how a structure of this kind could be brought under the authority of the emperor. Augustus refrained from taking the position of chief pontiff until the death of the former triumvir Lepidus in 12 BC.[9] Nevertheless, through his magistracies and membership of the senate he was in a position to introduce religious measures, such as the revival of the priesthood of the Arval brethren or the decision to hold the Secular Games in 17 BC.[10] He also became a member of seven priestly college – the four chief ones, the Arval brethren, the *fetiales* (who dealt with the religious aspects of war and peace), and the obscure Companions of Titius[11] – something as contrary to Republican principles as his combination of political powers. This had begun when, after becoming a pontiff in his teens under Caesar's dictatorship, he was also made an augur early in the Triumvirate.[12]

The religion over which the emperor came to preside consisted essentially of the cult of deities and the interpretation of signs from them. In Cicero's words, it was divided into rites, auspices, and the warnings which the interpreters of the Sibyl and the soothsayers (*haruspices*) derived from portents and prodigies.[13] Men in political or religious authority might advocate moral behavior, but, in so far as immoral behavior was held to be impious, this was a matter between the deity and the individual, for example the breaking of an a oath (the gods were expected to punish an individual for perjury).[14] Nevertheless, it was the duty of priests to ensure through appropriate procedures that, if any offense damaged the good relationship between the gods and the community, this should be remedied.

The Romans prayed to the gods, often as an accompaniment to sacrifice, they sacrificed, and they made vows of future gifts and sacrifices, should a desired result be achieved. More elaborate celebrations were the provision of feasts for divinities and the holding of games in their honor. One of our best pieces of evidence for many of these activities, though tediously repetitive to read, are the surviving fragments of the acts of the Arval Brethren,[15] which demonstrate the linking of vow and prayer with sacrifice, and how the priesthood were expected not only to perform according to a regular religious calendar but to react to special events and crises. Such events might be human fortunes and misfortunes – victories, defeats, plots, plagues, and events in the imperial family – they might also be unusual astronomical, physical, and physiological occurrences, such as lightning strikes, abnormal precipitation, and deformed births. These were reported as prodigies, and the priests were asked to decide the appropriate apotropaic response to these signs of divine displeasure.

While prodigies were treated as emergency messages from the gods, regular consultation was through augury – the examination of the heavens, especially the flight of birds, of the behavior of birds, and of the entrails of sacrificed animals. Roman magistrates undertook this before significant military and civil occasions, such as a battle, the leading out of an army, or the holding of an assembly or festival. They might also take notice of omens, such as a sudden thunderstorm, in the course of an event over which they were presiding. It could be argued against divination in general that, if events were predetermined, any information one received could not alter one's destiny and thus was in any case useless and potentially depressing: alternatively, if events were not so fixed, the information was *ex hypothesi* unreliable.[16] However, the results of augury were regarded not as predictions but as warnings, signs that an undertaking should be either abandoned entirely or postponed to a more favorable occasion: the art assumed that the auspice-taker was an agent with free will and the ability to affect the course of events.

Cicero placed the gods in three classes. First are the traditional deities; second are those whose achievements placed them in heaven, because they were benefactors of mankind, that is, Hercules, Liber/ Dionysus, Aesculapius, Castor, Pollux, and Quirinus (that is Romulus). The third he describes as the qualities which grant a man ascent to heaven, such as Mind, Virtue, Piety, and Good Faith.[17] This last group he describes elsewhere as "Utilities" and includes qualities which are not peculiar to a single human being, for example Concord, Liberty, and Victory.[18] These, he argues, are held to be divine, because they possess an especially potent force. The second and third categories of deity are of their nature open-ended, and it is easy to see how they left the way open for the deification of Julius Caesar and the Roman emperors on the one hand, and, on the other, of Rome itself in relation to its empire.[19]

The Roman calendar (*Fasti*) provides a catalogue of the various divinities whose cults were publicly acknowledged. In his poem entitled *Fasti* Ovid has left to us a commentary on the first six months of the year on an epic scale. It reveals how some festivals were so ancient and obscure that they baffled explanation, others had been integrated into Roman mythology, and yet others had a historical origin that could be documented. For example, no one knew the meaning of the Agonia on January 9, whereas the ancient Italian goddess Carmenta, celebrated on January 11, had been identified with the mother of Evander, the Arcadian exile who had come to settle on the Palatine before Aeneas' arrival.[20] By contrast, the Asian cult of the Great Mother, whose festival was on April 4, was known to have been introduced from Asia Minor in 204 BC.[21]

Figure 13   The so-called temple of Juno (perhaps in fact of Fortuna) at Gabii, twelve miles southeast of Rome, built in the middle Republic. It incorporated a crypt and had in its precinct a theater and a sacred grove.

The calendar had traditionally been the responsibility of the priests, to the extent that it was their authority which once officially settled the beginning and stage-points of the original lunar months. The political years of the Republic were solar years named after the pair of consuls, but for a long time they were awkwardly synchronized with the religious calendar. In the early Republic the political year apparently began in midsummer; by the late third century BC the consuls entered office on the Ides (15th) of March; only in 153 BC did January 1 become the beginning of the consular year.[22] The years continued to be named after the consuls who entered office on January 1, even under the emperors. The nature of the calendar reveals various reforms, including the change from a ten-month to a 12-month year, in that the last month December is in name the tenth: it was finally Julius Caesar who attemped, almost successfully, to reconcile the (in principle lunar) months with a solar year, in which there was no need to insert from time to time intercalary months in order to prevent misalignment with the seasons.[23]

When Ovid was explaining how March, the month of Mars, was originally made the first month by Romulus, he cited eight other Italian

Figure 14   Lucus Feroniae in Etruria, a colony of either Caesar or Augustus founded on the site of a shrine to the Sabine goddess Feronia. Here were the crossroads of the *via Tiberina*, leading to Rome, and the road to Capena (looking south). In the foreground are a late-Roman milestone and (in the center) a public lavatory.

calendars for the varying position of Mars' month in their years.[24] It is clear from the inscribed calendars that survive from the imperial period and their findspots that Augustus made a systematic effort to promote one festival year valid for all Italy. He was assisted by the antiquarian Verrius Flaccus, who wrote a commentary on the *Fasti* and was celebrated by a statue in the forum at Praeneste.[25] The fragmentary inscribed calendar found there is probably based on his work.[26] The new system combined ancient Roman festivals with celebrations connected with the imperial family. So on April 14 and 16 there were successively thanksgivings to Augustan Victory and the Good Fortune of the Empire in honor of Caesar Octavianus' first battle at Forum Gallorum and his first salutation as commander (*imperator*); on the other hand on April 15 there was the ancient festival promoting the fertility of cattle, the Fordicidia, on the 19th the games of Ceres, the goddess of earth and agriculture, while the 21st was the Parilia, originally in honor of Pales, patroness of shepherds, but also associated with Romulus and hence at present still celebrated as the birthday of the city.

Not all rites were conducted by magistrates or priests on behalf of the people. An important part of the festival of the Parilia was the fumigation of sheep in the countryside.[27] Families cultivated the *lares* and *penates* in their own homes.[28] The rites connected with the *lares* of the crossroads were performed at Rome by masters of guilds and later, as *lares Augusti*, by "masters of the wards" (*magistri vicorum*) (see chapter 4 above); shrines for this sort of worship have been found at Pompeii.[29] The cult of dead ancestors, which concluded on the day of the public festival of the Feralia (February 21), and that of the *lares* on the following day were matters for families, as was the expulsion of ghosts from the house on the Lemuria (May 9, 11, and 13).[30]

Traditional Roman religion was, in the words of Walter Pater (*Marius the Epicurean*, chapter 1), "a religion of usages and sentiment rather than of facts and belief." The "system of symbolic usages" developed "an impressibility of the sacredness of time, ... the circumstances of family fellowship, of such gifts to men as fire, water, the earth ... It was a religion for the most part of fear, of multitudinous scruples, of a year-long burden of forms." Yet it did foster an acceptance of, and joy in, life and the natural world. Nor was it exclusive: in principle men and women were free to seek other forms of religious and philosophical reassurance and in consequence many foreign cults found a home among the Romans. A recent work rightly has the title, *Religions of Rome*.[31]

Rome from its earliest years had imported cults not only from elsewhere in Italy but from beyond. The cult of Fortuna, established in the Forum Boarium under the Etruscan kings, is probably of oriental origin.[32] The cult of the Great Mother was officially adopted from Asia Minor during the second Punic war. New Greek rites were introduced into the cult of Apollo during the same war, as they had been earlier into the cult of Ceres.[33] Cults also entered Roman society unofficially, however. The classic instance of this remains the cult of Dionysus in rites which were termed Bacchanals, repressed in 186 BC. What appears from the restrictive measures taken against it is that the Roman authorities did not object to a cult of Dionysus/Bacchus in itself, but they did outlaw the societies that had formed around it, as potential centers of crime and political subversion, and rejected the secret form that rites took – they were held at night, often underground, and involved initiation.[34]

Cicero in his ideal code banned all nocturnal rites except those held on behalf of the people, that is, the celebration of the Good Goddess, and all initiation except that introduced into the cult of Ceres, which, according to him, was modeled on the Eleusinian mysteries.[35] The cult of the Egyptian deity, Isis, had for a long time an uncertain place at Rome – expelled in the late Republic, restored officially by the triumvirs, banned again from the city by Augustus and Tiberius (see chapter 4), and subsequently given official status.[36] This too involved initiation, and the deity seems to have claimed a universal, though not exclusive, power. This is illustrated above all in the celebration of the attributes of the goddess inscribed on the Greek island of Ios in the third century BC, where among other things the goddess is said to have separated heaven and earth, appointed the ways of the stars, made justice strong, linked woman and man, and enjoined the 10-month conception of children.[37] What clearly sustained this cult at Rome was its sheer popularity. The temple of Isis at Pompeii, rebuilt after the earthquake of 62 AD, seems to have been originally constructed in the first century BC.[38] Isis' consort Sarapis was similarly established both at Rome in the late Republic and at Puteoli on the bay of Naples before 105 BC.[39] Under the Principate more oriental cults would appear at Rome, such as the cults of Jupiter of Doliche and Mithras, and Christianity would find a niche in the already important Jewish community at Rome.[40] While the first two coexisted in a divine world with Rome's traditional deities, Christianity, like Judaism, rejected them entirely. However, it was to take many centuries for the ancient Roman religion to lose its significance and popularity.

For the educated elite there were the consolations of philosophy as well as, or in place of, the consolations of religion. Rome imported from the Greek world not only religious rites but aspects of rational thought. This may be said to have begun with the influence of Greek law on the Twelve Tables in the fifth century BC, but it is only in the second century that we have evidence of the impact on Rome of the Greek philosophical schools, part of a more general effect of Greek arts and sciences (see below). The philosophy was either idealist – Stoicism and some Academic philosophy – or materialist – Epicureanism – or skeptical. This last was the position of the current mainstream Academic philosophy which, because it held that philosophical ideas were only a matter of opinion, not of knowledge, allowed someone like Cicero to pick and mix his philosophical ideas. The Stoics, whose philosophy also derived from Plato and Aristotle, argued for the primacy of reason over the body and material appetites, and for the permanent reality of rational ideas, which in the Stoic view provided a channel for a divine power in the world. Epicureanism was ultimately descended from the Greek atomists Leucippus and Democritus: they argued that the world was essentially nothing more than a rain of atoms which made originally random con-

nections and evolved into the world we know. Hence Epicurus taught
that souls were mortal, ideas depended on sensation, and the aim of
ethics was pleasure or mental tranquillity. His gods lived in an Epicurean
world of their own, untroubled by human affairs.

Cicero himself, though an Academic skeptic, had a preference for Stoic
ethics, but he tells us of the large numbers of Roman Epicureans at the
time.[41] These included friends of his, ranging from the tyrannicide Gaius
Cassius to the apolitical foodie Lucius Papirius Paetus.[42] It was for this
receptive audience that Lucretius wrote his great epic *On the Nature of
Things*, an exposition of Epicureanism in Latin hexameters. This sought
to instill in his readers the mental tranquillity he held to be the highest
good, in particular to combat the fears of hell which sprang, as far as
we can tell, not from traditional Roman religion but from Greek ideas,
especially those associated with Pythagoras, Plato, and the Orphic
mystery religion.[43] Later, Horace admitted to being a "pig from the flock
of Epicurus"[44] and gave voice to his philosophical persuasion not only
in his didactic satires and epistles but in the lyrics of the *Odes*.
Epicureanism was still contesting its position in the melee of religious
and philosophical ideas which overtook the Roman world in the suc-
ceeding centuries, to judge from the inscribed exposition of Epicurean
doctrine set up, probably in the second century AD in the Asia Minor
city of Oenoanda by a local worthy, Diogenes.[45]

The Development of Arts and the Intellect

Education

The adoption of Greek philosophical systems was part of a general
importation of Greek intellectual culture. Horace famously claimed that
Greece after its capture captured the savage victor and brought the arts
(*artes*) into rustic Latium.[46] This is a pithy description of the impact of
Greece, but misleading in more than one way. First, it dramatizes as a
sudden movement what was in fact a long process of absorption from
the time Rome came into contact with the Greek world, first in southern
Italy and Sicily, then in Greece proper and the orient. Secondly, to select
Latium as the substantive to be qualified as "rustic" is unfair to other
Latin cities which during the Republic were in some ways more cultured
than Rome itself. Finally, the Latin word *artes* covers not only what we
understand as arts but all branches of knowledge, to the extent that it
can have moral connotations.

Traditionally, education was a matter for the family. According to Cicero, the Greek historian Polybius complained that it was passed over in Roman institutions; he himself admitted that there were no fixed rules laid down by law nor did the Romans desire uniformity in practice.[47] Under the Republic even the children of the most aristocratic families were educated by their fathers and mothers. Cato the Censor taught his son not only his letters and basic knowledge of the law but gave him physical training. He wrote out in his own hand his histories, and in large letters, so that his son could use it to learn Roman traditions.[48] The Gracchi brothers were educated in both Latin and Greek by their mother Cornelia, though they afterwards had the benefit of the Greek rhetor Diophanes of Mytilene and the Campanian philosopher Blossius.[49]

Educated freedmen or slaves might function as teachers in the more prosperous households; there were also professional teachers of letters, *grammatici* or *litteratores*. Some of these also taught rhetoric, but by the nineties BC there were specialized Latin teachers of rhetoric in Rome.[50] Cicero and his cousins, however, who were educated together at Rome by professional teachers under the ultimate supervision of the great orator and statesman Lucius Crassus, were taught Greek at an early age and advised that they should learn rhetoric also in Greek.[51] Apart from their formal education, the young men of the aristocracy would have been educated by accompanying their seniors about their business around the forum: indeed it was said that at one time they accompanied their fathers into the senate when still boys.[52] In the mature Republic and Principate the critical moment was when a Roman formally left boyhood. After receiving the toga of manhood from his father, Cicero was attached first to Quintus Mucius Scaevola (consul in 117) and then to another Scaevola, Publius (consul in 95), from whom he learnt jurisprudence by listening to the advice he gave in consultations.[53] The reception of this toga marked therefore not only the commencement of manhood but for the elite the beginning of public life. Augustus deliberately had himself elected consul for the years in which he gave the toga to his adopted sons, Gaius and Lucius Caesar.[54]

The sons and daughters of artisans and farmers learned from their fathers or mothers to perform their appropriate tasks.[55] There were, however, schools in Italy. Horace tells us that he, the son of a freedman debt-collector, might have gone to the school at Venusia, to which the sons of important centurions went with their satchels and slates slung from their left shoulders.[56] These would have been the children of the local elite: their fathers would become members of the colony's senate and perhaps donate a public building or a monument to the community.[57] The cost of the school was not great, two sesterces a month, so not beyond a reasonably prosperous farmer or tradesman. There, according to the poet, the pupils would have learnt what was profitable, rather than what was virtuous.[58] Instead, Horace's father took him to Rome, where he attended the schools of teachers there, not least that of "Orbilius the whacker" – Lucius Orbilius Pupillus of Beneventum, a former cavalryman who eked out a living as a *grammaticus* first at his home town, later at Rome. Orbilius made Horace learn the work of Livius Andronicus, the father of Latin poetry, by heart.[59]

Poetry and the theater

Greek philosophy and formal rhetoric came comparatively late to Rome: poetry, prose literature, and the theater all preceded them. Without Greek influence Latin poetry and the Roman theater would have been insignificant. A hymn sung by the Arval brethren under the Principate seems by its language archaic[60] and there are fragments of other early hymns, prayers, and epitaphs. We also hear of primitive comic performances with improvised dialogue, and of ancient songs sung at banquets praising famous men,[61] but of these nothing survives. It is clear, however, that Livius Andronicus, the slave brought to Rome on the fall of Taras (Tarentum) in 270 BC, introduced to Rome epic and tragedy. Subsequently Naevius and Ennius wrote epics on Roman themes and continued the tradition of translating Greek drama. Naevius also translated and adapted Greek New Comedy, *fabulae palliatae* (plays in Greek dress), and introduced the *fabula praetextata* or *praetexta*, a historical play on a Roman subject. Livius, Naevius, and Ennius are only known to us from quotations, but, thanks to his later popularity we have a rich supply of work of Plautus as of that of one of his successors, Terence (Publius Terentius Afer). Plautus adapted Greek New Comedy, a comedy of manners and character, into plays that were genuinely Roman, using extravagant language referring to Roman society, and exploiting farcical situations to get the maximum comic effect; Terence returned to the spirit of the Greek originals, while continuing to incorporate Roman language and values.[62]

The composition of tragedies continued through Pacuvius, Accius, and others; *fabulae praetextatae* were written by Ennius, Pacuvius, and Accius, and there were other Latin writers of Greek comedy, notably Statius Caecilius. However, specifically Roman genres of drama developed: the *fabula togata*, associated with Titinius, Quinctius Atta, and Afranius, was a form of situation comedy transferred, as its name implies, not only in language, but in dress and context, to Italy; the improvised farce from Atella in Campania was given literary texts by Pomponius and Novius. Moreover, the melodramatic mime was given a certain intellectual depth in the late Republic through the incorporation of reflections and pithy aphorisms (*sententiae*); its most renowned writers were Publilius the Syrian and the equestrian Decimus Laberius.[63]

Meanwhile the Latin hexameter had been turned to a new use in the writing of *Saturae*, a mixture of social, political, and literary comment on the Roman world. Gaius Lucilius was renowned for the freedom of expression with which he was not afraid to lampoon the great men of the late second century BC. The spirit may have been that of Greek Old Comedy of the fifth century, but as a genre it was a Roman invention, of which they were to be relatively few, but distinguished exponents. Satires, however, could be written in a variety of verse forms, as the productions of Cicero's contemporary, the polymath Marcus Terentius Varro, show.[64] The growth of legislation against defamation and the demise of the Republic meant that Lucilius' chief successors, Horace and Juvenal, could not attack powerful contemporaries in the way that he was able to. The first Latin elegiac love poetry, by Quintus Catulus (consul in 102), Valerius Aedituus, and Porcius Licinus, seems to have been written at the end of the second century BC, and in the same period Marcus Antonius (consul in 99) the great orator celebrated his success against the pirates on a monument at Corinth with an inscribed text in this meter.[65] Shortly after this the young Cicero wrote translations from the Greek, in particular a verse translation of Aratus' poem on astronomy, and probably composed his epic poem on Marius.[66] During Cicero's lifetime Lucretius' epic *On the Nature of Things* appeared, as did the lyric and elegiac poetry of Catullus; Cornelius Gallus was already writing elegiacs, and Helvius Cinna composed a massively learned miniature epic.[67] The earliest poems of Virgil, Horace, and Propertius follow closely on Cicero's death. In fact the late Republic and Augustan period saw a huge effusion of poetry, an almost invisible iceberg of which the great classical authors are peaks. As Horace wrote, "With or without talent, we write poems left, right and center."[68]

Lucilius and Catulus were members of the urban elite, as perhaps were Tibullus and the poet of Epicureanism, Lucretius. However, many of the great exponents of Latin literaure came from outside Rome – Propertius from Umbria, Ovid from Sulmo in Paelignian territory, Catullus and Virgil from Cisalpine Gaul. The writers of Latin drama, moreover, were mostly Italian rather than Roman – Naevius from

Campania, Plautus and Accius from Umbria, Ennius from Messapia, Pacuvius from Brundisium, and Afranius probably from Picenum. Caecilius and Terence are said to have been freed slaves. Latin literature and theater were a creation of the whole of Italy, not Rome alone or even Latium.

When Horace wrote a hexameter epistle on the art of poetry, addressed to an aristocrat, Calpurnius Piso, and his sons,[69] it was chiefly concerned with writing plays. The theater played a great part in the development of the Latin language and Roman culture, but during the Republic and early Principate it remained an object of suspicion in the eyes of the Roman elite. Professional actors, not the amateurs who performed Atellan farces, were treated as a degraded class without full citizen rights, even when they were free men. A decree of the senate of 19 AD, preserved on bronze at Larinum,[70] forbad the appearance of those of senatorial or equestrian family either in the arena or on the stage. It was Augustus, Suetonius tells us, who first abolished the right to coerce, that is, the right to imprison or flog, actors, except during the games and stage performances: this was to be interpreted under Tiberius as a total ban on flogging actors.[71] The cunning slave who manipulates the actions of his betters, notably Pseudolus in the Plautine comedy of that name, in some ways represents the humbler writers and actors of the plays. It is true that Quintus Roscius was made an equestrian by Sulla, but he was exceptionally privileged.[72]

The first stone theater at Rome was contracted for by the censors of 154 BC but demolished soon afterwards, at least in part, and a ban placed on the provision of temporary seating for games in the city and its suburbs.[73] We do not know how long this ban on temporary seating survived, but it was only in 55 BC that, thanks to Pompey, Rome once again possessed a stone theater. By contrast, towns in Latium and elsewhere in Italy were distinguished by their theaters. Rome's neighbors Praeneste and Tibur had theaters as part of the temple complexes of Hercules Victor and Fortuna Primigeneia (figure 15) .[74] Elsewhere we find, for example, theaters in the colony at Minturnae, and the then Oscan town of Pompeii, which antedate the War of the Allies.[75] Most remarkable is that which forms part of the shrine at Samnite Pietrabbondante, abandoned after that same war (figure 16).[76]

Theater allowed crowds to express their feelings about politics. In 59 BC, when the actor Diphilus declaimed the line, "At the cost of our misery you are great," he was compelled to repeat it by the audience, who understood it as a reference to Pompey. Similarly, "there will come a time when you will regret that very valor," and "if neither laws nor

Figure 15 Praeneste (Palestrina): temple of Fortuna Primigineia. View from the theater at the summit of the shrine south toward the Monti Lepini.

Figure 16 Pietrabbondante in the Molise, a shrine of the independent Samnite peoples, developed in the second century BC: view south over one of the temples with, below it, a theater.

Figure 17   Arausio (Orange) in the Rhône valley: the theater (probably Augustan epoch) of the colony founded by Julius Caesar for the veterans of his Second Legion. It was associated with a temple and altar, perhaps for the cult of the imperial family, which lie beyond the auditorium and stage-building at the rear of the picture.

morals restrain," produced cheers and boos. In 57, at the time when Cicero's recall from exile was being voted, the audience interpreted lines from Accius' *Eurysaces* and his *praetexta Brutus*, delivered by Aesopus, as praise of Cicero – in particular from the latter play, "Tullius who had made steadfast liberty for citizens," in the play an allusion to King Servius Tullius.[77] This freedom of speech survived the installation of monarchy. Nero is praised by Suetonius for ignoring many gibes against him, among them that by Datus, an actor of Atellan farces, who, when delivering the line "Farewell father, farewell mother!," accompanied the first half by eating, the second by swimming gestures – references to the deaths of Claudius and Nero's mother Agrippina.[78]

Historiography, letters, and technical knowledge

The arrival in Rome of philosophy and the study of rhetoric has already been mentioned. What was perhaps for the ancients the supreme prose art, the writing of history, had preceded them, even if 300 years of the Republic had to elapse before it produced Roman historians. The earliest of these were Fabius Pictor and Cincius Alimentus, both of whom held public office during the second Punic war and chose to write in Greek. By this time Naevius' poem on the Punic war had appeared and Ennius was composing his *Annals* in Latin. The historians' use of Greek in part reflected the lack of models of Latin prose, in part the international audience to which they hoped to explain Rome's origins and current greatness. Fabius and Cincius, like the epic writers, did not simply write contemporary history but traced an outline of Rome's development from its origins. The Romans termed such history "*annales*," because that was the term for the chronicle that preceded them: the annals of the pontiffs, we are told, were a register of the consular years in succession, to each of which seems to have been appended a note of the significant events of the year: battles, triumphs, food shortages, and portentous events such as eclipses.[79]

How far back such records were actually made at the time and hence are a sound framework for history is still debated. On any view Fabius, Cincius, and the writers of epic needed other material to produce something beyond mere chronography. This was supplied by Greek writers (Timaeus from Sicilian Taormina, active in the early third century BC, dealt with Rome in his work), by a few surviving early documents, and, above all, by aristocratic family tradition, perpetuated in funeral orations, and popular legend. A somewhat confused mythology about its origins had been growing at Rome for some time. For example, since around 300 BC at the latest, Rome was believed to have had in effect two foundations, one by Aeneas the Trojan, a second by Romulus and Remus. It was the historians and early writers of epic who first brought some coherence to the story by postulating a gap of 300 years or more between the two events, conveniently filled by a dynasty of kings from

Alba Longa. Rome could thus be presented to the Greek world in more than one way: in 194 BC Titus Flamininus claimed at Delphi to be a descendant of Aeneas, while about the same time a friend of Rome on the island of Chios engraved a genealogy of Romulus and Remus on stone and portrayed myths from Roman history on shields given as prizes.[80]

Soon afterwards Cato produced his history in Latin, entitled *Origins*, but one with a rich coverage of his own lifetime, to judge from the surviving fragments. It should be stressed that our knowledge of these historians depends on quotations and citations in the later writers whose works replaced theirs. The tradition of writing "annals" from the beginnings of Rome until the present continued until it reached its climax under Augustus with Livy's *From the Foundation of the City* in 142 books, of which we still have only 35. However, by that time other genres of historical writing had been introduced to Rome. There were biographies such as that written by Gaius Gracchus about his brother Tiberius, autobiographies such as Sulla's memoirs or the commentaries, which we possess, of Julius Caesar, and monographs on special topics, such as those we have by Sallust on Catiline's conspiracy and the war against Jugurtha. The word "*Historiae*" developed two senses – first, interpretative history beyond mere chronicle, secondly, contemporary history, as opposed to "annals" which were more ancient history (best illustrated in the titles of the two main works of the great historian of the Principate, Tacitus). All these works, although they embraced Rome's exploits abroad and the peoples with whom it came into contact throughout its imperial expansion, were centered on Rome. A Roman historian was termed "author" or "writer" "of Roman matters."[81]

An art which contributed to historical writing and was of great practical importance for the elite was that of writing letters. Roman commanders abroad were expected to communicate with the home city about their achievements and prospects. What probably were once short messages developed by the late Republic into elaborate briefings, especially important when the commander wished to put himself in the best possible light before a potentially critical audience, as we find in letters of Cicero from Cilicia.[82] Official letters were sent formally under the Republic to the consuls, praetors, tribunes, and senate. They would be read by a presiding magistrate to the senate.[83] Similarly, a commander might wish to brief influential friends about his achievements. Servius Galba sent Cicero his own version of the battle of Forum Gallorum in April 43 BC, but Cicero in the ensuing senate debate preferred to rely on the official version of the consul Hirtius.[84] Furthermore, consuls and praetors were required to draft on behalf of the senate and people letters to Rome's friends or enemies, which were diplomatic instruments: the importance of these grew with the expansion of the empire.[85]

On a personal level many letters were formal recommendations or requests, which lubricated the system of patronage.[86] Under the Principate letters to and from the emperor became the most important official forms of communication. A regular system of petitions developed, while imperial letters became a source of law.[87] The evidence shows that, by the late Republic, even men with no literary aspirations could write effective letters, perhaps with advice from slave or freedman secretaries. The art would have owed much originally to Hellenistic practices, where the letters of kings, officials, and cities provide an interesting comparison. The formula used to open official Roman letters, "If you are well, it is well. I and the army are well," derives from the correspondence of the monarchs of Syria and Pergamum and, even earlier, from that of Ptolemaic officials in Egypt.[88]

Works on rhetoric followed the appearance of formal instruction whether in Greek or Latin. The earliest that we possess, *Rhetorica ad Herennium*, transmitted in manuscript with the works of Cicero, is, to judge from its content, of the late eighties BC; Cicero's own *De Inventione*, on forms of rhetorical argument, is of the same period. Later in his life Cicero wrote a series of works on oratory, discussing content, style, and the practice of the law courts, and a review of the orators of the Republic, set against the background of their classical Greek predecessors. These were to be followed in the early Principate by works of the elder Seneca, Quintilian, and Tacitus. As for politics, in the late Republic treatises appeared on augury and constitutional matters.[89] A letter, the so-called *Commentariolum Petitionis*, purporting to be from Quintus Cicero to his brother, is in effect a manual on electioneering. However, the only known theoretical works on politics from the Republic are the dialogues *De Re Publica* and *De Legibus* of Cicero himself.

We have already had occasion to refer to treatises on agriculture, those of Cato the Censor and Varro. Works specifically on military matters, on land-surveying, and on aqueducts are not known until almost a century after Augustus. The first book we possess, dealing with art and what we now call technology, is Vitruvius' study of architecture. The Romans had been consumers of art from the regal period. Rome's conquests in Italy and abroad brought to Rome first Etruscan and then Greek sculpture. The earliest Roman fresco that we know is of about 300 BC (see chapter 2). However, although the Roman elite became connoisseurs of Greek painting and sculpture, we know of only a few sculptors under the Republic with a Latin name, Coponius and three freedmen Cossutii.[90] Italians were better represented in architecture, beginning with the Campanian Decimus Cossutius in the second century BC; a Gaius Mucius built the temple of Honor and Virtue for Marius, and the architect of the theater at Herculaneum was Publius Numisius.[91] Cicero's architect Vettius Cyrus, who believed that optics depended on rays of light (not filmy images, as supposed by Epicurus), was clearly a fashionable Roman practitioner of his time. To judge from his last name, he was either an enfranchised foreigner or of slave descent.[92]

Vitruvius served first Julius Caesar and then his son as a military engineer and subsequently an architect: his work was dedicated to Augustus.[93] It is based on a number of Greek theoretical works, combined with his own practical experience. What must strike a modern reader is that the treatise is not only on architecture but on a range of engineering topics (Books 9–10): water pumps and the management of water, water-clocks, sundials and the measurement of time, hoists, derricks, traction contrivances, machines for calibrating distance traveled, artillery, and siege engines. Vitruvius requires the good architect to be a polymath (Book 1), knowing mathematics, draftsmanship, history, physics, physical geography, law, and astronomy. He does not have to be a great theoretician in these disciplines: it is sufficient if he is good at using them in his work. It is to Vitruvius that we owe descriptions not only of typically Greek building and its orders of architecture, but also of Roman matters, for example the use of *pozzolana*, volcanic powder, with lime and rubble to create a form of concrete, and the shuttering of this with small stones to produce an irregular (*opus incertum*) or regular diamond-pattern (*reticulatum*) facing.[94] He also describes how Romans developed Greek town-planning to create the pattern of the forum with its surrounding basilicas and public buildings, the construction of theaters, baths (including the hanging heated floors, *suspensurae*), and harbors (Book 5).

Roman technological development was uneven. The organization of agriculture became sophisticated, but its instruments were for the most part basic – though it has been argued that the simple plough, first described by Hesiod in the seventh century BC, was more suitable for Mediterranean soils than heavier and more elaborate alternatives.[95] Roads were good but land transport primitive. At sea, vessels of great size were to be found but with an unsophisticated arrangement of sails, poor steering, and inadequate aids to navigation.[96] Vitruvius is good evidence for the growth of building technology, which was to be taken further through the use of fired brick to shutter concrete and the creation of arches and vaults out of concrete. One version of the hoists he describes can be found illustrated in a relief sculpture on the later tomb of the Haterii from the *via Casilina* outside Rome.[97] Apart from building, perhaps the greatest progress was made in the use of water, first for irrigation, secondly as source of power in water-mills and mines, and thirdly as an aid to the extraction of the ore itself .[98] As impressive as technology itself was the development of rational organization, to be seen on a grand scale in agriculture, the army, land survey, and the census, in microcosm in the deliberations of an individual. When Cicero tried to sum up the worsening political situation in 50 BC on the eve of civil war, he did so in what amounted to a written equivalent of a flow diagram.[99]

Relaxation, Ceremony, and Celebration

The number of festivals in the Roman calendar (see above), augmented in the late Republic and further increased during the Principate through the self-promotion of the imperial house, may give a misleading impression. Life was not a perpetual holiday for the average Roman. For the workers in the countryside some of the ancient festivals, such as the Parilia and the Fordicidia involving sheep and cattle respectively, would have retained their relevance, but what went on in Rome itself would have mattered little, unless they lived sufficiently close. The country towns were acquiring calendars similar to that of Rome, but are unlikely to have afforded celebrations as extensive as those in the city. For the city-dwellers themselves a festival meant a suspension of legal business, but the religious ceremonies were chiefly a matter for senators and priests and otherwise life went on. Scenic entertainment and gladiatorial shows could only be attended by a limited section of the citizen population at a time; it was the days devoted to chariot-racing in the Circus (17 a year in Augustus' reign) that were a holiday for the majority of the population.[100]

For the elite under the Republic there was a long adjournment of legal business in the spring from early April to mid-May and another in December at the time of the Saturnalia: Augustus, perhaps as a substitute, created a legal vacation at the end of the year of two full months.[101] Under the Republic the senate was treated as a council which was always available at short notice: it could even meet on days on which legal business was forbidden (*dies nefasti*). So, in theory, senators who were not absent on public business elsewhere, were expected to be living sufficiently close to Rome to be summoned.[102] In practice, they took advantage of legal vacations and the periods of the major games to escape from

Rome to a country or seaside villa. Under Augustus their opportunities would have been more frequent, since he restricted ordinary senate meetings to the kalends and the ides of each month and reduced participation in September and October each year to an allotted quorum, sufficient for the passage of decrees.[103]

In the city, work followed closely on daylight, as did the morning visits of friends to friends and clients to their patrons (*salutationes*). For many the working day effectively stopped at noon and lunchtime.[104] Legal and political business, however, might last until sunset. A full day also was probably worked by the porters, construction-workers, and others at the lower end of the social scale, as it was for those who worked on the land.[105] Those who had the leisure might take exercise and visit the baths in the afternoon, and dinner often began as early as the ninth hour of the day.[106]

Drinking followed dinner and for the elite took place at someone's home, sometimes at a different house to that of the dinner, as was the practice for Greek *symposia*. Various kinds of entertainment were provided, ranging from listening to poetry or rhetoric to dicing and other board games. Suetonius has great satisfaction in quoting letters of Augustus to Tiberius and his daughter Julia in which he refers to the gaming that regularly accompanied his dinners.[107] Dinner parties took place in a room with three couches (*triclinium*), which could normally accommodate nine, at a maximum, 12 diners. On special family occasions more rooms would have been used, also when there were special guests. When Cicero entertained Caesar during the Saturnalia in December 45, he needed three dining rooms for Caesar's staff, including his superior slaves.[108]

From the early second century BC onward there was a series of sumptuary laws, in particular aimed at restricting expenditure on dinners. When the question of luxury was raised in the senate in 22 AD, the emperor Tiberius pointed out that all the laws, including those of Caesar and Augustus, had been disregarded with impunity.[109] The sumptuary laws were one of Lucilius' subjects for mockery, and luxury in eating remained a favorite topic of later Roman satirists. However, the legislation had not aimed to restrict culinary ingenuity and conspicuous expenditure on food so much as its use for the cultivation of political support.[110] The limitation of the number of dinner-guests by the *lex Orchia* of 182 BC suggests a tradition of giving public meals, perhaps in the open air. This custom may have returned in the early Principate. Augustus, we are told, gave formal dinners but to a select clientele; Nero decided to ban public banquets, replacing them with distributions of food. However, Domitian abolished public food distributions and brought back formal dinners.[111] These were held in the huge banqueting hall he incorporated into his palace on top of a more restricted dining complex constructed by Nero. Here, according to the poet Statius, the emperor entertained members of the senate and equestrian order en masse.[112]

There were a number of occasions for family celebrations, some obvious to us, others less so. Birthdays were an occasion for sacrifices, parties, and presents. If you happened to have been born in an intercalary month under the old Republican calendar (which occurred only every three or four years), you celebrated on the last day of February.[113] The Caristia on February 22, the day following those of the cult of the dead, was a day when relatives dined together; another family day was the Matronalia on March 1, the festival of the goddess of childbirth.[114] The Saturnalia on December 17–19 were a form of carnival, in which normal restrictions were lifted, children and slaves went unpunished, and masters and slaves exchanged roles. The Compitalia, which followed at the end of December or the beginning of January, were another celebration for slaves in their households, as well as for freedmen and other members of the plebs in their societies (*collegia*).[115] Weddings led to a series of entertainments: the father of the bride gave a party at the betrothal, when originally a legally binding promise was made, later something less formal; a further party occurred at the wedding itself, when the contract was signed, presents given, the bride handed over, and then taken in procession to her husband's home; finally, the day following the wedding the bridegroom entertained at the couple's home.[116]

The funerals of the elite were designed to impress the population at large and for this reason praised by the Greek historian of Rome's rise to power, Polybius.[117] The corpse was carried to the Rostra in the Forum, accompanied by mourners in chariots, dressed as his ancestors in the appropriate robes for their rank, and wearing the masks representing their features (*imagines*), which were preserved in the family home. In the Forum a son or close relative delivered the formal eulogy, before the procession departed for the place of cremation or tomb. However, in general since the time of the Twelve Tables and, to judge from the archeological evidence, even earlier, there had been regulations restricting mourning and ostentatious expenditure on funerals. When his friend Servius Sulpicius Rufus died on an embassy to Mark Antony in 43, Cicero urged the senate that in addition to other honors these restrictions should be lifted. We discover some of these in Cicero's discussion of his ideal law code.[118] Women were not permitted exaggerated mourning or

Figure 18   The tomb of an aristocratic lady, Caecilia Metella, on the Appian Way.

the tearing of the cheeks, there was to be a maximum of 10 pipers, and "drinking around" was forbidden. Nor were expensive grave goods allowed, such as gold, except for the person, "whose gold was linked with teeth." The funeral was followed by nine further days of family mourning, at the end of which a sacrifice was made to the deceased.[119] Most of the corpses were cremated in the period up to Augustus but the families of the Cornelian clan inhumed: the tombs of the Scipiones are outside the Republican wall on the Appian Way. By Augustus' time wealthy families, although they practiced cremation, sought increasing monumentality in the tomb for the ashes. So we find major mausolea, among them Augustus' own, that of Caecilia Metella on the Appian Way (figure 18), and that of Lucius Munatius Plancus near Gaeta.[120] The most exotic is the pyramid of the senator Gaius Cestius, a friend of Agrippa and Valerius Messala Corvinus, outside the Ostian gate.[121] Even a comparatively undistinguished knight who had held the post of military tribune, Marcus Lucilius Paetus, built for himself a mausoleum, about 33 meters in diameter, on the *via Salaria*.[122]

Another striking form of celebration, the Roman triumph, does not receive an extensive description in what survives of Polybius, and its general importance has perhaps been overestimated by modern scholarship.[123] This seems essentially to have been the formal return of a victorious commander and his army into the city, obviously an occasion for particular rejoicing by not only his family and friends but those of the surviving soldiers. The procession, led by the commander in a chariot, followed an anti-clockwise circuit round the center of the city, ending at the temple of Jupiter on the Capitol. Booty and prisoners were displayed, and in the later Republic placards recorded and floats illustrated the army's success. Various conventional elements were incorporated into the ceremony, perhaps accretions over time rather than part of an original ritual. Permission had to be sought from the senate for a triumph – an understandable restriction in view of the frequency of Roman campaigning and the eagerness of the elite for prestige.[124] At the end of the Republic the triumphs of the dynasts became grandiose shows. Pompey held a two-day triumph after his eastern campaigns in 61, Julius Caesar five triumphs, four in one month, in 46 BC, Augustus a three-day triumph in 29 BC.[125] The last triumph held by a man not a member of the imperial house, Lucius Cornelius Balbus, was in 19 BC:[126] thereafter commanders who were not Caesars were granted the right to the dress worn on this occasion. Inevitably under the Principate an actual celebration became relatively uncommon.

Public celebration and entertainment combined in the games. The Roman games in September, dedicated to Jupiter, were said to have been introduced by the first Etruscan king, Tarquinius Priscus, in the sixth century BC.[127] By Augustus' time they lasted 15 days. Major festivals created in the Republic were those dedicated to the Great Mother and to Ceres in April, those of Flora at the end of April and the beginning of May and of Apollo in July, and the plebeian games in November, also dedicated to Jupiter. There were 57 days of games at the beginning of the first century BC, which were gradually increased by Sulla, Caesar, and the imperial house, until eventually they were to fill over a third of the year. Although some public money seems to have been deployed on certain necessities of the Republican games, since the third century at least they were occasions on which the magistrates charged with their peformance, originally the aediles and the urban praetor, spent their own money in order to enhance their popularity and future electoral prospects.[128] This did not cease with the Principate, but the expenditure of the regular magistrates was dwarfed by that of Augustus who gave games in his own name four times and 23 times in place of the regular magistrates.[129]

The greater part of the days of the games was devoted to theater and other forms of spectacle. Among the latter were competitive pipe-playing, boxing, and rope-dancing.[130] Theatrical performances were for most of the Republic on a small scale in temporary theaters with compara-tively few seats. Plautus imagines some of his spectators sitting, others on their feet.[131] It was only the construction of Pompey's theater and later that dedicated by Augustus to Marcellus and the theater of Balbus that permitted an audience comparable to one in a major Greek theater.[132] Athletics, similar to those in Greek games, were claimed to have formed part of the "Roman Games" from its inception: they were treated with respect by Augustus, though he was most interested in watching boxing.[133]

Gladiatorial shows, first held in 264 BC, were said to have adopted by the Romans from Etruscan practice, but more probably came from Campania and south Italy.[134] They were originally a tribute to someone recently dead and until Julius Caesar's dictatorship were usually only given as part of a funeral or a commemoration. In Rome they were still held on occasions in the Forum until Augustus' time (see above).[135] No permanent amphitheater was constructed at Rome until that of Augustus' friend, Statilius Taurus – probably on the southern side of the Circus Flaminius.[136] However, a number of Italian towns, for the most part in Campania, already possessed one in the Republican period: two of the best preserved are those at Pompeii and Puteoli.[137]

Gladiators were armed in various ways.[138] They also came from dif-ferent sources. Some were prisoners-of-war or condemned criminals, who would have been normally doomed anyhow; later under the Principate we find men being sentenced to enter a gladiatorial school as a lesser punishment than death or long-term labor in the mines. Other gladiators were slaves sold to a trainer. Finally, there were free men who committed themselves to gladiatorial service either under compulsion, usually economic, or out of sheer bravado and excitement. Nevertheless, gladiatorial service was degrading and a disqualification for public office.[139] In the time of Augustus and Tiberius the number of young men and even women of senatorial or equestrian rank who turned themselves into gladiators became a scandal and it was formally forbidden by decrees of the senate in 11 BC and 19 AD (a bronze copy of the latter decree was found at Larinum).[140] Successful gladiatorial fighting created celebrity and sexual attraction;[141] with good fortune it also led to honor-able discharge both for the free and the former slaves. We find already in the satires of Lucilius a gladiator, Pacideianus, who was the supreme professional in the second century BC.[142] Gladiatorial training, moreover, might become in effect a qualification. In the late Republic in particular, when engagements in the arena were less frequent than under the Caesars, many trained gladiators were also employed as bodyguards or as members of gangs.[143]

Figure 19   Alba Fucens: the amphitheater provided according to the provisions of the emperor Tiberius' will by Naevius Sutorius Macro, his prefect of the guard – now used for football practice.

It was an Etruscan king who was said to have inaugurated the Roman Games, and it is likely that their climax, chariot-racing, had also been introduced from Etruria: a circus is pictured in the Tomb of the Chariots at Tarquinia,[144] and chariot-racing is depicted on terracotta decorative plaques from the archaic period found at Velletri (Velitrae) in Latium.[145] The chariots were two-horse originally, later for the most part four-horse. Their drivers were normally professionals, originally no doubt financed by wealthy aristocrats, as was the rule in the Greek world, but by 214 BC apparently financed at least in part by the Roman people.[146] Gaius Antonius, Cicero's consular colleague, apparently drove a chariot in Sulla's victory games, as did other men of rank, but this seems to have been an exception and later even the appearance of Nero at the games on a chariot dressed as a charioteer was a scandal.[147] It may be that the origin of the four factions, named after colors, is to be found also in the middle Republic.[148] The Circus was used, furthermore, from the second century BC onwards to exhibit wild beasts and for hunts.[149] The hunters were professionals like gladiators, and in the Principate we find the animals being given names as if they too were a kind of gladiator.

The Circus Maximus, the location of these games, lay between the Palatine and the Aventine hills. Originally, it was little more than a leveled valley floor, just over 600 meters long, from which the water was drained into a sewer which debouched into the Tiber; the spectators watched the races from the slopes on either side. This space, however, was gradually monumentalized during the Republic. The starting gates are said to have been first constructed in 330 and rebuilt in 174 BC.[150] In this latter year there was also work on the central *spina*, the turning-posts, and "eggs" to mark the laps covered. We hear of further work by Julius Caesar [151] and Agrippa. By the time Dionysius of Halicarnassus, writing during Augustus' reign, described it,[152] it had acquired on three sides a ditch separating spectators from the track and stands with three levels (the lowest of stone, the upper two of wood): the stand at the opposite (eastern) end to the gates was curved. There was also an entrance building with shops from which stairs led to the stands. The starting gates were arched and opened by a rope controlled by a machine. The laps were counted by a system of eggs and dolphins installed by Agrippa.[153] We hear of a kind of imperial box (*pulvinar*) installed for Augustus, but he often watched from the houses of his friends and freed-men which would have overlooked the course from the Palatine.[154] Otherwise the seating was apparently open to all with, until Claudius' reign, no separate enclosures for men and women[155] – hence for an atten-tive reader of Ovid an opportunity for seduction (see chapter 5).

Such was the center of the Roman empire, a source of wonder to foreign visitors. The empire's strength lay elsewhere, in the Italian coun-tryside and, more importantly, in the provinces and on the frontiers. A survey of the whole Roman world is beyond the scope of the present volume. However, we cannot leave a society built on military success without considering how that success was being maintained by the emperor.

The Armed Services and the Frontiers

"The empire was bounded by the ocean or distant rivers; the legions, the provinces, the fleets were all linked with each other; there was the rule of law among citizens and discipline among allies." So Tacitus described how the admirers of Augustus summarized his achievement after his death.[1] The emperor himself had left his successor Tiberius a short guide (*breviarium*). It contained the public resources, how many citizens and allies were under arms, how many fleets, the allied kings, the provinces, direct or indirect taxes, and both regular expenditure and occasional largesse.[2] The empire with its defense forces and revenues, these texts suggest, was an organized system.

We have no evidence for any long-term or forward planning about the size or shape of the empire under the Republic. For a long time the Romans, although they enjoyed the profits of their victories, were happy if their subject allies obeyed orders when required, but remained cautious about assuming direct control of territory outside Italy with its resulting commitment in men and money.[3] During the second century BC this attitude changed: the Romans decided that their empire was there to be exploited and its profits could provide for not only military and administrative expenditure but positive benefits for themselves – notably, land distribution at home or abroad and subsidized grain at Rome itself. The consequent military requirements remained, however, a deterrent against the excessive expansion of direct rule. A change came in the last generation of the Roman Republic through the ambition of the great commanders – Lucullus, Pompey, and Caesar – and perhaps through the availability of a united Italy as a recruiting ground for the core of the army, the legions. Lucullus reached Armenia, Pompey the Caucasus and northern Arabia, Caesar the Rhine and Britain; both Caesar and Mark Antony planned to invade the Parthian empire. The notion of an empire without an end was created.[4]

Augustus did not overtly reject this ideology. He claimed to have "pushed forward the boundaries of all provinces bordered by peoples who did not obey our command (*imperium*)."[5] Many of the instances he then lists are dubious. In Gaul and Spain it was more a matter of suppressing dissension. His armies did reach the Elbe but at the time of his death had been effectively forced to return to the Rhine after the defeat of Quinctilius Varus in 9 AD. The expeditions into Ethiopia, i.e. the Sudan, and Arabia, did not lead to any permanent annexations. Control of Armenia, as he admits, had to be exercised indirectly through a compliant king.[6] As for the Parthians, no military force invaded Mesopotamia, but a diplomatic agreement was reached, through which Crassus' standards were recovered, and this was celebrated by a triumphal arch.[7] The most remarkable permanent expansion consisted in the conquest of the Alps and the Balkans, which moved the frontier of the empire to the Danube and even led to expeditions beyond it.[8]

How far military activity under Augustus was a matter of "grand strategy" or the traditional pursuit of wealth and glory is a subject of debate.[9] The advance to the Danube looks after the event the most rationally calculated, since it not only created a clear frontier, but greatly improved east–west communications by means of a road system beyond the Alps: it also allowed the subjugation of the Balkans southwards by means of the routes up the tributaries of the Danube.[10] However, in the absence of good geographical information it is not clear how soon this advantage was perceived by Augustus and his commanders. The best evidence for calculation about expansion comes from the geographer Strabo, who was a friend of the imperial family. After describing how the chieftains of Britain had voluntarily become friends of Augustus he points out that, coupled with their readiness to pay import and export duties in Gallic harbors, this obviated any need to garrison the island. It would have required at a minimum a legion and some cavalry if tribute were to be demanded, and the expenditure on the army would have counterbalanced any financial returns.[11] This implies that Romans by the end of Augustus' reign at least were employing what we call cost-benefit analysis. Such analysis would have been also an argument against any attempt to reconquer systematically the territory between the Rhine and the Elbe after the defeat of Varus.

The Roman army under the Republic was originally composed of conscripted Roman citizens. Fit adult males were expected to serve, depending on their status, either six annual campaigns in the infantry or ten in the cavalry.[12] After this they could serve for further campaigns voluntarily but could only be compulsorily conscripted in an emergency (*tumultus*), when there was a threat to Rome and the homeland. Those below a minimum property qualification (*proletarii*) were only permitted to serve in the legions in an emergency, but regularly served in the navy.[13] Marius was famous for recruiting volunteers for the legions in 107 BC, not only the financially unqualified but time-served and experienced soldiers.[14] It would have been the regular re-enlistment of the latter which contributed most to the army becoming professional in the late Republic. Nevertheless, the armies which resisted the Germanic tribes, fought the Allies, and sustained the civil wars were largely created from levies, indeed from emergency levies. Even after this, conscription remained the foundation of the legions throughout the late Republic and persisted in the early Principate.[15]

Augustus made massive demobilizations of the forces which fought the civil wars in 30 BC and of those which campaigned in the early Principate in 14 BC, leaving himself a citizen army of originally 28 legions, of which three were to be lost with Varus in 9 AD.[16] He is said to have introduced standard long terms of service for soldiers in 13 BC – 16 years for legionaries, 12 for the praetorian guard – and it is generally assumed that this implied the recruitment of volunteers.[17] However, levies were still required in the Pannonian and German crises of 6 and 9 AD,[18] and in 6 AD freedmen were used as reinforcements for the armies fighting the Pannonians, including slaves exacted from their owners and liberated.[19] Shortage of volunteers remained a problem under Tiberius.[20]

In the long term this was to be solved through recruitment from Roman citizens in the provinces, notably those settled in citizen colonies. Under the Principate legionary soldiers are identified frequently on their tombstones, and occasionally on surviving military documents, by their town of origin.[21] The statistics assembled by G. R. Forni show that under Augustus, Tiberius, and Caligula those recruited from Italy outnumbered those from the provinces in the proportion of three to two; the balance had already swung in favor of the provinces under Claudius and Nero, while in the Flavio-Trajanic period (over 100 years into the Principate) the proportion was over three to one in favor of the provinces.[22] Even under Augustus the bulk of the Italians came from Cisalpine Gaul, the regions north of the rivers Arno and Rubicon, which was not completely incorporated into the Roman citizen body until Caesar became master of Rome; the same regions were later the only Italian source of legionaries. Essentially, peninsular Italy became the recruiting ground for the praetorians and the urban cohorts alone.

Rome's military success under the Republic would have been impossible without the assistance of allies, originally those in Italy (which doubled or trebled its forces), later a variety of contingents from abroad, especially cavalry and light-armed troops. The unification of Italy meant that many allied forces now became Roman, but the contribution from abroad seems to have become greater with the wider recruiting ground for the so-called auxiliary troops (*auxilia*). Under the Republic it had been usually a matter of a king or a community, whether a city or people, sending soldiers to the Romans. Under the Principate the Romans themselves seem to have recruited their auxiliaries into established units. Like the historian Dio Cassius,[23] we have no means of estimating their number under Augustus, but globally it is likely to have matched the number of legionaries.

Rome is said to have first paid her soldiers during the wars against Veii in about 400 BC.[24] In Polybius' time an ordinary legionary was paid a *denarius* every three days; when the silver coin was retariffed, this became roughly five bronze *asses* a day. Caesar doubled this in the Gallic wars, and ten *asses* was still the ordinary soldier's pay at the end of Augustus' reign.[25] The money would have been little more than a contribution to subsistence until Caesar's time. Even under Caesar and Augustus the basic pay, which was diminished by deductions,[26] would not have been tempting. However, promotion multiplied salaries, and victories brought the prospect of booty, an important factor under the Republic. Above all, eventual demobilization led to more substantial rewards from the time of Marius onward, both in bounties and land. The civil wars led to temporary promises to soldiers in order to obtain their support, which were vast by comparison with ordinary pay, such as Caesar Octavianus' offer of 500 *denarii* a man in 44 BC.[27] However, such large inducements to sign on could not be maintained for long. As for the prospects for the demobilized, Augustus ceased to distribute land himself after 14 BC, but paid bounties amounting to 400 million sesterces instead, expecting soldiers to return to their home towns.[28] In 6 AD he created a military treasury (*aerarium militare*) to pay these benefits, making an initial contribution from his patrimony of 170 million sesterces. The treasury was to be fed in the future by a 5 percent tax on legacies and gifts and a 1 percent (later 0.5 percent) tax on sales.[29] The sums set were 20,000 sesterces for a praetorian and 12,000 for a legionary, deliberately high to encourage recruiting.[30]

The last paragraph encapsulates a fundamental problem for the Augustan Principate, how to raise adequate funds to pay the forces which protected the empire in circumstances where further conquest would rarely yield dividends: the richest prizes lay east beyond the Euphrates, but Augustus could see no chance of success there. In the later Republic the regular income of the treasury was chiefly derived from their subject allies overseas. Citizens had been liable to direct taxation (*tributum*) until

167 BC, their Latin and Italian allies until the War of the Allies.[31] There were also indirect revenues in Italy: transit dues (*portoria*), temporarily abolished in 60 BC; rents on public land, which were greatly reduced as the land was rendered private property by distribution; and a 5 percent tax on the proceeds of manumission.[32] There was no attempt to reimpose direct taxation under the Principate but, as we have seen earlier, new indirect taxes designed to fill the gap between income and expenditure. So, when Cappadocia was made a province in 17 AD, the 1 percent sales tax was reduced to 0.5 percent.[33]

A new factor was the contribution of the patrimony of the imperial house to public finance. Augustus claimed that the total of the money that he gave to either the treasury, or the Romans plebs, or demobilized soldiers was 2,400 million sesterces. This was apart from money spent on buildings, aqueducts, and roads, and the incalculable sums spent on entertainments and support for cities struck by natural disaster or indigent individuals among his friends and senators.[34] Tacitus remarks with light irony that in Augustus' will his legacies were not outside the range of those made by ordinary citizens, except that he left 43,500,000 sesterces to the Romans plebs, 1,000 sesterces to each praetorian, and 500 sesterces to each member of the three urban cohorts – that is 10,500,000 sesterces more – and 300 sesterces to each Roman citizen in a legion or cohort, about a further 40 million sesterces.[35] Augustus' wealth has been estimated at over 1,000 million sesterces. Its sources cannot be known exactly. Victory in the civil wars brought him not only cash but estates in Italy and abroad. The property of those with no legitimate heirs and some condemned men fell to the emperor also.[36] In addition, Augustus received large sums from the legacies of his friends – allegedly 1,400 million in the last 20 years before he wrote his will in 13 AD. However, he claimed to be leaving only a clear 150 million to his heirs. This is perhaps the cash figure and takes no account of his estates.[37]

These enormous sums may give the impression that the emperor financed Rome. However, even if the public treasury (*aerarium*) did not accumulate capital to the same extent as the emperor's patrimony and thus have large sums available for emergencies, its budget was on a different scale. The actual sums involved can only be a matter of very rough estimate. Pompey claimed in 61 BC, for example, that his eastern campaigns brought an extra 340 million sesterces into the treasury in taxation beyond the existing 200 million; four years earlier Cicero argued that the income of the Egyptian king was 300 million sesterces.[38] The historian Velleius claimed that the income derived by Julius Caesar from Gaul almost matched that from the rest of the world, while the sum contributed to the public treasury by Egypt after Augustus' conquest almost matched that of Gaul.[39] These totals, designed to impress or persuade, are not accountant's figures, nor can we tell how far the taxation systems of the Republic survived intact under Augustus or whether all the royal income from Egypt did go in fact into the Roman public treasury. However, this evidence does suggest that in Augustus' time Rome may have derived as much as 1,000 million sesterces a year from provincial taxation and spent a similar amount.[40]

By far the greatest element in public expenditure would have been the army, including the auxiliaries, and the navy. It is clear from the reaction to the mutinies at the beginning of Tiberius' reign in 14 AD that a general increase in soldiers' pay could not be countenanced; even Germanicus' concession, that the term for demobilization originally laid down by Augustus should be respected, was accepted at Rome only to be revoked the next year because of the cost of bounties.[41] It might be thought that the Romans could have easily raised provincial taxes to meet their needs. However, the system of taxation was a longstanding one, often inherited from previous rulers: increasing rates might lead to unrest.[42] Moreover, even under the Principate indirect taxes were farmed out in five-year contracts, which precluded rapid changes in terms.[43]

In 22 AD the senate debated luxury at Rome and the sumptuary laws which, according to the aediles, had fallen into contempt. Tacitus gives a version of the emperor Tiberius' speech, in which he declined to intervene, because he would make enemies over nothing.

> How small the matter is, of which the aediles remind us, how negligible, if you have due regard for the wider picture! But by heaven no one raises the topic of the dependence of Italy on foreign aid, the fact that the means of life of the Roman people is daily tossed by stormy seas. And if the resources of the provinces do not support us landowners with our slaves and properties, our garden villas and country estates are going, I suppose, to keep us secure.[44]

Tacitus' Tiberius may have underestimated the economic self-sufficiency of the Italian countryside, but there is no doubt that the city itself was heavily dependent on imported grain. Moreover, the social and political elite, who were the economic *raison d'être* of the city, were themselves subsidized by the rents and taxes from abroad, which arrived in the public treasury or swelled the patrimonies of the emperor and other wealthy Romans. It was an economic model that in fact worked, so long as it was not subject to excessive strains and so long as the Roman right to rule remained unquestioned. This in turn was heavily dependent on Roman military superiority.

I have sought elsewhere to analyse the coherence of the Roman empire and question the view that it became a universal society.[45] The ultimate justification of the empire for the Romans of the Augustan period was that it existed: that was what heaven had decreed. However, the basis of its existence was at least as much in the barrack-blocks of forts and camps as in the streets of Rome. It was this tension between the city and the Italian countryside on the one hand and the frontiers on the other, which was to threaten from time to time the stability of Roman society and eventually to subvert it.

Notes

1 INTRODUCTION

1 Dio Cassius 54.9.9–10; Strabo 15.1.73 (719–20).
2 *RG* 31.1; Pliny, *Natural History* 6.100–6; Dihle 1978.
3 Momigliano 1975.
4 EJ² 261, 360a–b = Braund 494, 735a–b; Pliny, *Natural History* 6.103, cf. 84 for Annius Plocamus the tax-collector of the trade.
5 See ch. 7 below and Wilkes 1996.
6 Welles 1934, no. 75.
7 Pliny, *Natural History* 6.82; Casson 1971.
8 *ILLRP* 460a; *L'Année Épigraphique* 1973, no. 492.
9 Strabo 4.6.11 (208).
10 EJ² 290, 294 = Braund 801, 805.
11 Matthew 5.41.
12 Mitchell 1976; Braund 552; Levick 1985, no. 91.
13 EJ² 301 = *RGE* 86.
14 Millar 1993.
15 Cicero, *To his Friends* 15.4.3; *To Atticus* 5.18.2.
16 Memnon, *Fragmente der Griechischen Historiker* (ed. Jacoby) III B 424, F22.
17 Cicero, *To Atticus* 5.13.1.
18 Dörner and Gruben 1953; Herrman 1960: 71–2, 105ff.
19 Bowersock 1965: 95–6.
20 Strabo 5.3.8 (236).

2 THE GROWTH OF AN EMPIRE

1 For comprehensive general surveys of early Rome see *CAH* VII.2²: 1–112; Cornell 1995: 1–214.
2 Angelelli and Falzone 1999.
3 Claridge 1998: 128–34.
4 Smith 1996; Cristofani 1990.
5 Terrenato 2001, with references to possible parallels.

6   Cristofani 1990: 18–25. Greek is found as early as *c.* 800 BC.
7   Cristofani 1990: 182–91; *ILLRP* 1271, 1271a.
8   Peter 1914: 1–66; Wiseman 1979: 9–53 and 2004.
9   Gruen 1993: 6–51.
10   Livy 8.40.4–5; Cicero, *Brutus* 62.
11   Lintott 1999a: 30–1.
12   Ibid.: 31–9.
13   Crawford 1996a, II, no. 40.
14   Lintott 1999b: 6–10.
15   Cornell 1989a, 1989b, and 1995: 369–98; *Roma medio-repubblicana* (1973).
16   Lintott 1993: 7, 195 n. 3.
17   Franke 1989; Scullard 1989a and 1989b; Lazenby 1978; Lancel 1995 and 1998.
18   Lancel 1995: 131–3.
19   *ILLRP* I, 319.
20   Polybius 1.63.4–9.
21   Crawford 1985: 1–51.
22   Errington 1989a; Derow 1991.
23   Polybius 3.9.6–12.6, 15.12–13.
24   Polybius 6.1.1–3.
25   Crawford 1985: 52–61.
26   Errington 1989b; Derow 1989; Gruen 1984 II.
27   Polybius 1.4.1, 8.2.3–4.
28   The case restated in Coarelli 2005.
29   Preisigke and Bilabel 1926 III, no. 7169.
30   Harris 1989.
31   *Misurare la terra* 1983: 99.
32   Lancel 1995: 404–27.
33   Lintott 1992: 53–5, 1994: 27–8.
34   E.g. Sallust, *Catiline*.10.1; *Histories*.1.11.

3 THE CRISIS OF THE LATE REPUBLIC

1   For overviews of the problems and historians' approaches to them see Brunt 1988: 1–92 and Lintott 1994a, 1994b, and 1994c.
2   Lintott 1972: 632–4. The general principle of an external threat producing political discipline is found in Cato's speech for the Rhodians (*ORF* no. 8, fragments. 163–4) of 167 BC.
3   1 Maccabees 8.2–3.
4   Polybius10.15, cf.18.3.4; Lintott 1972: 635–7.
5   Polybius 36.9.5–8.
6   Lintott 1972: 629–32.
7   Lintott 1992: 22, 198; Derow 1979; Richardson 2008.
8   Lintott 1990.

9   Lintott 1999b.
10   Earl 1967: 12–43.
11   Lintott 1999b: 121–8.
12   Polybius 6.57.5–9.
13   Brunt 1971: 269ff; 1988: 240–75; Lintott 1994b: 16–19; 1994c: 53–8.
14   Polybius 6.14.2.
15   Appian, *Civil Wars* 1.7.26–8.34; Lintott 1992: 34–52.
16   Gabba 1989; Brunt 1988: 93–143.
17   Purcell 1994.
18   See for the new identification of the building Cozza and Tucci 2006 with criticisms of the earlier re-identification by Tuck 2000.
19   See *L'Année Épigraphique* 1991, no. 138 = Friggeri 2001: 49 for a mid-first century BC funerary *cippus* for three freedmen, two of whom have Semitic *cognomina*. The significance of the Jewish community in Rome in 59 BC is shown by Cicero, *For Flaccus* 66–9.
20   Garnsey and Rathbone 1985.
21   Lintott 1994c: 40–89 with further bibliography.
22   Lintott 1994b: 36–9; 1994c: 90–103.
23   Gabba 1994; Brunt 1988: 93–143.
24   Hind 1994; Seager 1994a: 165–80.
25   Seager 1994a: 181–207.
26   Seager 1994b; Sherwin-White 1984: 149–223; 1994; Lintott 2008: 81–100.
27   Sherwin-White 1984: 159–223; 1994; Wiseman 1994a; 1994b; Seager 2002; Lintott 2008: 129–280.
28   Gelzer 1968: 195–333; Rawson 1994a; 1994b; Lintott 2008: 281–424; Pelling 1996; Syme 1939: 97–300; Osgood 2006.
29   *RG* 1.1, the language recalling his father's official justification for the outbreak of civil war in 49 (Caesar, *Civil War* 1.22.5).
30   *RRC* no. 508.
31   *RRC* no. 524.
32   EJ² 22 15.
33   *RG* 25.2.

4 THE EMPEROR AND HIS PEOPLE

1   Rich and Williams 1999.
2   Zanker 1988: 92-6 for this and the coin representations.
3   Eck 2007.
4   Crook 1996a and 1996b.
5   Strabo 10.5.3; Agathias 2.17; *RGE* 96.
6   Dio Cassius 51.20. 6–9; EJ² 122 = Braund 149; *SEG* 26.1243.
7   *POxy* 1453; Rea 1982.
8   Rowe 2002.
9   Polybius 6.53–4; Lintott 1999a: 169.

10   Crook 1967: 98ff; Andreau 1999.
11   Dio Cassius 53.28–31.
12   Suetonius, *Augustus* 100; Zanker 1988: 73–7; Claridge 1998: 181–4.
13   Suetonius, *Augustus* 28.
14   Crook 1996a with further references.
15   Wiedemann 1996: 198–202.
16   On "friends" see Gelzer 1969: 101–10. On Caesar's cabinet of friends see Lintott 2008: 319–23.
17   Dio Cassius 53.23.5–7; EJ[2] 21= Braund 425.
18   Dio Cassius 53.21.4–5.
19   Tacitus, *Annals* 1.6.
20   *POxy* 2435 verso; EJ[2] 379 = Braund 556.
21   Suetonius, *Augustus* 29, 72; Crawford 1996a I, no. 37 *Tab.Heb* = EJ[2] 94a,1; Claridge 1998: 128ff; Zanker 1988: 51ff.
22   *To Atticus*.13.52.
23   Dio Cassius 54.21.3–8. Others are in Suetonius, *Augustus* 67, 101; EJ[2] 147, 157 = Braund 300, 316.
24   EJ[2] 158 = Braund 317.
25   *POxy* 44.3208; Brown 1970.
26   Suetonius, *Augustus* 101.
27   Tacitus, *Annals* 4.5.
28   Dio Cassius 56.23.4; Suetonius, *Augustus* 49; Tacitus, *Annals* 1.24; Speidel 1994.
29   See e.g. *ILS* 1717–30, 2081.
30   Beloch 1886: 507, accepted by Hopkins 1980: 118–19.
31   Nicolet 1980: ch. 2.
32   Crawford 1996a I, nos. 37-8; *Tab. Heb.* 6ff.; EJ[2] 94a–b.
33   Dionysius of Halicarnassus, *Antiquities* 4.15; Crawford 1996a I, no. 24, 142ff.
34   Illustrated in Bianchi Bandinelli 1970: 52-6; Nicolet 1980.
35   Varro, *Latin Language* 6.86; Cicero, *To Atticus* 1.18.8.
36   Crawford 1996a I, no. 24, 142ff.
37   Suetonius, *Augustus* 37; Tacitus, *Annals* 2.30; EJ[2] 209 = Braund 375.
38   See the waxed tablets from Egypt, *FIRA* III, no. 2 (= Braund 697), cf. no. 3; Crook 1967: 46–8.
39   *FIRA* III, no. 4; *THerc* no. 5.
40   *RG* 8.2–4. An apparently discrepant figure in the Fasti of Ostia for 14 AD (EJ[2]: 40) should be explained as the result of a small error in engraving (Nicolet 2000: 189ff.).
41   Beloch 1886: 370f.; Brunt 1971: 1–25; Nicolet 2000: 189ff.; Scheidel 2004: 5–9; *contra* Lo Cascio 1994.
42   Suetonius, *Augustus* 41.
43   Brunt 1971: 376ff. – with a low estimate of slaves.
44   Suetonius, *Augustus* 35; cf. Appian, *Civil Wars* 1.35 and 100.
45   Cf. Dio Cassius 53.28.3–4.

46 Dio Cassius 54.17.3. On the figures of 800,000 and 1,200,000 in Suetonius, *Augustus* 41, see Nicolet 2000: 178ff. and 1984: 90ff.
47 Suetonius, *Augustus* 38; Dio Cassius 59.9.5.
48 Ovid, *Amores* 3.15.5–6; *Tristia* 4.10.5ff.
49 *Tristia* 2.89f.
50 *Tristia* 2.93ff.; 4.10.27ff.
51 Nicolet 1966–74 I; Wiseman 1970.
52 Polybius 2.24.
53 Sallust, *Jugurtha* 95.1.
54 Caesar, *Gallic War* 7.65.5.
55 Nicolet 2000: 163–87.
56 See n. 48 above; Nepos, *Atticus* 1.1; Horace, *Epistles* 1.1.57.
57 *Satires* 1.6.24–5, 45–8, and see below.
58 Dio Cassius 54.23.1–6; *ILS* 109; Tacitus, *Annals* 1.10; Syme 1979 II, 518ff.
59 EJ² 358 = Braund 709.
60 Pliny, *Natural History* 33.32–3.
61 Brunt 1988: 144ff.
62 Nepos, *Atticus* 6.3–4.
63 Varro, *Rural Matters* 2.2.1ff.
64 Cicero, *On the Manilian Law* 17–18.
65 Lintott 2008: 219–21, 431–2.
66 Nicolet 2000: 26ff.
67 Cf. Cicero, *To his Friends* 1.9.24.
68 See the prosopography in Nicolet 1966–74 II.
69 Nepos, *Atticus* 12.4; Cicero, *To his Friends* 13.6.2–3.
70 *To his Friends* 12.29; Lintott 2008: 177; *To Quintus* 2.12.2.
71 D'Arms 1981: 27–8; Cicero, *For Rabirius Postumus*, esp. 22, 40; cf. *ILS* 4404 for a funerary monument outside Rome of a putative freedman of Rabirius', associated with a priestess of Isis.
72 Cicero, *To his Friends* 13.56. See also Bispham 2000 on N. Cluvius.
73 Vitruvius 7.11.1; D'Arms 1981: 49–55.
74 Cicero, *To his Friends* 13.75, 79; 7.23; D'Arms 1981: 28. For a family even more deeply involved in the production of sculpture and architecture, the Cossutii, see Rawson 1991: 189ff.
75 *Amores* 3.15.6.
76 EJ² 270 = Braund 503; cf. Nicolet 1966–74 II, no. 233. See on upward mobility in general Osgood 2006: 251–97.
77 Coarelli 1980: 226–7.
78 Meiggs 1973: 39–40, 475–8.
79 EJ², 242–3, 245, 247 = Braund 475–6, 480.
80 Tacitus, *Annals* 1.24; Dio Cassius 57.19.6; EJ² 220.
81 EJ² 370 = Braund 458.
82 Horace, *Odes* 1.29; *Epistles* 1.12.
83 Purcell 1983.

84 Crawford 1996a I, no. 14.
85 Mommsen 1887–8 I: 332ff.; Jones 1960: 154–8.
86 Suetonius, *Life of Horace* 1; cf. Purcell 1983: 138ff.
87 Friggeri 2001: cover photo and p. 51 = *CIL* VI, 1820. See n. 106 below for a group of four freedmen, two of whom are *viatores* and two record-keepers, one for the quaestors, the other for the tribunes.
88 *L'Année Épigraphique* 1973, no. 283; Horsfall 1976.
89 Horace, *Epistles* 1.8.1–2.
90 Taylor 1961: 118; Mouritsen 2005: 38–63, with further bibliography.
91 A similar high proportion of freedmen is found among magistrates' attendants other than scribes; see Purcell 1983: 146ff.
92 For the texts see Camodeca 1999 and the articles cited in Rowe 2001.
93 *CIL* I², 1259 = *ILLRP* 80; 3018a = Friggeri 2001: 60.
94 Taylor 1961: 130–1; Calza 1940: 44 with figs. 9 and 10; Graham 2006: 88ff.; Carroll 2006: 69ff.
95 Juvenal, *Satires* 3.21ff.
96 Horace, *Epistles* 1.7.46–95.
97 Horace, *Epistles* 1.13.15.
98 *On Electioneering* 29, 34–7; cf. Cicero, *For Murena* 71.
99 Taylor 1960: 132ff.
100 Watson 1967: 185ff.
101 Ibid.: 197.
102 Pliny, *Natural History* 33.32, and see above, p. 87.
103 Suetonius, *Augustus* 40.
104 Gaius, *Institutes* 1.18–47; Buckland 1908: 533ff; Gardner 1986: 138ff., 223ff.
105 *CIL* X, 4811 = Chioffi 2005: no. 264.
106 *CIL* VI, 1815 = EJ² 151 = Braund 304.
107 Lintott 2002: 560ff.
108 See Lintott 2002: 557 for the activities of Hesuchus, the slave of an imperial freedman, in the grain trade.
109 *Digest* 14.3.5.1, citing Ser. Sulpicius Rufus; Aubert 1994: 52–7, 76.
110 *ILLRP* 799.
111 Cicero, *To Atticus* 4.18.4.
112 *CIL* I², 3005 = Friggeri 2001: 61.
113 *ILLRP* 101ff.
114 EJ² 360a–b, 363 = Braund 735a–b, 825.
115 Cicero, *To his Friends* 13.45 – probably during the civil war in the early forties BC.
116 Cicero, *To his Friends* 6.1.6; 9.15.1.
117 *To Quintus* 1.2.1–2; *To Atticus* 2.18.4, 19.1.
118 Lintott 2002: 558–9.
119 Suetonius, *Augustus* 67.
120 Hinard and Dumont 2003: 18, lines 8ff.
121 Buckland 1908: 36–8.

122   Gaius 1.145ff.; Watson 1967: 146ff.
123   Gaius 1.145.
124   *Digest* 16.1.2.
125   Cicero, *For Caecina passim.*
126   Tacitus, *Annals* 13.21; *TPSulp* 46, 79; D'Arms 1981: 76, 78.
127   *CIL* I², 3011a = Friggeri 2001: 52.
128   *ILLRP* 805a; Friggeri 2001: 63.
129   Livy 39.9ff; Gellius 4.14.1–6.
130   Cicero, *To Atticus* 4.15.6; Horace, *Satires* 1.10.77.
131   *ILLRP* 803 = Wiseman 1985: 30–5.
132   Sallust, *Catiline* 25.
133   *ILLRP* 973.
134   Suetonius, *Augustus* 73.
135   *ILS* 8393; EJ² 357 = Braund 720; Friggeri 2001: 64.
136   Valerius Maximus 8.3.3; Appian, *Civil Wars.* 4.32.136–33.144.
137   Cicero, *To Atticus*, 15.11.1–2; *To Brutus* 26.1–2.
138   Suetonius, *Gaius* 23.2; Seneca, *Clemency* 1.9; Dio Cassius 55.14–21.
139   Cicero, *To Atticus*, 5.1.3–4.
140   Tacitus, *Annals* 3.33–4.
141   *Annals* 3.55.
142   *RG* 15–18; Suetonius, *Augustus* 41–2.
143   Suetonius, *Augustus* 40; EJ² 92 = Braund 111.
144   Asconius 7, 45, 75C; Dionysius of Halicarnassus, *Antiquities* 4.14–15;
       Lintott 1999a: 177–8; 1999b: 78–82, with the bibliographies cited there;
       Wallace-Hadrill 2008: 264–90.
145   Suetonius, *Augustus* 30, 57; EJ², Fasti 7 BC, and nos. 41, 139–40 = Braund
       773, 170–1; *ILS* 99, 3611–12, 9250.
146   *FIRA* I, no. 46; III, nos. 32–3, 35–8.
147   Bispham 2007.
148   Syme 1979 I, 88–119; Wiseman 1971: 221, 228, 232, 262–3.
149   EJ² 196, 198, 205, 211 = Braund 359, 361, 370, 382; Wiseman 1971:
       253–5, 270.
150   Catullus 39.10–13.
151   Crawford 1996b; Wallace-Hadrill 2008: 95–6.
152   Torelli 1975: fragment 1, photo also in Pallottino 1974 (pl. 15).
153   *Inscr.Ital.* xiii, 2, nos.5ff.
154   Suetonius, *Grammarians* 17; Fasti illustrated in Calabi Limentani 1968:
       400ff.; Wallace-Hadrill 2008; 239–48.
155   Horace, *Odes* 3.5.9.
156   *ILLRP* 515, p. 34, line 6, i.e. line 3 of third column of lower inscription;
       CIL I², 3107.
157   Lintott 1993: 163–4.
158   Syme 1958: 455–6.
159   Tacitus, *Agricola* 4.1; EJ² 371.
160   Cicero, *For Flaccus* 66.

161   *L'Année Épigraphique* 1991, no. 238 = Friggeri 2001: 49.

162   Philo, *Embassy to Gaius* 568–9; Horace, *Satires* 1.4.143.

163   *ILLRP* 951; *L'Année Épigraphique* 1973, no. 283.

164   *Satires* 3.60–80.

165   Dio Cassius 54.6.6; cf. 40.47.3–4, 42.26.2; 53.2.4.

166   Suetonius, *Augustus* 42.

167   Tacitus, *Annals* 2.85, 87; Josephus, *Antiquities* 18.65–84, explaining this as a reaction to corruption among the priests of Isis and embezzlement among the Jews.

168   Tacitus, *Annals* 15.44.

169   Sallust, *Catiline* 31.7, cf. Cicero, *For Sulla* 23; Tacitus, *Annals* 4.3.

170   Statius, *Silvae* 4.5.45–8.

5 TOWN AND COUNTRY

1   Horace, *Epistles* 1.7.46ff.; *Satires* 1.9; Cicero, *On the Orator* 2.283; Polybius 6.53.1.

2   Vitruvius 5.1.1; Coarelli 1980: 78–9; 1985: 222ff. Welch (2007: 38–42) has argued that the passages were for beasts rather than gladiators.

3   Claridge 1998: 215ff.

4   *LTUR* I, 183, following Purcell, 1989: 161.

5   Crawford 1996a II, no. 40, Table VI, 6–7 = 8–9, VII. 6–7, regarding common walls and the width of streets – at least 8 feet wide and 16 feet on bends. Tacitus, *Annals* 15.43; Livy 5.55.3–5. See also Robinson 1992: 33ff.

6   Cicero, *On the Agrarian Law* 2.95; Suetonius, *Augustus* 30; Vitruvius 2.8.18–20.

7   Claridge 1998: 111–12, 135.

8   Suetonius, *Augustus* 100; Pliny, *Natural History* 36.72–3; Claridge 1998: 181–4, 190–1; Heslin 2007: 1–20 with earlier bibliography. Heslin has shown that the interpretation of the monument as a sundial goes far beyond the evidence: it merely showed the time of year through the length of the midday shadow.

9   *RG* 12.2; Claridge 1998: 184–9.

10   Horace, *Satires* 1.8; Carroll 2006: 69ff.; Graham 2006: 68ff.

11   *To his Friends* 5.6.2; cf. *To Atticus* 1.13.6 (on one emendation); Pliny, *Natural History* 36.103.

12   Cicero, *Academica* 2.70; Festus 120L; Coarelli 1985: 140ff.; *LTUR* I, 309–14. The view of the *comitium* is updated in Morstein-Marx 2004: 42–51.

13   Vitruvius 5.1.1–10.

14   Livy 44.16.10–11.

15   Coarelli 1985: 237–57.

16   Ibid.: 258ff.

17   Zanker 1984.

18   *THerc*.13–15, 89.
19   *RG* 20.2; Suetonius, *Augustus* 30; Dio Cassius 49.42–3.
20   Cicero, *For Roscius of Ameria* 18; *For Caelius* 61.
21   On the origins of Roman baths and bathing see Fagan 2001: 403–26 with earlier bibliography; Wallace-Hadrill 2008: 169ff.
22   Dio Cassius 53.27.1; 54.29.4; Rodriguez Almeida 1981: pl. 31; *LTUR* V, 40–2.
23   Tacitus, *Annals* 15.43; Carettoni, et al. 1960; Rodriguez Almeida 1981; Wallace-Hadrill 2008: 301–12.
24   *Aeneid* 1.148–53.
25   Suetonius, *Augustus* 42; cf. 84 for his use of a herald.
26   Suetonius, *Augustus* 35; Dio Cassius 55.3.1–4. Cf. Horace, *Satires* 2.6.19.
27   *FIRA* I, no. 40, nos.I and IV; cf. EJ² 30 = Braund 768.
28   Gai.*Inst*.1.2.4, cf. e.g. the *Senatus Consultum Calvisianum* (EJ² 311, no. V = Braund 543E).
29   Lintott 1999a: 94ff.
30   *Ex Ponto (From the Black Sea)* 4.9.3–56.
31   Dio Cassius 53.2.1, 32.2; Suetonius, *Augustus* 36; EJ² 207 = Braund 373.
32   Dio Cassius 54.2.4.
33   Suetonius, *Augustus* 37.
34   EJ² 278A, 295–6 = Braund 789A, 806.
35   Dio Cassius 54.1.4; Tacitus, *Annals* 1.7; EJ² 212, 215, 278A = Braund 383, 386, 789A.
36   Dio Cassius 55.8.6–7, 26.4; Suetonius, *Vespasian* 5.3.
37   Tacitus, *Annals* 1.77; 6.47; 16.26; *Histories* 4.9.
38   Dio Cassius 55.8.7.
39   Dio Cassius 54.26.7.
40   Suetonius, *Titus* 6; Dio Cassius 66.10; *Digest* 1.13.1.2 & 4; Mommsen 1887–8 II, 569–70.
41   Tacitus *Annals* 4.27; Suetonius, *Claudius* 24.
42   Dio Cassius 54.26.6–7.
43   *Tristia* 2.93ff.; 4.10.27ff.
44   Dio Cassius 55.8.6–7; Suetonius, *Augustus* 30; EJ² 41,139–40 = Braund 773, 170–1.
45   *ILS* 6073.
46   *Annals* 1.9.
47   Lintott in D. Johnston (ed.) *Cambridge Companion to Roman Law*, ch.15, forthcoming.
48   Lintott 1999a: 148; 2004: 62–3.
49   Lintott 2001–3; Rutledge 2001.
50   Tacitus, *Annals* 4.22.
51   Horace, *Satires* 2.6.34–5; *Epistles* 1.19.8.
52   Coarelli 1985: 24–6, 166ff, preferring the former.

53 Vitruvius 6.5.2.
54 Gaius, *Institutes* 4.11ff. For civil procedure in the later Republic and Augustan period see Crook 1967: 73ff.
55 Lintott 2008: chs. 4 and 5.
56 Lintott 2002.
57 *Digest* 17.2.59 preface.
58 Crook 1967: 118ff. For a sociological treatment see Champlin 1991.
59 Suetonius, *Julius* 26.3; Crawford 1985: 143ff.
60 *RRC* II, 633ff.
61 Crawford 1978: 187–8.
62 Mark 12.15–17.
63 Crawford 1985: 152ff.
64 Burnett 1992 I, nos. 688ff.; Gölitzer 2004.
65 Cicero, *To Atticus* 5.13.2, 15.2; *For Rabirius Postumus* 40; Lintott 1993: 48–9. In addition, major financial transactions among the Roman elite were book transfers of credit and debt, as Harris (2006) has recently stressed in a discussion of what constituted "money" at Rome.
66 Vitruvius 5.1.2.
67 Livy 41.27.12; Cicero, *Philippics* 6.15; Horace, *Satires* 2.3.18-19; *Epistles* 1.1.52ff.; Coarelli 1985: 181ff.
68 Horace, *Epistles* 1.20.1.
69 Coarelli 1985: 146ff.; Claridge 1998: 154–5.
70 Horace, *Satires* 2.3.229.
71 *ILS* 5592; Haselberger 2002: 163.
72 Horace, *Satires* 2.3.18-19.
73 Lintott 1993, 76–7, 86–91; Nicolet 2000: 297ff.
74 For the customs law of Asia, see Cottier et al. 2008.
75 Crawford 1996a I, no. 24, lines 56–67; Juvenal 3.232–8.
76 Suetonius, *Vespasian* 18.
77 Cicero, *To Quintus* 2.9.2; Catullus 10.15ff.; Juvenal 3.239–42, 4.75.
78 Laurence 1994: 55–66.
79 Suetonius, *Augustus* 57, cf. *ILS* 7547; Varro, *Latin Language* 6.14. Another shoe-maker, however, worked by the *Porta Fontinalis* on the saddle between the Capitoline and Quirinal hills (*ILS* 7544).
80 Cicero, *Against Catiline* 1.8; *For Sulla* 52.
81 *ILLRP* 110; *ILS* 7685, 7692–3; *CIL* I²: 3005; Friggeri 2001: 61, 141. On the funerary commemoration of trades see Carroll 2006: 248–9.
82 *ILS* 7602, 7708; *CIL* VI: 9435; *ILS* 7610; *CIL* VI: 9795.
83 *L'Année Épigraphique* 1923: 59 = Friggeri 2001: 85; *CIL* VI: 7597.
84 *ILS* 7485, 7487. An allusion perhaps in Horace, *Satires* 2.3.229.
85 *Digest* 9.2.52.2, my translation adapted from Frier 1989: 76–8.
86 *Ars Amatoria* 1.67–162.
87 Pliny, *Natural History* 3.17; Nicolet 1990: esp. 95ff.
88 Suetonius, *Augustus* 43 and see ch. 1.
89 Barker and Rasmussen 1998: 151ff.

90   See Gros and Torelli 1992: 127ff.; Torelli 1999: 43ff.
91   Vitruvius 5.1–2.
92   Richardson 1998: 141ff.; Duprè i Raventos 1997.
93   Lancel 1979; Gros 1985.
94   Lintott 1993: 132–45. For variations in this pattern in the municipaliza-
     tion of Italy see Bispham 2007: 205ff.
95   See Lintott 1992: 34ff. for a fuller discussion of what follows.
96   Livy 5.30.8.
97   Appian, *Civil Wars* 1.7.26–7.
98   Varro, *Rural Matters* 1.10; Livy 8.21.11; Frontinus, *Boundaries* 13–14
     Thulin.
99   *ILLRP* 517, 32ff.
100 Frayn 1979: 34ff., 57ff.
101 *Lex agraria* (Crawford 1996a) I, no. 2: 14; Lintott 1992: 216–17.
102 *Lex agraria* 14–15, 24–5.
103 Lintott 1992: 237–8.
104 Columella 1.7.3–6; De Neeve 1984.
105 See the entries in Shatzman 1975.
106 Cotton and Métraux 1985: 78ff.
107 Marzano 2007.
108 Coarelli 1973; Stewart 1977.
109 Arthur 1991: 58f., pls.VIII–IX.
110 Lintott 1994c: 53ff.
111 Cicero, *Duties* 2.89.
112 *Agriculture* 1.7. See Spurr 1986: 5ff. on types of cereals and cultivation,
     119ff. on crop regimes.
113 Ibid. 5.8, cf. 30.
114 Ibid. 3, 10, 11.
115 Ibid. 20–2.
116 Ibid. 4.
117 Ibid. 2. 2,4,7; 4; 5.4.
118 Ibid.14–15.
119 Cato, *ORF* no. 8, fragment 182 = Festus 282L. Punic pavements were a
     pattern of blocks, *opus sectile*, of yellow marble veined with red from
     Chemtou in Tunisia.
120 Cotton 1979: Cotton and Métraux 1985.
121 Cato, *ORF* no.8, fragment 174 = Gellius 13.24.1; Cicero, *Laws* 2.3.
122 Cotton and Métraux 1985; Carandini 1985.
123 E.g. *Rural Matters* 1.18.1, 19.1, 22.3.
124 E.g. Ibid. 1.16.5, 18.2, 19.1.
125 Ibid. 1.1.10.
126 Ibid. 1.17.3.
127 Ibid. 1.13.6–7; 2. pref. 2; 3.2.5–10.
128 Ibid. 2. pref. 4 & 6; 2.2.9.
129 Ibid. 3.16.

130   Ibid. 3.3ff.; 13–15; 17ff.
131   Ibid. 3.5.9–17. The villa was confiscated by Caesar and taken over by Mark Antony in 44 BC, according to Cicero, as a venue for drunken orgies (*Philippics* 2.103–5).
132   *Rural Matters* 1.2.6–7; 2.1.3.
133   Rathbone 1981; Barker, Lloyd, and Webley 1978; Terrenato 1998.
134   Lintott 1992: 56–8.
135   Keppie 1983.
136   *RG* 16.
137   Cato, *Agriculture* 144–6; *CIL* IV:6672; Suetonius, *Vespasian* 1.
138   *ILS* 6509 and 6675; Smallwood 1966: nos. 435–6.
139   Horace, *Odes* 2.18.19ff.; cf. 15.1–4; 3.24.1–4.
140   Horace, *Satires* 2.6.1–3, 7.118; *Epistles*. 8.4–6; 14.1–3; 16.1–10.
141   *Eclogues* 1.64ff.
142   Tacitus, *Annals* 14.27.

6 CUSTOMS, CULTURE, AND IDEAS

1   *RDGE* 34; *RGE* 8. The most convenient introduction to this subject is Beard, North, and Price 1998. See also North (1989) and Beard 1994.
2   E.g. Horace, *Odes* 1.2; 3.6; Propertius 3.13.
3   Cicero, *Laws* 2.15–16.
4   Ibid. 16, 26.
5   Ibid. 19–22.
6   Homer, *Odyssey* 3.143–7.
7   Lintott 1999a: 63.
8   Ibid.: 49, 182ff.
9   *RG* 10.2.
10   *FIRA* I, no. 40; *ILS* 5050; Braund 768–9.
11   *RG* 7.3.
12   *MRR* under the years 47 and 42 BC.
13   Cicero, *Nature of the Gods* 3.5.
14   Cicero, *Laws* 2.19, 22; Tacitus, *Annals* 1.73.
15   *CIL* VI: 2074–83, 32371–8; translated extracts in Braund, 250, 259–60, 286; Beard, North, and Price 1998: 87–8, 151.
16   Cicero, *Divination* 2.15–25.
17   Cicero, *Laws* 2.19.
18   Cicero, *Nature of the Gods* 2.61–79; Clark 2007.
19   See Gradel 2002 with earlier bibliography. Gradel argues (30–1) that god and man were distinguished in ritual practice, but there were no absolute criteria. Divine and human were antonyms, but not mutually exclusive.
20   Ovid, *Fasti* 1.323ff.; 467ff.
21   Ibid. 4.247ff.
22   *MRR* II: 637ff.

23   Michels 1967.
24   *Fasti* 3.87–98.
25   Suetonius, *Grammarians* 17; Macrobius 1.10.7, 12.15; Wallace-Hadrill 2008: 240ff.
26   *Inscr.Ital.* xiii, 2, no. 17.
27   Ovid, *Fasti* 4.735ff.
28   Beard, North, and Price 1998 II: 30–1, 32–3.
29   Ibid. I, 185–7; Laurence 1994: 39–42.
30   Ovid, *Fasti* 2.533ff.; 5.419ff.
31   Beard, North, and Price 1998; reviewed by Linderski (2000).
32   Cornell 1995: 146–8.
33   Lintott 1999a: 187–8.
34   Lintott 1999a: 189–90; Beard, North, and Price 1998 II: 288–9.
35   *Laws* 2.21, 35–6.
36   Beard, North, and Price 1998 I: 230–1,250, 264–5.
37   *Syll.*³ 1267.
38   Richardson 1988: 281–5.
39   Catullus 10.26; *ILLRP* 518, 5.
40   Beard, North, and Price 1998 I: 275ff.
41   Cicero, *On Moral Principles (De Finibus)* 1.25; 2.44.
42   Cicero, *To his Friends* 15.16–18; 9.15–26.
43   For the Orphic underworld see Kern 1922 fragment 32, p.104ff.; West 1983: 78.
44   *Epistles* 1.4.16.
45   Chilton 1971; Smith 1982
46   *Epistles* 2.1.156-7. On "hellenization" see now Wallace-Hadrill 2008: 17–37, 96–143.
47   Cicero, *Rep.*4.3.
48   Plutarch, *Cato maior* 20.6–7.
49   Cicero, *Brutus* 104, 211; Plutarch, *Tiberius Gracchus* 8.6.
50   Suetonius, *Grammarians* esp. 4; Cicero, *On the Orator* 3.93; Suetonius, *Rhetoricians* 1–2.
51   Cicero, *On the Orator* 2.1–2; Suetonius, *Rhetoricians* 2.
52   Polybius 3.20.3; Gellius 1.23.
53   Cicero, *Friendship* 1; *Brutus* 306.
54   Suetonius, *Augustus* 26.
55   Horace, *Odes* 3.6.37ff.
56   Horace, *Satires* 1.6.71–5.
57   E.g. EJ² 247–8, 254 = Braund 480–1,487.
58   Horace, *Epistles* 1.1.53–6.
59   Suetonius, *Grammarians* 9; Horace, *Epistles* 2.1.68–72.
60   *ILS* 5039.
61   Livy 7.2; Cato fragment 118P = Cicero, *Brutus* 75. On popular culture see Wiseman 2004: 84ff, 323.

62 See Beare 1964; Beacham 1991; Rawson 1991: 468–87.

63 Fragments of early Latin poetry can be found in *Remains of Old Latin* I–III, ed. E. H.Warmington (Loeb, 1935–8); fragments of Greek mimes in D. L. Page, *Select Papyri* III (Loeb), 323ff.

64 For Lucilius see *Remains of Old Latin* III; Horace, *Satires* 1.4.1–12; 10.1–4; 53–71; 2.1.15–33; 62–83; on the origins of satire and Varro see now Wiseman 2009: 131–51.

65 Gellius 19.9–14; *ILLRP* 342.

66 Fragments edited by Traglia (1962); Courtney 1993: 212ff.

67 Hollis 2007: 11ff., 219ff.; Courtney 1993: 259ff.; Wiseman (1974) 44ff.; Catullus 95.

68 *Epistles* 2.1.117.

69 Horace, *Ars Poetica* 6, 24.

70 Levick 1983 = Braund 724.

71 Livy, 7.2.11–12; Suetonius, *Augustus* 45; Tacitus, *Annals* 1.77.

72 Macrobius 3.14.13.

73 Livy, *Periochae* 48; Valerius Maximus 2.4.2; cf. Appian, *Civil Wars* 1.27.125.

74 Hanson 1959: 29ff.; Sear 2006; Gros 1987: 161ff.

75 Coarelli 1984: 371–4; Richardson 1988: 75ff.

76 Torelli 1999: 130.

77 Cicero, *To Atticus* 2.19.3; *For Sestius* 120–3.

78 Suetonius, *Nero* 39.3.

79 Peter 1914 esp. I, 1–66; Frier 1979; Cornell et al. forthcoming.

80 Plutarch, *Flamininus* 12.6–7; *SEG* 16.486. See in general Gruen 1993: 6ff.; Galinsky 1969.

81 See the essays in Dorey 1966; Rawson 1991: 245–71.

82 *To his Friends* 15.1–2.

83 Sallust, *Histories* 2.98.10; Plutarch, *Caesar* 30.3.

84 Cicero, *To his Friends* 10.30; *Philippics* 13.25–9.

85 See *RDGE* for texts of these, found in the Greek world, and *RGE* for translations.

86 See esp. Cicero, *To his Friends* 13 *passim*.

87 Lintott 1993: 116.

88 Welles 1934 nos. 56–61, 71–2; *Select Papyri* ed. A. S. Hunt and C. C. Edgar, (Loeb) I, nos. 88, 92, 96–7, 99.

89 Gellius 13.15.3–16.3; *Digest* 1.13.1 pref.; Gellius 14.7.1.

90 Pliny, *Natural History* 36.41; Rawson 1991: 195–9; Gruen 1993: 134.

91 Vitruvius 7 pref., 15, 17–18; Gruen 1993: 132–3; Rawson 1991: 190–2; *ILS* 5637a–b.

92 Cicero, *To Atticus* 2.3.3; *To Quintus* 2.2.2; *To his Friends* 7.14.1; *For Milo* 46, 48.

93 Vitruvius 1 pref. 2–3; Frontinus, *Waters* 23. For an appreciation of Vitruvius see Wallace-Hadrill 2008: 144–210.

94 Vitruvius 2.6 & 8.
95 White 1970: 174ff.; Spurr 1986: 23ff. On technology in general see the essays in Oleson 2008.
96 Casson 1971, and see ch. 1.
97 Vitruvius 10.2.7; Bianchi Bandinelli 1970: 217.
98 Wilson 2002 and 2008.
99 Cicero, *To Atticus* 7.9.
100 Balsdon 1969: 244–8, 267–9.
101 Suetonius, *Augustus* 32.
102 Lintott 1999a: 74–5.
103 Suetonius, *Augustus* 35.
104 Balsdon 1969: 17–26.
105 Ibid., 54–5.
106 Ibid., 26–33.
107 Suetonius, *Augustus* 71.
108 Cicero, *To Atticus* 13.52.
109 Tacitus, *Annals* 3.52–5.
110 Gellius 2.24; Macrobius 3.17; Lintott 1972: 631–2. On Roman luxury and the "discourse of luxury" see Wallace-Hadrill 2008: 315–55.
111 Suetonius, *Augustus* 74; *Nero* 16.2; *Domitian* 7.1.
112 Statius, *Silvae* 4.2.18–44; Claridge 1998: 136–9; Gibson, DeLaine, and Claridge 1994.
113 *Digest* 50.16.98.1.
114 Ovid, *Fasti* 2.617ff.; 3.245ff.
115 Balsdon 1969: 124–5.
116 Treggiari 1991: 138–53, 161–70.
117 Polybius 6.53.
118 Cicero, *Philippics* 9.15-17; *Laws* 2.58–62.
119 Marquadt 1886: 343–85.
120 *ILS* 881, 886; Claridge 1998: 341–2; Coarelli 1984: 357–9.
121 Claridge 1998: 364–6; *ILS* 917, 917^a.
122 Coarelli 1980: 226–7.
123 Beard 2007.
124 Richardson 1975.
125 Pliny, *Natural History* 7.97–8; Plutarch, *Pompeius* 45; Suetonius, *Julius* 37; Plutarch, *Caesar* 55; *RG* 3; Suetonius, *Augustus* 22.
126 EJ^2: 36.
127 Livy, 1.35; Dionysius of Halicarnassus, *Antiquities* 3.68.
128 Balsdon 1969: 244ff.
129 Suetonius, *Augustus* 43; cf. *RG* App. 4.
130 Polybius 30.22; Terence, *Hecyra* 33–6.
131 Plautus, *Captivi* 12. For temporary constructions see Crawford 1996a I, no. 24, 77–9; for the exploitation of temples Goldberg 1998 esp. 1–8.
132 Claridge 1998: 214, 243–5; Coarelli 1980: 244–5, 254–7.

133 Dionysius of Halicarnassus, *Antiquities* 7.72.2–3; 73.3; Suetonius, *Augustus* 44–5.

134 Livy, *Periochae* 16; Barker and Rasmussen 1998: 294.

135 Welch 2007.

136 Haselberger 2002: 44–5.

137 Bomgardner 2000: 39ff., 59.

138 Balsdon 1969: 294ff.; Dunkle 2008.

139 Crawford 1996a I, no. 24: 112–13.

140 Ricci 2006; Levick 1983.

141 Hopkins 1983: 1ff.

142 Lucilius IV.172–5, cf. n. 63.

143 Lintott 1999b: 84–5.

144 Barker and Rasmussen 1998: 294; Pallottino 1974: 179f.; Humphrey 1986: 12–17.

145 Cristofani 1990: 201–3, and pl. XXI.

146 Pliny, *Natural History* 21.50; Livy 24.18.10.

147 Asconius 88C; Tacitus, *Annals* 15.44.

148 Rawson 1991: 389–407.

149 Pliny, *Natural History* 8.17, 53, 70f.; Plautus, *Persa* 199; Livy 44.18.8; *Periochae* 51.

150 Livy, 8.20.2; 41.27.6.

151 Suetonius, *Julius* 39; Pliny, *Natural History* 36.102.

152 Dionysius of Halicarnassus, *Antiquities* 3.68.

153 Dio Cassius 49.43.2.

154 *RG* 19.1; Suetonius, *Augustus* 45.

155 Dio Cassius 60.7.3; Tacitus, *Annals* 15.32.

7 THE ARMED SERVICES AND THE FRONTIERS

1 Tacitus, *Annals* 1.9.

2 Ibid. 1.11; Suetonius, *Augustus* 101.

3 Lintott 1993: 5–12; Derow 1979.

4 Virgil, *Aeneid* 1.278–9; cf. Horace, *Odes* 4.15; Lintott 1993: 12–15, 41–2.

5 *RG* 26.1.

6 *RG* 26.2.–27.2.

7 *RG* 29.2; arch - EJ[2] 26–7; Claridge 1998: 72, 99; Haselberger 2002: 51.

8 *RG* 30.

9 Gruen 1996; Luttwak 1976.

10 Wilkes 1996: 545–53.

11 Strabo 4.5.3, 200–1C.

12 Polybius 6.19.2, with the unamended manuscript text.

13 Polybius 6.19.3; Brunt 1971: 402, 668–9.

14 Sallust, *Jugurtha* 84.2, 86.2.

15 Brunt 1971: 408–15.

16   *RG* 16; cf. Tacitus, *Annals* 4.5; Parker 1928: 72–92.
17   Dio Cassius 54.25.5–6.
18   Velleius 2.111.1; Dio Cassius 56.23.2; EJ² 368 = Braund 428.
19   Dio Cassius 55.31.1–2.
20   Tacitus, *Annals* 4.4; Velleius 2.130.2; Suetonius, *Tiberius* 48.2.
21   E.g. EJ² 255, 257–9, 261 = Braund 488, 490–2, 494.
22   Forni 1953: 159ff.; 1974: 366ff.
23   Dio Cassius 55.24.5, writing 200 years later.
24   Livy 4.59.11–60.6; Diodorus Siculus 14.16.5.
25   Polybius 6.39.12; Suetonius, *Julius* 26.3; Tacitus *Annals* 1.17.
26   Tacitus, *Annals* 1.17.
27   Cicero, *To Atticus* 16.8.1.
28   *RG* 16.
29   *RG* 17.2; Dio Cassius 55.25.2–5; Tacitus, *Annals* 1.78; 2.42.
30   Dio Cassius 55.23.1.
31   Lintott 1993: 70–96; Nicolet 2000: 93–103.
32   Cicero, *To Atticus* 2.16.1; Dio Cassius 37.51.3–4; Lintott 1993: 83–4.
33   Tacitus, *Annals* 2.42.
34   *RG* Appendix.
35   Tacitus, *Annals* 1.8, cf. Suetonius, *Augustus* 101.
36   Tacitus, *Annals* 2.48; 6.2, 19; Brunt 1990: 145–6.
37   Suetonius, *Augustus* 101; Shatzman 1975: 357–71.
38   Plutarch, *Pompeius* 45.4; Cicero, *On the Alexandrian King*, fragment 13 Puccioni = Strabo 17.798C.
39   Velleius 2.39.1–2.
40   See Hopkins 1980 for a theoretical calculation of what might have been plausibly extracted.
41   Tacitus, *Annals* 1.17, 36, 52, 78.
42   Brunt 1990: 325–6, 343–4, reviewing Neesen 1980.
43   Lintott 1993: 85ff.
44   Tacitus, *Annals* 3.54.
45   Lintott 1993: 186–94.

References

Andreau, J. (1999). *Banking and Business in the Roman World*. Cambridge.

Angelelli, C. S., and S. Falzone. (1999). "Considerazioni sull' occupazione protostorica nell'area sud-occidentale del Palatino, *Journal of Roman Archaeology* 12.1: 5–32.

Arce, J., E. Ensoli, and E. La Rocca, eds. (1997). *Hispania Romana*. Milan.

Arthur, P. (1991). *Romans in Northern Campania*, British School at Rome, Archaeological Monographs 1. London.

Aubert, J. J. (1994). *Business Managers in Ancient Rome. A Social and Economic Survey of Institores 200 B.C.– A.D.250*. Leiden.

Balsdon, J. P. V. D. (1969). *Life and Leisure in Ancient Rome*. London.

Barker, G., J. Lloyd, and D. Webley (1978). "A Classical Landscape in Molise," *Papers of the British School at Rome* 46, 35–51.

Barker, G., and T. Rasmussen (1998). *The Etruscans*. Oxford.

Beacham, R. C. (1991). *The Roman Theatre and its Audience*. London.

Beard, M. (1994). "Religion," *CAH* IX²: 729–68.

— (2007). *The Roman Triumph*. Cambridge, Mass. and London.

Beard, M., J. North, and S. Price (1998). *Religions of Rome*. Cambridge.

Beare, W. (1964). *The Roman Stage*. 3rd edn. London.

Beloch, K.- J. (1886). *Die Bevölkerung der griechisch-römischen Welt*. Leipzig.

Bianchi Biandinelli, R. (1970). *Rome: the Centre of Power*. London.

Bispham, E. (2000). "Carved in Stone. The Municipal Magistracies of N. Cluvius," in A. Cooley (ed.), *The Epigraphic Landscape of Roman Italy*, *Bulletin of the Institute of Classical Studies* Suppl. 73: 39–75.

— (2007). *From Asculum to Actium: the Municipalization of Italy from the Social War to Augustus*. Oxford.

Bomgardner, D. L. (2000). *The Story of the Roman Amphitheatre*. London and New York.

Bowersock (1965). *Augustus and the Greek World*. Oxford.

Brown, V. (1970). "A Latin letter from Oxyrhynchus," *Bulletin of the Institute of Classical Studies* 17: 136–43.

Brunt, P. A. (1971). *Italian Manpower 225 B.C.–A.D.14*. Oxford.

— (1988). *The Fall of the Roman Republic and Related Essays*. Oxford.

— (1990). *Roman Imperial Themes*. Oxford.

Buckland, W. W. (1908). *The Roman Law of Slavery*. Cambridge.
Burnett A., et al. (1992). *Roman Provincial Coinage* I. London.
Calabi Limentani, I. (1968). *Epigrafia Latina*.
Calza, G. (1940). *La Necropoli del Porto di Roma dell'Isola Sacra*. Rome.
Camodeca, G. (1999). *Tabulae Pompeianae Sulpiciorum*, Vetera 12. Rome.
Carandini, A. (1985). *Settefinestre. Una villa schiavistica nell'Etruria romana*. 3 vols. Modena.
Carettoni, G., A. M. Colini, L. Cozza, and G. Gatti (1960). *La pianta marmorea di Roma antica*, 2 vols. Rome.
Carroll, M. (2006). *Spirits of the Dead: Roman Funerary Commemoration in Western Europe*. Oxford.
Casson, L. (1971). *Ships and Seamanship in the Ancient World*. Princeton, N. J.
Champlin, E. (1991). *Final Judgement. Duty and Emotion in Roman Wills 200 B.C.–A.D. 250*. Berkeley and Los Angeles, Calif.
Chilton, C. W. (1971). *Diogenes of Oenoanda. The Fragments*. London, New York, and Toronto.
Chioffi, L. (2005). *Museo Provinciale Campano di Capua. La Raccolta Epigrafica*. Capua.
Claridge, A. (1998). *Rome*. Oxford.
Clark, A. (2007). *Divine Qualities: Cult and Community in Republican Rome*. Oxford.
Coarelli, F. (1973). "Sperlonga e Tiberio," *Dialoghi di Archeologia* 7: 97–122 = *Revixit Ars* (Rome, 1996) 470–500.
— (1980). *Guida Archeologica di Roma*. 2nd edn. Milan.
— (1984). *Lazio*. Rome and Bari.
— (1985). *Il Foro Romano: periodo repubblicano e augusteo*. Rome.
— (2005). "L'Agora des Italiens: lo statario di Delo?," *Journal of Roman Archaeology* 18: 196–212.
Cornell, T. J. (1989a). "Rome and Latium," *CAH* VII.2²: 264–323.
— (1989b). "The Conquest of Italy," *CAH* VII.2²: 351–91.
— (1995). *The Beginnings of Rome: Italy and Rome from the Bronze Age to the Punic Wars (c. 1000–264 BC)*. London and New York.
— et al. (forthcoming). *Fragments of the Roman Historians*. Oxford.
Cottier, M., M. H. Crawford, C. W. Crowther, J.-L. Ferrary, B. M. Levick, O. Salomies, and M. Wörrle, (2008). *The Customs Law of Asia*. Oxford.
Cotton, M. A. (1979), *The Late-Republican Villa at Posto, Francolise*, British School at Rome Suppl. London.
Cotton, M. A., and G. P. R. Métraux (1985). *The San Rocco Villa at Francolise*, British School at Rome Suppl. London.
Courtney, E. (1993). *The Fragmentary Latin Poets*. Oxford.
Cozza, L., and P. L. Tucci (2006). "Navalia," *Archeologia Classica* 57: 175–202.
Crawford, M. (1978). *The Roman Republic*. London. 2nd edn. 1992.
— (1985). *Coinage and Money under the Roman Republic*. Cambridge.

— ed. (1996a). *Roman Statutes, 2 vols., Bulletin of the Institute of Classical Studies* Suppl. 64. London.

— (1996b). "Italy and Rome from Sulla to Augustus," *CAH* X²: 414–33 and 979–89, App.1–7.

Cristofani, M. ed. (1990). *La Grande Roma dei Tarquinii*. Rome.

Crook, J. A. (1967). *Law and Life of Rome*. London.

— (1996a). "Political History, 30 B.C. to A.D. 14," *CAH* X²: 70–112.

— (1996b). "Augustus: Power, Authority, Achievement," *CAH* X²: 113–46.

D'Arms, J. H. (1981). *Commerce and Social Standing in Ancient Rome*. Harvard, Mass.

De Neeve, P. W. (1984). *Colonus, Private Farm Tenancy in Roman Italy during the Republic and Early Principate*. Amsterdam.

Derow, P. S. (1979). "Polybius, Rome and the East," *Journal of Roman Studies* 69, 1–15.

— (1989). "Rome, the Fall of Macedon and the Sack of Corinth," *CAH* VIII²: 290–387.

— (1991). "Pharos and Rome," *Zeitschrift für Papyrologie und Epigraphik* 88: 261–70.

Dihle, A. (1978). "Indienhandel der römischen Kaiserzeit," *ANRW* II.9.2: 546–80.

Dorey, T. A. ed. (1966). *Latin Historians*. London.

Dörner, F. K., and G. Gruben (1953). "Die Exedra der Cicerones," *Mitteilungen des Deutschen Archaeologischen Instituts, Athenische Abteiling* 68: 63–76.

Dunkle, R. (2008). *Gladiators: Violence and Spectacle in Ancient Rome*. Harlow.

Duprè i Raventos, X. (1997), "Il Foro nelle Province Ispaniche," in Arce et al. 1997: 156–60.

Earl, D. C. (1967). *The Moral and Political Tradition of Rome*. London.

Eck, W. (2007). *The Age of Augustus*. 2nd edn. Oxford.

Errington, R. M. (1989a). "Rome and Greece to 205 B.C.," *CAH* VIII²: 81–106.

— (1989b). "The East after the Peace of Phoenice," *CAH* VIII²: 244–89.

Fagan, G. G. (2001). "The Genesis of the Roman Public Bath: Recent Approaches and Future Directions," *American Journal of Archaeology* 105: 403–26.

Forni, G. R. (1953). *Il recrutamento delle legioni da Augusto a Diocleziano*. Milan and Rome.

— (1974). "Estrazione etnica e sociale dei soldati delle legioni," *ANRW* II.1: 339–91.

Franke, P. R. (1989). "Pyrrhus," *CAH* VII.2²: 456–85.

Frayn, J. M. (1979). *Subsistence Farming in Roman Italy*. Fontwell.

Frier, B. W. (1979). *Libri Annales Pontificum Maximorum: The Origins of the Annalistic Tradition*, Papers and Monographs of the American Academy 27. Rome.

— (1989). *A Casebook on the Roman Law of Delict*. Atlanta, Ga.

Friggeri, R. (2001). *The Epigraphic Collection of the Museo Nazionale Romano*. Rome.

Gabba, E. (1989). "Rome and Italy in the Second Century B.C.," *CAH* VIII²: 197–243.

— (1994). "Rome and Italy: the Social War," *CAH* IX²: 104–28.

Galinsky, G. K. (1969). *Aeneas, Sicily, and Rome.* Princeton, N. J.

Gardner, J. F. (1986). *Women in Roman Law and Society.* London.

Garnsey, P., and D. Rathbone (1985). "The Background to the Grain Law of Gaius Gracchus," *Journal of Roman Studies* 75: 20–5.

Gelzer, M. (1968). *Caesar: Politician and Statesman*, trans. P. Needham. Oxford.

— (1969). *The Roman Nobility*, trans. R. Seager. Oxford.

Gibson, S., J. Delaine, and A. Claridge (1994). "The *Triclinium* of the *Domus Flavia*: a New Reconstruction," *Papers of the British School at Rome* 62: 67–93.

Goldberg, S. M. (1998). "Plautus on the Palatine," *Journal of Roman Studies* 88: 1–20.

Gölitzer, E. (2004). *Entstehung und Entwicklung des alexandrinische Münzwesen von 30 v.Chr. bis zu Ende der jülisch-claudische Dynastie.* Berlin.

Gradel, I. (2002). *Emperor Worship and Roman Religion.* Oxford.

Graham, E.-J. (2006). *The Burial of the Urban Poor in Italy in the Late Roman Republic and Early Empire*, British Archaeological Reports international series 1565. Oxford.

Gros, P. (1985). *Byrsa III*, Collection de l'École Française de Rome 41. Rome.

— (1987). *Architettura e Società nell' Italia romana.* Rome.

Gros, P. and Torelli, M. (1992). *Storia dell'urbanistica.Il mondo romano.* Rome and Bari.

Gruen, E. S. (1984). *The Hellenistic World and the Coming of Rome*, 2 vols. Berkeley and Los Angeles, Calif.

— (1993). *Culture and National Identity in Republican Rome.* London.

— (1996). "The Expansion of the Empire under Augustus," *CAH* X²: 148–97.

Hanson, J. A. (1959). *Roman Theatre Temples.* Princeton, N. J.

Harris, W. V. (1989). "Roman Expansion in the West," *CAH* VIII²: 107–62.

— (2006). "A Revisionist View of Roman Money," *Journal of Roman Studies* 96: 1–24.

Haselberger, L. (2002). *Mapping Augustan Rome, Journal of Roman Archaeology* Suppl. 50.

Herrman, P. (1960). "Die Inschriften römischer Zeit aus dem Heraion von Samos," *Mitteilungen des Deutschen Archaeologischen Instituts, Athenische Abteiling* 75: 68–183.

Heslin, P. (2007). "Augustus, Domitian, and the so-called Horologium Augusti," *Journal of Roman Studies* 97: 1–20.

Hinard, F., and J. Dumont (2003). *Libitina.* Paris.

Hind, J. G. F. (1994). "Mithridates," *CAH* IX²: 129–64.

Hollis, A. S. (2007). *Fragments of Roman Poetry c.60 BC–AD 20.* Oxford.

Hopkins, K. (1980) "Taxes and Trade in the Roman Empire," *Journal of Roman Studies* 70: 101–25.

— (1983). *Death and Renewal*. Cambridge.

Horsfall, N. (1976). "The 'Collegium Poetarum,'" *Bulletin of the Institute of Classical Studies* 23: 79–85.

Humphrey, J. H. (1986). *Roman Circuses. Arenas for Chariot-Racing*. London.

Jones, A. H. M. (1960). *Studies in Roman Government and Law*. Oxford.

Keppie, L. (1983). *Colonisation and Veteran Settlement in Italy 47–14 B.C.*, British School at Rome Suppl. London.

Kern, O. (1922). *Orphicorum Fragmenta*. Berlin.

Lancel, S. ed. (1979). *Byrsa I*, Collection de l'École française de Rome 41. Rome.

— (1995). *Carthage: A History*, trans. A. Nevill. Oxford.

— (1998). *Hannibal*, trans. A. Nevill. Oxford.

Laurence, R. (1994). *Roman Pompeii. Space and Society*. London and New York.

Lazenby, J. F. (1978). *Hannibal's War*. Warminster.

Levick, B. (1983). "The Senatus Consultum of Larinum," *Journal of Roman Studies* 73: 97–115.

— (1985). *The Government of the Roman Empire–A Sourcebook*. London.

Linderski, J. (2000). Review of Beard, North, and Price 1998, *Journal of Roman Archaeology* 13.2: 453–63.

Lintott, A. (1972). "Imperial Expansion and Moral Decline in the Roman Republic," *Historia* 21: 626–38.

— (1990). "Electoral Bribery in the Roman Republic," *Journal of Roman Studies* 80: 1–16.

— (1992). *Judicial Reform and Land Reform in the Roman Republic*. Cambridge.

— (1993). *Imperium Romanum*. London.

— (1994a). "The Crisis of the Republic: Sources and source-problems," *CAH* IX²: 1–15.

— (1994b). "The Roman Empire and its problems in the late second century," *CAH* IX²: 16–39.

— (1994c). "Political history, 146–95 B.C.," *CAH* IX²: 40–103.

— (1999a). *The Constitution of the Roman Republic*. Oxford.

— (1999b). *Violence in Republican Rome*. 2nd edn. Oxford.

— (2001–3). "*Delator* and *Index*. Informers and Accusers at Rome from the Republic to the early Principate," *Accordia Research Papers* 9: 105–22.

— (2002). "Freedmen and Slaves in the Light of Legal Documents from First-Century A.D. Campania," *Classical Quarterly* 52: 555–65.

— (2004). "Legal Procedure in Cicero's Time," in J. Powell and J. Paterson, eds,. *Cicero the Advocate*, 61–78. Oxford.

— (2008). *Cicero as Evidence: A Historian's Companion*. Oxford.

Lo Cascio, E. (1994). "The Size of the Roman Population: Beloch and the Meaning of the Augustan Census Figures," *Journal of Roman Studies* 84: 23–40.

Luttwak, E. N. (1976). *The Grand Strategy of the Roman Empire from the First Century* AD *to the Third.* Baltimore.

Marquadt, J. (1886). *Das Privatleben der Römer.* Leipzig. Repr. Darmstadt 1964.

Marzano, A. (2007). *Roman Villas in Central Italy: A Social and Economic History*, Columbia Studies in the Classical Tradition 31. Leiden and Boston, Mass.

Meiggs, R. (1973). *Roman Ostia.* 2nd edn. Oxford.

Michels, A. K. (1967). *The Calendar of the Roman Republic.* Princeton, N. J.

Millar, F. (1993). *The Roman Near East 31BC–AD 337.* Cambridge, Mass.

Millar, F. and E. Segal eds. (1984). *Caesar Augustus: Seven Aspects.* Oxford.

Misurare la terra (1983). *Misurare la terra: centuriazione e coloni nel mondo romano*, exhibition catalogue. Modena.

Mitchell, S. (1976). "Requisitioned Transport in the Roman Empire. A New Inscription from Pisidia," *Journal of Roman Studies* 66: 106–31.

Momigliano, A. (1975). *Alien Wisdom.* Cambridge.

Mommsen, Th. (1887–8). *Römisches Staatsrecht*, 3 vols. Leipzig.

Morstein-Marx, R. (2004). *Mass Oratory and Political Power in the Late Roman Republic.* Cambridge.

Mouritsen, H. (2005). "Freedmen and Decurions: Epitaphs and Social History in Imperial Italy," *Journal of Roman Studies* 95: 38–63.

Neesen, L. (1980). *Untersuchungen zu den direkten Staatsabgaben der römischen Kaiserzeit (27 V.CHR–284 N.CHR.).* Bonn.

Nicolet, C. (1966–74). *L'Ordre équestre à l'époque républicaine (312–43 av.J.-C)*, 2 vols, Bibliothèque des Écoles Françaises d'Athènes et de Rome 207. Paris.

— (1980). *The World of the Citizen in Republican Rome*, trans. P. S. Falla. London.

— (1984). "Augustus, Government, and the Propertied Classes," in Millar and Segal 1984: 89–128.

— (1990). *Space, Geography and Politics in the Early Roman Empire.* Ann Arbor, Mich.

— (2000). *Censeurs et publicains: Économie et fiscalité dans la Rome antique.* Paris.

North, J. A. (1989). "Religion in Republican Rome," *CAH VII.* 2^2: 573–624.

Oleson, J. P. ed. (2008). *The Oxford Handbook of Engineering and Technology in the Classical World.* Oxford.

Osgood, J. (2006). *Civil War and the Emergence of the Monarchy.* Cambridge.

Pallottino, M. (1974). *The Etruscans.* London.

Parker, H. M. D. (1928). *The Roman Legions.* Oxford. Rev. edn. G. R. Watson, 1971.

Pelling, C. (1996). "The Triumviral Period," *CAH* X^2: 1–69.

Peter, H. (1914). *Historicorum Romanorum Reliquiae*, 2 vols. 2nd edn. Repr. Stuttgart 1993.

Preisigke, F., and F. Bilabel (1926). *Sammelbuch Griechischer Urkunden aus Ägypten* III. Berlin and Leipzig.

Purcell, N. (1983). "The *apparitores*: a study in social mobility," *Papers of the British School at Rome* 51: 125–73.

— (1989). "Rediscovering the Roman Forum," *Journal of Roman Archaeology* 2: 156–66.

— (1994). "The City of Rome and the *Plebs Urbana* in the late Republic," *CAH* IX²: 644–88.

Rathbone, D.W. (1981). "The Development of Agriculture in the *Ager Cosanus* during the Roman Republic," *Journal of Roman Studies* 71: 10–23.

Rawson, E. (1991). *Roman Culture and Society. Collected Papers.* Oxford.

— (1994a). "Caesar: Civil War and Dictatorship," *CAH* IX²: 424–67.

— (1994b). "The Aftermath of the Ides," *CAH* IX²: 468–90.

Rea, J. R. (1982). "Lease of a Red Cow called Thayris," *Journal of Egyptian Archaeology* 68: 278–82.

Ricci, C. (2006). *Gladiatori e attori nella Roma giulia-claudia: studi sul senatus consulto di Larino.* Ledonline. (www.ledonline.it)

Rich, J. W., and J. H. C. Williams (1999) "*Leges et iura p.r. restituit*: a new aureus of Octavian and the settlement of 28–7 B.C.," *Numismatic Chronicle* 159: 169–213.

Richardson, J. S. (1975). "The Triumph, the Praetors, and the Senate in the Early Second Century BC," *Journal of Roman Studies* 65: 50–63.

— (1998). *The Romans in Spain.* Oxford.

— (2008). *The Language of Empire.* Cambridge.

Richardson, L. jnr. (1988). *Pompeii. An Architectural History.* Baltimore and London.

Robinson, O. (1992). *Ancient Rome. City Planning and Administration.* London.

Rodriguez Almeida, E. (1981). *Forma Urbis Marmorea: Aggiornamento generale 1980*, 2 vols. Rome.

Roma medio-repubblicana (1973). *Roma medio-repubblicana. Aspetti culturali di Roma e del Lazio nei secoli IV e III*, exhibition catalogue. Rome.

Rowe, G. (2001). "Trimalchio's World," *Studia Classica Israelica* 20: 235–42.

— (2002). *Princes and Political Cultures: the New Tiberian Senatorial Decrees.* Ann Arbor, Mich.

Rutledge, S. (2001). *Imperial Inquisitions.* London and New York.

Scullard, H. H. (1989a). "Carthage and Rome," *CAH* VII.2²: 486–572.

— (1989b). "The Carthaginians in Spain," *CAH* VIII²: 17–43.

Seager, R. (1994a). "Sulla," *CAH* IX²: 165–207.

— (1994b). "The Rise of Pompey," *CAH* IX²: 208–28.

— (2002). *Pompey the Great.* 2nd edn. Oxford.

Sear, F. (2006). *Roman Theatre: An Architectural Study.* Oxford.

Scheidel, W. (2004). "Human Mobility in Roman Italy," *Journal of Roman Studies* 94: 1–26.

Shatzman, I. (1975). *Senatorial Wealth and Roman Politics*, Collection Latomus 142. Brussels.

Sherwin White, A. N. (1984). *Roman Foreign Policy in the East*. London.

— (1994). "Lucullus, Pompey, and the East," *CAH* IX²: 229–73.

Smallwood, E. M. (1966). *Documents Illustrating the Reigns of Nerva, Trajan, and Hadrian*. Cambridge.

Smith, C. (1996). *Early Rome and Latium: c. 1000–500 BC*. Oxford.

Smith, M. F. (1982). "Diogenes of Oenoanda: New Fragments 115–121," *Prometheus* 8: 193ff.

Speidel, M. (1994). *Riding for Caesar: the Roman Emperor's Horse Guards*. London.

Spurr, M. S. (1986). *Arable Cultivation in Roman Italy c.200 B.C. – c. A.D.100*, *Journal of Roman Studies* Monographs 3. London.

Stewart, A. F. (1977). "To Entertain an Emperor: Sperlonga, Laokoon and Tiberius at the Dinner-Table," *Journal of Roman Studies* 67: 76–90.

Syme, R. (1939). *The Roman Revolution*. Oxford.

— (1958). *Tacitus*, 2 vols. Oxford.

— (1979). *Roman Papers* II, ed. E. Badian. Oxford.

Taylor, L. R. (1960). *The Voting Districts of the Roman Republic*, American Academy Papers 20. Rome.

— (1961). "Freedmen and Freeborn in the Epitaphs of Imperial Rome," *American Journal of Philology* 82: 113–32.

Terrenato, N. (1998). "*Tam firmum municipium*: the Romanization of Volaterrae and its Cultural Implications," *Journal of Roman Studies* 88: 94–114.

— (2001). "The Auditorium Site and the Origin of the Villa," *Journal of Roman Archaeology* 14.1: 5–32.

Torelli, M. (1975). *Elogia Tarquiniensia*. Florence.

— (1999). *Tota Italia. Essays in the Cultural Formation of Roman Italy*. Oxford.

Traglia, A. ed. (1962). *M. Tulli Ciceronis Poetica Fragmenta*. Milan.

Treggiari, S. (1991). *Roman Marriage*. Oxford.

Tuck, S. L. (2000). "A New Identification of the Porticus Aemilia," *Journal of Roman Archaeology* 13: 175–82.

Wallace-Hadrill, A. (2008). *Rome's Cultural Revolution*. Cambridge.

Watson A.(1967). *The Law of Persons in the Later Roman Republic*. Oxford.

Welch, K. (2007). *The Roman Amphitheatre from its Origins to the Colosseum*. Cambridge.

Welles, C. B. (1934). *Royal Correspondence of the Hellenistic Period*. New Haven. Repr. Chicago 1974.

West, M. L. (1983). *The Orphic Poems*. Oxford.

White, K. D. (1970). *Roman Farming*. London.

Wiedemann, T. E. J. (1996). "Tiberius to Nero," *CAH* X²: 198–255.

Wilkes, J. J. (1996). "The Danubian and Balkan Provinces," *CAH* X²: 545ff.

Wilson, A. (2002). "Machines, Power, and the Ancient Economy," *Journal of Roman Studies* 92: 1–32.

— (2008). "Hydraulic Engineering and Water-Supply," in *Oleson* 2008: 285–336.

Wiseman, T. P. (1970). "The Definition of 'eques Romanus' in the late Republic and early Empire," *Historia* 19: 67–83.

— (1971). *New Men in the Roman Senate 139 B.C.– A.D.14*. Oxford.

— (1974). *Cinna the Poet and other Roman Essays*. Leicester.

— (1979). *Clio's Cosmetics*. Leicester.

— (1985). *Catullus and his World. A Reappraisal*. Cambridge.

— (1994a). "The Senate and the *Populares*, 69–60 B.C.," *CAH* IX²: 327–67.

— (1994b). "Caesar, Pompey and Rome, 59–50 B.C.," *CAH* IX²: 368–423.

— (2004). *The Myths of Rome*. Exeter.

— (2009). *Remembering the Roman People: Essays in Late-Republican Politics and Literature*. Oxford.

Zanker, P. (1984). *Il foro di Augusto*. Rome.

— (1988). *The Power of Images in the Age of Augustus*. Ann Arbor, Mich.

Index

Certain well-known Romans are indexed under their familiar names; others under their *nomen*, their main family name, e.g. **Cicero**, but his brother, Q. **Tullius** Cicero.